JULIUS **ERVING**

WITH KARL TARO GREENFELD

18 17

HARPER

www.harpercollins.com

Dr. J

THE AUTOBIOGRAPHY

HarperCollins books may be purchased for educational, business, or sales promotional use. For information, please e-mail the Special Markets Department at SPsales@harpercollins.com.

FIRST EDITION

Designed by William Ruoto

Frontispiece by Neil Leifer/NBAE/Getty Images

Library of Congress Cataloging-in-Publication Data

Erving, Julius.
Dr. J : the autobiography / Julius W. Erving with Karl Taro Greenfeld.
p.   cm.
ISBN 978-0-06-218792-5
1. Erving, Julius. 2. Basketball players—United States—Biography. I.
Greenfeld, Karl Taro. II. Title.
GV884.E78A3   2013
796.323092—dc23 [B]   2013027874

14 15 16 17   OV/RRD   10 9 8 7 6

In loving memory of my parents, Julius Sr. and
Callie Mae; my brother, Marvin Vincent; my sister,
Alexis Alfreda; my stepfather, Dan Lindsay; and
my son Cory Marvin Erving

Contents

Preface

Mine is an American life, fully lived, rich with the spoils and temptations of success, and rife with the failings and shortcomings of succumbing to those same temptations. I believe that while what I achieved is only possible in the United States, my faults are my own, singular and personal. I am born with great genetic gifts of speed and strength and dexterity, and the opportunities of my country allowed me to gain wealth and fame through basketball. Yet my journey is more than that of an athlete. I am an African-American, living through tumultuous times in our country, navigating a cultural landscape that has been very much divided for much of my life; I am a husband, trying and not always succeeding to live up to vows of fidelity amid the seductions of celebrity and fame; I am a father, seeking to impart values and my belief in America to my sons and daughters, pulled too often by the demands of professional sports away from those children; I am a businessman, believing deeply in the system that rewarded me and now seeking to build another legacy.

I am, of course, an athlete, a former basketball player, and while my achievements in that arena are my best known, they are only the mythic part of my story. My other accomplishments—of completing my college degree, of the pride I take in my children, of rising up and out of the Hempstead, Long

Island, projects to become Julius Erving, founder and CEO of Dr. J Enterprises and the Erving Group, partner in the first minority-owned NASCAR team in the modern era, board member of corporations such as Saks Fifth Avenue, Meridian Bank, Williams Communications, and Sports Authority, and institutions including Thomas Jefferson University Hospital and Philadelphia's Fairmont Park Commission—are those I wish to be measured by.

I am an American man whose journey has been blessed by the great gifts that America offers—wealth, fame, championships, awards—and also scoured by the tragedies that are a part of the human experience. I have lost too many loved ones.

I ask for no pity; I only want to relate what I have felt and seen.

I have hurt too many people.

For that I ask forgiveness.

An American life, after all, is the sum of its parts, the successes and the failings, and mine has been rich with both.

I want to be candid about my life. I want to recall with you everything that I have seen and done, and try to make sense of this ongoing journey. I am living a bountiful life, and while it has not always been easy, it has been exciting and, I believe, emblematic of our time.

Mine is an American life, fully lived.

1.

Rise.

I jump.

I reach up both hands, my brown corduroys sagging, and I take flight, my blue Keds leaving the linoleum floor and my fingers reaching above the sill. I can't see out the window. Jump again. Higher. I can touch the glass. And every time I jump, I know, I jump higher.

But I can't see out the window.

"June, what are you doing?"

"Nothin'." I sit down on the floor. "Jumpin'."

I can smell what Mom is cooking: chicken, lima beans, spinach. The steam coming from the kitchen, the wet grassy smell of the greens. My mother's voice singing a hymn:

> *At the cross where I first saw the light*
> *The burdens of my heart rolled away*
> *It was there by faith that I first received my sight*
> *And now I'm happy all the day.*

Freda. Marky. Mom and me. We're four of us. I'm the man of the house, Mom told me. I'm older than Marky, my younger brother, Marvin. He's a baby, in his crib, wheezing. Still in a diaper. If I stand on tiptoes, if I jump, I can see through the slats to where he's sleeping.

And Freda—my older sister, Alexis Alfreda—she's three years older than I am and she's faster and stronger than I am and thinks she can tell me what to do but I'm the man of the house, I want to tell her. Can't tell *me* to stop jumping, or take off my shoes or get up off the carpet or help Mom in the kitchen. Or she can, and she does, but I'm still the man of the house.

"Jumpin'!" I tell Mom.

We live on the third floor of 50 Beech Street, a brick public housing building called Parkside Gardens. Freda, Marky, and I all share one bedroom, a corner, with windows facing Beech and Laurel and I want to look out them, to see the kids playing in the sandlot across Laurel or roller-skating and riding bikes in the street. Because if Freda won't take me out to play, I can't go by myself, Mom said, 'cause I'm too small—but I want to see out that window so I jump.

And every time I jump, I jump higher.

I rise.

Callie Mae Abney is Mom. She comes from Batesburg, South Carolina, third youngest of fourteen siblings, received her teaching degree from Bettis Academy, married a Batesburg boy: Julius Winfield Erving Sr., my dad, and then they left Batesburg, moved to Chicago, and then Hempstead, Long Island. They had me at Meadowlark Hospital, just two miles from here. My parents divorced when I was three. I've seen my dad about a half-dozen times since. But we live surrounded by family. There's another family of Abneys, my mom's people, right down the hall. There are kids in every apartment, and plenty of them don't have fathers.

Mom doesn't have a teaching credential for New York State, so she cooks and cleans for a family that I never see. She comes home in the afternoon, and then cooks and cleans for us.

Freda and I are in charge when she's gone. Marky stays in his crib. We can't go play until Mom comes back and so we watch TV, *The Little Rascals*, and then finally Mom is back and cooking and she brings out the plates and we say grace and eat, chicken and spinach and beans. I used to be chubby, but now I'm getting longer. My arms and my hands are stretching, my fingers long like Popsicle sticks, and Mom and Freda are talking about school, and I'm going to start school soon, Prospect Elementary, just a mile away, but right now, after we eat and drink our milk, I hear Joe Farmer in the hall. He's two years older than I am and can go outside without anyone, without Freda, and I ask Mom if I can go play after supper because it's still light and she says, "Go on, but stay with Freda and Joe," and we're gone, out the door, down the zigzagging steps. Joe and Freda can jump them but I can only take two at a time, leaping, and then we're down on the ground floor, the concrete entryway with the benches and Joe and Freda are jumping over them onto the lawn and I have to slow down and climb them but soon, I know, I can't wait, soon I'll be jumping them, too.

I will jump everything.

There are at least twenty kids out in front of the building, in the play area with the strange basketball hoop, a metal rim mounted on a pole with three hoops in an inverted pyramid beneath it. The hoop on top is high up, and little kids can only throw a tennis ball through the bottom. Occasionally, I can throw a tennis ball through the top and then it falls and I

Dr. J 5

have to chase it. The bigger kids play basketball on this rim, without a backboard, dribbling in the bald patch of dirt. No out of bounds.

This community is mixed. There's Ray, Richard, and John: they're white kids. And then Joe, Juanita, Sonny Boy, Levi, Cleveland, and the rest of us black kids. We all play together, every game is both black and white and nobody picks teams by white or black or even boy or girl but by who's good and who isn't. Freda is good. She's the fastest kid in the whole project, boy or girl, so she's picked for everything first. I'm fast, I tell the captains. I'm a good jumper. But they say I'm still too small and I never get picked for the real basketball games.

Tonight, though, we're playing Hot Buttered Peas 'cause Joe has got a strap and he says he's gonna hide it and we all have to count. Everyone can play.

"What do I do, Freda?" I ask.

She says, "June, when somebody finds that strap they're gonna say, 'Hot Buttered Peas; come and get your supper,' and you're gonna run fast as you can back to the pole."

She points to our strange hoop.

"You got that?" she says. "You *run*."

It's finally getting dark and the heat of the day breaks, loses its hold, so that it is cool now and we are all huddled near the pole, hands over our eyes or heads leaning against a shoulder in front, like a congregation bowing to a basketball rim. We count. I feel my forehead against Freda's hard shoulder blade, keeping my head pressed at an angle to keep the part on the right side of my hair, and I'm looking down, between her back and my front, to the dirt. Someone is counting. How high?

I can count past ten, but I'm not sure how far past.

And whoever is counting goes way past ten. I follow to

twenty, which I know, and to numbers higher and it takes forever.

"Freda," I whisper. "How long?"

"Shhhh," she says.

Finally, the huddle breaks up and we rise.

"We run?" I ask Freda.

"Nah, June, now we look. We look for the strap." She turns to me, squinting. "Now June. When someone finds it, when someone says, 'Hot Buttered Peas; come and get your supper,' what do you do?"

"When I find it, I'm gonna run!" I tell her.

"June, when *anybody* finds it, you run, okay?"

"I run!"

Everybody is walking all around the front of the projects, combing over the earth clear up to Beech Street. They are looking down at the ground, behind benches, near the swings, in the bushes, behind the garbage cans. But they are also looking around, measuring their distance from each other, from the pole. I wander this way and that, imitating the other kids. But I don't remember what I'm looking for. What does it look like? Who lost it?

I kick at the ground with my Keds, poke my toe at a bottle cap, a rock, part of a nail, a Tootsie Roll wrapper. Someone once found a fossil of a clam in the sandlot across the street, the impression in the stone like the shape left by a spoon in a mound of mashed potatoes. Joe Farmer once found a mouse skeleton, and a quarter. With a quarter you can go to the movies and have enough left to buy pop, popcorn, and Mike and Ikes. Or that's what Freda told me, but I don't understand how the pennies, nickels, dimes, and quarters add up, how you can divide a quarter into smaller parts. I only know that a quarter is the biggest coin, beside a Franklin half-dollar.

"Hot buttered peas! Come get your supper!"

I hear it and it seems like the commotion of everyone running at the same time. There is the patter of sneakered feet against dirt and concrete, of kids leaping over the benches and running. I begin running, too, but too late. Robert, who everyone calls Bo, has the strap and he is swinging it, shouting, whipping kids, stinging their legs. He looks like a pirate waving his cutlass, a cowhand flailing a whip. The kids are shouting as the strap makes a wicked, snipping noise against their pant legs, their backs. He goes easy on a few of the girls, takes care to avoid punishing those boys who might retaliate, and lets the strap fly on those poor little kids like me.

"Come on, get your supper!" he's shouting as he swings.

I stop. I'm the only kid still standing, and between me and the safety of the pole is Bo and his strap. He lifts the whip from a boy's back and turns to see who is left.

No one but me.

"Run, June!" Freda is shouting.

Bo is smiling. "Can't hide, June. Get your supper!"

"Don't wanna."

He swings the strap. "Supper!"

Then he comes toward me.

Bo is older than I am, bigger than I am, and faster than I am. He is stronger than I am, too, and he is looking forward to whipping me.

I see Freda coming toward us. She is going to tell him to leave me alone.

"Freda, don't," I say. I'm the man of the house, I think, and I can't have my sister save me.

She stops, seeming to understand, and now all the kids whose hands are reaching in, touching the pole for safety, are either looking at me and Joe Farmer or are rubbing their backs and behinds where they've been lashed.

Bo smiles and takes a step toward me. I juke left, go right, he swings.

I duck beneath the lash.

I run. He swings again.

I jump.

I rise.

Over the strap, and run to the pole where Freda hugs me safe.

2.

As soon as I can jump high enough to look out that window onto Laurel, I see what everyone is talking about. They are plowing up the sandlot. With each jump, I see the backhoes and diggers and dump trucks. There are rumors about what they are going to build. A swimming pool. An ice rink. A tennis court. A boxing gym.

Mom just shakes her head when I tell her what I hear. What Joe Farmer or Juanita Hayden told me. Joe lives two doors down and he is an only child and he always has every toy as soon as we see it advertised on TV, a GI Joe, Tonka trucks, roller skates that shoot sparks, a Hula-Hoop. Juanita lives across the hall and besides my sister she might be the fastest girl in the projects.

"They're making a park, June, for you to play."

"How long's it gonna be?"

She tells me a few months and I'm disappointed. That sounds like forever. More than today, tomorrow, the day after that, more than until Sunday and church at South Hempstead Baptist Church down the block where my mom is deaconess.

"When they finish the park, we all can play?"

"Of course, June, every child can play there."

Marky is walking around, wheezing, chewing on a blanket. When he breathes, you can hear the inside of his chest crackling, like his lungs are made of paper. I tell him about the new park and how we won't have to walk the mile to go to Kennedy Park anymore. I tell him what I see when I jump.

"Can I play, too?" Marky says.

"'Course," I say. We all can play. There's gonna be an ice cream saloon and a hockey rink and a race car track. Everything a boy could dream of will be in that park. Marky thinks this over, wheezes, nods. "Okay June," then he goes back to chewing on his blanket.

I walk along the wall, beneath the framed photo of Martin Luther King Jr. He's a pastor like W. C. Evans at our church, who reads the psalms to us every Sunday while Freda, Marky, and I sit in the pews and I wear my best jacket, a blue blazer with gold buttons. The church ladies come by and pinch me and Marky, and pat Freda, admiring her fair skin. I'm the darkest and Marky is in between. Freda, if she had to, could pass, is what they say. Pass for what?

But all I think about is the park. We can play football and baseball in the sandlot behind the house, and basketball on the strange rim in front of the projects, but with a park, then we might have a football field with lines on it, or a baseball diamond, or basketball rims with backboards.

I jump again, to look out the window, at the men working

there. They wear yellow hard hats and green uniforms with their sleeves rolled up, black pants, brown boots. They push and pull at levers controlling yellow and green bulldozers and diggers, the mechanical jaws of these machines ripping up the sugar maples and sedge and rush, the ground there I know littered with cigarette butts and broken glass. I've walked the trail in the shade of those maples with Freda, when she's been sent on an errand to borrow a sweater from the Costa family. They have six girls, and plenty of hand-me-downs. When Mom is cooking she'll shout out, "Freda, Freda, go on to Miss Pete's and get a loaf of bread."

Miss Pete's is a store down the path that looks like a house.

And Freda will sigh and get up from the TV and I'll jump up, too, because I want to jump down those stairs with her and we'll go.

That night, though, Freda says she doesn't wanna go. "Evlith is coming on."

Mom chooses me instead.

"June, *you go to Miss Pete's*. We need bread."

She hands me a quarter and I look at her and at Freda, unsure if this is something that I can really do.

"You're the man of the house," Freda says, staring at me with her big hazel eyes.

That's right. I pull on my sweater, put on my sneakers, go out the door, and take off down the stairs, jumping as far as I can but still not reaching the bottom. I turn, jump down some more. Turn, jump. Turn, jump. And then I'm out the door and across Beech and running alongside the idling diggers and dozers, the silent machines still smelling of gas and oil and somehow seeming like sleeping monsters but I'm not afraid. I run. There are a few older kids coming toward me.

"Hey, June."

Dr. J 11

I nod and keep going, crashing over sticks, stumbling in gouges in the ground. Berries grow here in the summer, black and red, and the red are sweeter but the black more common. Trees jut above, the branches pointing skyward in thickets. I run between the trunks like I do grown-ups' legs after church. Those berry bushes will be torn up. Those trees ripped up. Everything. All of it torn, flattened, and the passage of time marked by gone trees, missing berries, a sheared section of high sedge that in summer can hide a boy.

Up ahead I see Miss Pete's, the blue ICE sign, the red and blue Crown Royal poster, and there in the window is Miss Pete, wrapping cheese up in brown paper. Miss Pete's got a mean-ass dog, a little black-and-white mutt that's all growl and snarl and snap. He's usually fenced in, but if he's loose he'll eat your shoe before he lets you into that store. I look both ways. Hound's asleep.

When I run into the store I am blasted by the white light, the smell of bread and pickles and fruit and cheese, the warmth of the interior after the cool of outside, the grown-ups smiling down at me. I pause by the baked goods, studying the cookies and cakes for a moment before remembering my mission. I wander down the aisle and then find the bread and bring it to the counter where Miss Pete stands, her brown eyes behind oval-shaped lenses, like pennies at the bottom of a glass of water, and makes change. I put the coins in my pocket, take the loaf, wrapped and soft, and I run back.

Our building ahead is lit up, the rectangular windows in even rows like boxes of cereal on Miss Pete's shelves, and I plunge back into the woods where the diggers haven't yet dug and above me is the sky and below me is the dark ground and my sneaker sole against the earth is like the slap of a card laid down in the pitty pat card games my mom plays with Uncle Brunson and Aunt Estelle. I breathe, the cool air filling me, and soon, soon I will be faster than Freda and Juanita and Joe Farmer and no one in the projects will be able to catch me.

I look both ways, run across Beech and down the concrete path, beneath the three bare rims and through the ajar glass doors of the entrance of Parkside Gardens and then make the turn and jump.

I make it to the fourth step from the top.

And I turn and jump, turn and jump.

I burst into 3D, into the overwhelming warmth, the smell of something frying, the hot-breath smell of meat roasting and the metal and steam smell of vegetables boiling in a pot. The kitchen blasts with heat, the hiss of gas, sweat coming off Mom's brow, her apron wet with whatever she's wiped off her hands, the pans rattling and sending forth even more heat.

"We're eating soon," Mom says, smiling down. She lifts me, sets me on the counter, takes a cloth and wets it with warm water and wipes my face, my upper lip, picks a bit of leaf out of my hair. "There." She puts a hand over my heart and she detects the hard, fast beating and she smiles. I move my face close to my mom's face, so close I can feel her breath coming out, smell the soapy smell of her skin and the perfume of her hair.

She sets me down.

She gives me a pile of plates that I am to bring out to the yellow-linoleum-topped table under Dr. King's photo. I lean against the chrome legs, which are cool through my pants. "Freda, Marky," I say.

Freda ignores me. Marky looks up.

"Let's eat."

I return to the kitchen, collect forks, spoons, and knives,

cloth napkins, glasses, and a third-full milk bottle. Marky comes over, breathing hard, his face squished and serious. Marky is a sickly child, I've heard Mom tell Uncle Al. If anything is going around, Marky will catch it twice.

Al tells Mom that Tonk, that's my dad, was a sickly child. He grew out of it.

"But the asthma," Mom says. "That's a fright."

Marky comes over, climbs onto a gray cushioned chair. "You wash up?" Freda asks.

Marky shakes his head. I help Marky down, take him by his hot, soft hand to the bathroom where I stand him on the inverted milk crate and pull his arms out so his hands are under the cold water.

I rub the hard rough soap over his hands under the stream, flick a few drops into his face, which makes him flinch, then laugh, and then tell him to dry himself with the brown towel.

Now Mom and Freda are both seated, waiting for us before Mom says the blessing—*As you have provided for us in the past, so you may sustain us throughout our lives, while we enjoy our gifts, we may never forget the needy and those in want. Lord, we thank you—* and we bow our heads and Freda and I look at each other and she rolls her eyes like she does whenever Mom takes too long with the blessing.

Then Freda adds, "And thank Evlith!"

"Hush," Mom says, ladling out the chicken and mashed potatoes. I eat my food in steady bites. We've never missed a meal, never didn't have clean clothes. There's kids who don't get breakfast, kids who wear the same clothes every day. Kids down on Franklin Avenue, in the Wilklow Projects, who are no-food poor. Mom won't let that happen to us. But I know we're not as well off as some. Mom used to take us down to

Hempstead Assistance where we would pick up government cheese, a block of pinkish brown ham, some powdered milk, and she called it the subsidy. But we didn't like the cheese, wouldn't drink the powdered milk, so she said there was no reason to keep going back.

Mom says there are holes everywhere. Everyone's got a hole in their life somewhere, missing something, someone who's not there, some soul gone up to heaven and left behind a hole. We have a hole, I think, and that's Tonk, my dad, who's not here, who lives with Uncle Al, only we don't see him as much as we do Uncle Al. But we don't compare ourselves, we're not trying to copy anyone else's life because we have us four. Freda. Marky. Mom. Me. Look at how we're all growing so fast. Especially me.

"June, you're gonna be taller than I am before you know it," Mom says.

The man of the house. I'm getting longer and longer.

Jumping higher and higher.

We clear the kitchen, pile the plates by the sink in a teetering castle of white enamel, silverware threatening to slide off the top, empty milk glasses standing guard. Freda has pulled the milk crate into the kitchen and she stands next to Mom, whose slippered feet are on the braided cloth rug. Mom is washing, steam rising up from the sink, and Freda is in a hurry, grabbing each plate out of Mom's hand and running the dishcloth over it too quickly, so that one of the plates slips and crashes into the sink, and the shatter causes Marky to yelp.

"Freda!" Mom shouts.

Freda is rushing because of Evlith.

I don't know who or what Evlith is, but it's on *The Ed Sullivan Show* tonight and Freda has been talking about it all day

Dr. J   15

and Marky and I are excited because Freda is so excited, but now she dropped a plate, smashed it in the sink, and Mom is shaking her head, angry at Freda, and I wonder if she's going to take the belt to Freda like she does me when she's angry at me but, no, Freda doesn't get hit, she stands there quiet and still as Mom collects the shards piece by piece and drops them in the white metal bin by the Frigidaire.

We all gather around the TV. Freda, Marky, and I sit on the rug, watching some children's choir sing, and Marky and I are wondering what Freda was so excited about and we ask, "That's Evlith?"

I still have my lisp.

"No!" Freda says. "That's not Elvis."

After the children in their gray robes shuffle off, Ed Sullivan comes back on and he introduces the next act and this man comes on in a slick suit, with a guitar strapped around his neck, and he starts singing, and there's the sound of girls screeching underneath him and even Freda starts screaming and Marky and I turn to see her and she jumps up, and while Elvis is wobbling back and forth, swinging his hips around, Freda goes up and kisses the TV screen.

3.

At home I'm June, short for Junior. Outside the house I'm June or Jule.

Julius Winfield Sr. walks with me, my hand in his big hand, his fingers wrapped all the way around my wrist. He wears a green cap, a mechanic's uniform, blue with oil stains, a patch on his chest, cuffed pant legs above black work shoes with soft soles. He says that when the new park is done, he'll play ball with me, and dominoes, and teach me Tonk, his favorite game, a card game popular in South Carolina where he grew up.

"And they call you Tonk!" I say.

He nods, smiles down at me. "Yes they do."

Tonk. Tonk. Tonk. I roll the word around in my mouth. That's Daddy.

"I'm the man of the house," I tell Daddy.

He shrugs. Something about what I've said seems to make him unhappy and his expression goes stern.

We are walking toward Hempstead Village, where we are going to get haircuts, my first in a real barbershop.

"Have to look sharp to feel sharp," Daddy says.

I nod.

"I can jump three steps," I tell him. "I can jump out of the swings. I'm the fastest boy. I can jump over the benches." The last part isn't true, but I want it to be true so much that it feels true.

He looks down at me again. His smile is back. "Your momma could jump. Played ball at Bettis Academy back in South Carolina. Callie could play."

I've seen a photograph of my mother, seated at the front of a group of black women in basketball uniforms. Mom is in the center holding the ball, a serious expression on her face.

"How's Marky doin'?" Dad asks.

I shrug. "Wets the bed. He's wheezy."

"Boy has the asthma," Daddy says.

I nod, trying to look thoughtful.

I'm proud to be with my daddy; I want everyone to see.

We're out of the projects, walking down the hill where the bigger kids race soapbox derby cars, and then I jump up on the curb and we are walking down Peninsula toward the Calderone and Rivoli, the movie theaters where for a quarter we can see the movies, even the Elvis movies my sister likes, and then Robert Hall, and then we are at the barber where my father puts me in a seat and a white cloth is thrown around my chest and neck and my father tells the barber to cut my hair so there's a part in it down the right side. The smell of menthol and camphor is so strong I can feel it in my eyes, a stinging, and the sound of the scissors swishing is like sword fights in a movie, and I close my eyes as he trims above my forehead and I turn and I see my father, his cap off, smiling, trying to make the barber laugh at something. He turns to me, and he looks at me serious and stern, and then winks.

The barber brushes the back of my neck with powder that smells sweet like soap and I try to see how I look different with my new side-parted hair. I had imagined a change, and that a more grown-up boy would be in the mirror, but looking back is the same me who walked in. I glance at the men in the barbershop, cigarettes sending up ribbons of smoke, collars opened at the necks revealing gold chains and crosses. A fat man chews gum and looks at a newspaper. There are magazines in a stack near the entrance, brightly colored illustrations of soldiers and sailors and athletes on the covers.

Daddy pays the barber a half-dollar and then says he is going to get Mom some groceries, and takes me into the Grand Union where he lets me pick out a box of animal crackers that I struggle to open and Tonk finally reaches down and opens for me while we walk around the store, gathering milk, bacon, potatoes, bread, butter. He carries the two large sacks in his long arms, his hands bearing the weight under each bag, a smile on his face. I am proud. I have heard Mom complain to her pitty pat friends that Tonk doesn't pull his weight, doesn't contribute enough to his kids, loses his money playing cards. But here he is, with two bags of groceries and Mom will have to let him in now, not lock the door the way she sometimes does when Dad comes over and wants to see us, shouting through the door, "You don't give us nothing, nothing. You can't see them."

And Marky and me crying to Mom to let Dad in.

And one time he climbed down from the roof to our window ledge, tapping at it so we would let him in. He crawled inside and hugged us both and said, "Don't tell Mom I'm here." Mom heard us in there laughing and came in and told him, "You had your fun, now get out."

We climb the hill to Parkside Gardens and he's humming a song and I try to make out the tune but I can't and he smiles down at me and I tell him, "Dad, when we get to the Gardens I'm gonna show you something."

He nods.

Here is what I want to show him. I am going to sit in the swings, and pump myself up higher and higher, and then Geronimo out as far as I can. I can already jump higher and farther than any other boys my age. Dad sets down his groceries, shakes out a cigarette, and lights it, nodding.

"So let's see June, let's see."

I pump my legs and the swing rises back and forth and I climb higher than I've ever gone, higher than anyone has ever gone, as high as you can go and not flip over the entire swing set, and at the highest point I jump, both sneakered feet in front of me, my hands in the air. I jump as high and as far as any child in the history of the world, so far that my father's cigarette stops midair in his hand on its way to his lips and his mouth drops open because he can't believe how far I can jump.

4.

One morning Mom doesn't go to work. She says, "Get up, we goin' to Batesburg," and I rub my eyes and Marky begins jumping up and down in his bed and Freda sniffs his diaper to see if he peed and then says, "Good, Marky, you're dry."

Mom was up late last night, the kitchen hot from the oven and pots of frying oil as she prepared chicken and biscuits in a pile I could stick my arm in up to my elbow. She's already packed three suitcases, one for each of us, and told us we don't need much more because it's summer and we won't hardly wear nothing playing in the dirt next to Gilbert and Bertha's house. We washed up quickly, and Marky and Freda ate a boiled egg and I had cereal and Mom told us to go to the kitchen and grab some empty pop bottles to pee in on the way.

"I don't like stopping," she said.

She takes a tin pot filled with chicken and then comes back for another filled with biscuits and then the three of us follow, Freda carrying her and Marky's suitcases while I carry my own. We climb into the blue Oldsmobile 98 and Mom noses it out onto Beech and says, "It's summer, time for seeing family."

She drives, angry at every stop for the time we are losing, the money pouring into the gas tank, the sodas we demand because we are parched from chicken and biscuits. She doesn't want us drinking too much because then we'll want to stop some more. She says, "Save the bottles for the car," so we don't have to stop.

She tries finding side ways and stone bridges and cat roads, making failed attempts to skip tolls, but this ends up with us lost on back roads and I have to pee so bad I pull it out and fill up a bottle and toss it out of the car. Then Marky tries the same thing but pees on the seat and himself and looks at me, shaking his head, begging me not to say nothing about it to Freda or Mom and I keep it quiet and Marky sits in his own pee until Mom sniffs it and says, "Might as well stop."

"Marky wet himself."

We don't have air-conditioning and the cities pass on the radio dial in crackles and screeches as we slide down Route 1, Newark, Elizabeth, New Brunswick, Trenton, and then into Pennsylvania where we pick up Uncle James Simpear Abney, or Simp, and Aunt Margaret, who will share the driving with Mom and who hates stopping just as much. Simp takes a look at me and nods his head.

"Growing big!" he says to Mom.

"Chicken?" she offers.

Simp takes the wheel in one hand and in the other manages to hold a thigh piece while he fiddles with the dial till he finds a station playing the Platters' "Twilight Time."

"Is this Evlith?" I ask.

"Elvis!" Freda shouts. "With an S. And no!"

We make this drive every summer, and every summer, at some point in the drive, Mom and whoever she's sharing the driving with become real quiet because they say we are passing a certain line.

"The Mason-Dixon Line," says Mom.

Dr. J

Below this line colored folks were slaves.

And I know from previous visits that below this line is where we can't use the same bathroom as white people or drink from the same water fountains or even eat at the same restaurants. In Hempstead, we can eat wherever we want and pee in all the same bathrooms. My school, Prospect Elementary, is half-white and half-black and the only rule is boys can't go into the girls' bathroom, which my friend Archie Rogers once did on a dare but that I told him he shouldn't do, because, well, that's the rules.

Where we live, white kids and black kids play together. Down around my grandma's house in Batesburg, we never see a white child.

We follow Route 1 all the way through Maryland, Virginia, North Carolina, deeper and deeper south through hot, buggy air that leaves our windshield splattered with carcasses. We sleep in fits, our mouths dry and hanging open, waking up when we feel a bug stuck to our tongues or when the thirst is so powerful that separating our tongues from the roof of our mouths makes a sound like an STP sticker coming off a school notebook. An afternoon. A sunset. And then the road signs coming up out of the night, the leaping red Mobilgas horse, the inviting orange roof of a Howard Johnson's, the walking bear in nightcap of a roadside motel, and then crossing into North Carolina a sign that says WELCOME TO KLAN COUNTRY.

Mom and Simp stop at the shoulder to switch seats, us kids climbing out to pee and then quickly back in, the operation as efficient as a pit crew.

"When we gonna get there?"

"Soon," Mom says, "morning."

Freda sleeps. Marky sleeps. I sleep.

The car pulls up onto the tall grass in front of Gilbert and Bertha Abney's and the bump of the car over dirt and rocks wakes us all and we can see Gilbert sitting on the porch and standing and waving and here are my cousins, Bobby and Vincent and Shirley, and there's Uncle Melvin and Melvin Jr. and Aunt Chloe and her kids Charles and Cynthia, and we emerge from the car, smelling of chicken and exhaust. The summer sun is high and we are surrounded, hands and fingers rubbing our hair, men picking us up, women giving us hugs, dogs barking and sniffing at us and getting their noses into the pot where the chicken had been.

"Look at you, June!" Uncle Melvin says. "You taller than Bobby!"

Bobby is Lucinda's boy, he's a year younger than I am, and whenever we come down here, he's who I run with.

"You playing ball, June?" Bobby asks.

I nod.

"What?"

"Football, basketball, baseball," I tell him. "I play anything."

They made a park near our house, I tell Bobby, a big park with a clubhouse where we can check out balls and bats and roller skates and whatever we want.

"Bobby, watch out," Freda says. "June is fast. The boy can run."

"And jump!" I add.

Gilbert and Bertha's house is yellow and brown, the foundation resting on cinder blocks. A whole mess of chickens live in coops in the shade under the house. In back is a copse of dogwood and beech trees that we run through and play cowboys and Indians, Bobby showing us how to take a mop handle and turn it into a cowboy horse by tying string around it for the reins. He takes me fishing by the pond where we sit on the sloped bank and cast over water lilies and cattails. We catch bass and perch that Bobby shows me how to kill by taking the tail and thumping it against a flat rock. Crows watch us from the crook in the dogwoods, their feathers so black they're reflective. My grandma breads the fish in flour and fries them and we eat in the backyard, our hands greasy and tasting of our own sweat and the pond water.

Our days are unbroken by the intrusion of school or work or schedule. Mom visits all day with her brothers and sisters, processions of relatives driving up from Atlanta or down from Chicago or over from Ward, and the women sit and drink iced tea while the men smoke and drink whiskey. Nobody pays us kids more mind than every now and then pointing out how the heat doesn't seem to bother us.

Bobby's one of my favorite cousins. He's dark skinned with short hair and a squeaky voice. He's the youngest of four, with two brothers and a sister, so when I visit he likes for me to tag along with him the way he's always tagging along with his older siblings. But this year, when we play basketball on the dirt court in front of Melvin's, I can dribble right past Bobby. And I can outjump him.

Bobby takes out a baseball and a bat and says, "Here, I'll pitch you a few." I can barely hit the ball out of the driveway and Bobby laughs and says, "See, Junior, you ain't better than me at everything."

We get a dollar from Mom and Aunt Lucinda and walk two miles into Batesburg with Freda. We walk past a drugstore and I tell Bobby I want to get a cold Coke and he reminds me we can't go in there.

"Whites only," Bobby says.

And Freda and I become real quiet because this doesn't seem right or fair and then, when some white people come walking down the street, Bobby pulls me by the arm and tells me to cross.

"Why do we have to cross the street?" I ask.

"Don't want no trouble," Bobby says.

"What's the trouble? We're walking."

"White people'n black people don't mix," Bobby says. "That's how it is."

I tell Bobby, "I got white friends in Hempstead. There's Ray, Richie, John, Miss Pete's boy."

"I think white people are devils," Bobby says. "Don't mean nothing but evil for colored folks."

I nod, but I don't understand.

Freda shrugs. We buy Cokes from a gas station vending machine. A machine can't tell the difference between black and white.

"Why is it like that?" I ask Mom, but she says, like Bobby, that's just how it is. "There's folks trying to change it," Mom says, "like Dr. Martin Luther King Jr."

His picture hangs in our hall, over our dining table.

"But that's why we don't live here," she says.

"Bobby says white people are the devil," I tell her.

"June, all people are the same," Mom tells me. "Black. White. We're all the same. There's good and bad people among white and black. You remember that."

I tell Bobby what Mom says. "Good and bad. White and black."

Bobby runs in and hits me on the side of the head and says I'm it and goes running off again, into the woods. I catch him.

My cousins have been bragging about me. Telling their neighbors up and down Batesburg that June from New York is faster than any kid down here. My cousins hatch an idea without telling me. They set a race against this older boy, a running back for the local middle school. He's built like a man with a big chest and thick arms and he's got facial hair on his upper lip. They're calling him the Manimal.

Fifty yards down this trail, Bobby is telling me, that's all. "I seen you, June. You're faster than him."

"He looks like a freight train," I tell Bobby.

"June, he's big, not fast."

We line up. They shout, "Go."

All I see is dust. The Manimal tears off ahead of me. I don't even run. I'm just standing there.

"June, what the hell is that?"

I shrug. I'm frightened.

"We set this up because we know you can get him."

"Get him? I don't ever wanna see that dude again."

Bobby loses his money.

5.

Time steals in. One moment, I'm dreaming about playing in the new park and jumping up to see over the sill and the next I can stand flat on my feet and look out the window at the completed park, the basketball court with six hoops so that you can play two small games simultaneously or run one big game the long way. I can jump up four steps, then five, then up the whole half-flight. I leap the benches and my toe catches, tumbling me to the grass. Then I leap again and I clear them. I can barely get a ball up through the top of the round rim in front of the project and then I begin shooting on the new baskets in the park and I never shoot on that strange little rim again.

I like Prospect Elementary. We have a gym where we can play ball and a field where we can play football. And every day, we play. In the fall we play football and in the winter we play basketball and in the spring we play baseball and my best friend is Archie and we try to be on the same team if we can. We talk about how far we can jump and how fast we can run and Archie admits that I'm the fastest runner and highest jumper, but I can't hit a baseball and Archie can.

Class is all about sitting behind a desk, next to girls like Sharon, and we sometimes share a book if she forgets hers and we sit so close that my leg is against hers and she smiles at me. But I have trouble talking to girls. I can talk to Freda, but the girls in my class, the girls in the projects, I don't know what to say to them so sometimes I just run past them rather than have to stop and talk. I am embarrassed about my lisp. I don't raise my hand. But I can sound out every word I read, and the teacher, Mr. Hairston, even tells me, "Julius, I'm sending a note home to your momma," and I worry about it, but all it says is that I'm doing fine and would it be okay with my mom if I could mow his lawn on Sundays. He says he'll pay me five bucks.

I do my homework every day. Some kids in the building don't like school, don't do their work. Lorenzo Knight, Sonny Boy, doesn't do his homework. He hollers up to me from the street for help and I fill out the answers on a piece of paper and then toss it down, but the next day in class, he's still empty handed. While I'm at my desk I can see the kids beginning to play in the park across the street, the first pickup games on the sideways courts, kids lining up to be chosen, a game begins, and from where I sit I can hear the dribble, the bank off the wood, the thunk of ball on rim. I force myself to concentrate on my homework. Mom says if I do my homework first, then I can play. I have to keep quiet in class. I must go to school. I should respect my elders.

I stand by the rules, move with care and respect and wariness, and agree to abide by the penalties of failure and rewards of success. Despite what I have seen in the Jim Crow South, the injustice that makes Bobby hate, and even the violence of our own Parkside Gardens, where even as a child I can get a sense that some lives just aren't valued as highly as others, I seek shelter in the security of rules, the snugness of being tucked into a line, of being a number in a column rather than a soul out of place, alone.

I enjoy rules, and games have rules. A basketball court has rules and order and laws and requirements; it is regulated. I like that aspect of it: the predictability of a universe, the basketball court, the football field, where we are all set in motion by the same strictures and standards. My basket is worth no more or less than yours.

Finally, my homework completed, I can slide on my sneakers and run out to join my peers, Marky trailing after me. There is Archie and Juanita and Juanita's brother Rob and Joe and Cleveland and Levi. They've already signed out the ball from the park attendant and we line up to choose and I'm one captain and Archie is the other and we pick and I pick Juanita. She's a girl but she can dribble and cut faster than most of the boys. Archie chooses Levi and then I choose Marky, because otherwise short and wheezy Marky won't be selected. We play five on five, short court, Juanita bringing the ball up and then, maybe because she's a girl, she doesn't shoot but instead passes it and in this game, everyone else shoots as soon as they get the ball. But, and this is astonishing, I notice beneath Juanita's T-shirt an up-and-down motion, two budding breasts bobbing, the sight mesmerizing and immediately causing every boy who guards Juanita to focus his glare at her chest instead of the ball, allowing Juanita to dribble with ease past boys who are slower-footed anyway. And even when I'm playing defense or pushing someone out of the way for a rebound, I can't get that image of the movement beneath Juanita's T-shirt out of my mind. It causes me to not only look at her differently, but to see the world differently, as if there were now two worlds: the one all around us and the one bobbing beneath Juanita's T-shirt.

We play hundreds of games and score thousands of points, we play until balls are worn bald and then the black rubber bladder beneath the leather tumors and bubbles, dribbling so often and furiously that my hands become dirtier than the court and when there is snow on the ground we take shovels to clear the court and when there are puddles we splash through them. We play in winter, spring, summer, fall, in the afternoon and the night and the morning on Saturday and after church on Sunday. I gather millions of rebounds. Launch millions of shots. Block millions of attempts. I am long, but not the longest on the court, strong but not the strongest, but what I have is a powerful and easily observed love for the game. I admire the rules, the ledger of points that add up in my head on each side, the simplicity of makes or misses. I will play by myself, one-on-one, two-on-two, or a million on a million, and I will keep playing until I hold the court and can say, "Next."

One afternoon, after I've been playing, I come inside and Mom tells me to go into my room and pack because we have to drive back down south, now, tonight.

"But it's not summer," I say.

"Bobby died," Momma says.

He slipped down the embankment into the lake where he used to fish. Bobby couldn't swim.

"Where do people go?" I ask Mom, but I know her answer is heaven. I can't see that or feel that. All I know are the holes they leave behind.

6.

Basketball is my favorite game, but in the fall we play football. Archie and I will play one-on-one in the sandlot on the other side of the projects from the park, punting to each other and then returning the kick. John Mackey of the Syracuse Orangemen and later the Baltimore Colts went to Hempstead High, he was a Hempstead Tiger, and our dream is to play for Hempstead and be Tigers. We're evenly matched, Archie and I; we score hundreds of touchdowns.

On cold autumn days the projects empty out and boys and girls troop to the sandlot and we can play five-on-five or nine-on-nine. I'm usually quarterback and Archie is wide receiver and we play until streetlights come on and our parents are shouting our names and then we say, "Next touchdown wins!" and it will be me throwing a high, long one to Archie who runs under it and spikes the ball like John Mackey.

But one afternoon when we're playing in the sandlot and Archie is playing quarterback and I'm wide receiver, he throws a short pass to me, at the edge of the dirt, where the pavement begins, and I catch it and then my sneakers slide out from under me on the dry dirt covering the pavement and I fall forward, my right knee dragging behind me through broken shards of glass.

I sit up and look at my knee and I can see, through the pulses of blood, something aspirin white.

"You ripped up," Archie says, bending over me.

I pull off my sneaker and slide off my sock and wrap it around my knee and try to stand and can't put any weight on it, blood is streaming down my leg, and I hop around across the street and around the building and then up three flights to our apartment where my mom opens the door.

"I fell, I cut it," I tell her. "I can see into my knee."

Mom's eyes get wide and she begins breathing hard and that's the first time I become frightened because I can see that Mom is scared. "Oh, June."

She sits me down on a dining room chair and squints at the cut. She goes into the kitchen for rubbing alcohol and comes back and pours it over my knee, trying to dab with a cotton swab, but I jerk so hard and start screaming and knock over a chair. Marky comes running out of his room and now he starts crying. Mom is shaking her head and carries me downstairs and loads me into the 98 to take me to Doc Richards and he takes a look at my knee and says I have to go to Meadowbrook Hospital, where I was born.

"Is it bad?" Mom asks him.

He shrugs. "He's torn something."

The hospital smells like soap and alcohol, and while I am sitting in the emergency ward, I pass out waiting for the doctor, and when I wake up, it is with a doctor telling me don't worry, they're going to numb my right knee and then they are going to operate. My ligaments have been torn clean through, severed, and I need surgery to put them back together. Otherwise, I won't even be able to stand up.

"Where's Mom?" I ask.

"She's in the waiting room."

"You have to cut me open?"

"We have to put your knee back together."

"So I can jump?"

The doctor is now making marks on my knee with a black marker. He tells me to lie down and that I will feel a little prick, and when I wake up my mom will be there.

I wake up stitched. Mom is in the room, and Freda and Marky, and they are all smiles and Mom keeps saying, "Oh, June, we thought you'd lose your leg."

I look down. My leg is still there.

"But can I jump?"

She shakes her head. "You're gonna be in a cast. Doctor says you may have a limp for, well, for a long time."

"Limp?" That can't be. I'm going to be a Hempstead Tiger, a football and a basketball player. I can't do that if I'm . . . limping. If I can't jump. If I can't run.

"Can I play ball?"

"First you gotta walk," Mom says.

7.

I am fitted with a cast from my ankle to my hip and when I walk it is with a straight-legged limp so that everyone calls me Peg Leg. I sit with Marky in our room and I watch everyone else playing basketball in Campbell Park and worry that I will never be able to jump or run again. I can see Archie guarding Juanita and Sonny Boy shooting and I want to be on the court running instead of here, with my leg in a cast and the doctors telling me they don't know if I will ever be able to run again.

"The fastest boy," I tell the doctor when he checks on my knee. "Only my sister was faster and I was almost catching her."

He doesn't respond. "Get some rest, and then when the cast comes off, we'll see if you can walk."

Walk? No. I'm going to run.

"Oh, June," Mom says, hugging me to her when we are back home. "I know you wanna run—"

"Jump!"

"—jump, but maybe it's not meant for you."

"What do you mean?"

She turns away. And I can see Freda in the kitchen, spreading peanut butter on bread for Marky and she's staring down and not looking at me.

"I'm gonna jump," I tell her.

I'm determined. I limp to my room and lie down. On the dresser across from me are photos—of Tonk, of Bobby, of my grandparents. I want to tell someone that this doesn't make sense, this isn't fair. I haven't done anything wrong, I did my homework, paid attention in school, listened to my mom and big sister, and never stole anything or knocked the heads off parking meters the way I've seen some kids in the neighborhood do as they searched for change. I looked out for Marky and younger kids. My life has been orderly. I've followed the rules. Yet here, in my knee, is this betrayal.

And there was Bobby, who did no wrong, and he fell in a lake and drowned. I don't understand.

"June, June." I hear Marky's voice and he comes up beside my bed. "June, I think you'll jump again."

"Thanks, Marky."

"Even higher. You'll jump even higher." Marky nods. "I know it."

I smile at Marky. I believe him.

I watch basketball, from the window where in the afternoon I pay more attention to how older kids are playing. In the early evening, the court is taken over by high schoolers and grown men. They run us off the court. Sometimes, when they are short a man or two, they let me and Archie play with them. We're the only kids who can occasionally run in the grown-up games, to play under the lights, and I know it's because I can jump. Could jump.

I watch them from my window and I see how the men play. They sweep the ball down from the rim and begin dribbling up court in one motion. They seldom pass, not on this court, and the action really begins after a shot is put up, with men pushing and banging and leaping for rebounds and loose balls. The game is played primarily from the basket to the foul line, a scrum for the ball from which a player will emerge with the basketball as if he's starving and it's a loaf of bread. Then he will turn, launch another shot, and the battle reboots. The game lacks . . . charm, grace. It is a war of attrition, of hard-fought baskets. When there is a player with a good shot or ball-handling skills, the game changes, it opens up as players move away from the basket or leave men open to slow down the fast, skillful dribbler. But I notice something else, in this game where few players pass: those who get the ball more than anyone else are those who can rebound the ball themselves, not those who battle in the scrum for the ball but those who take the ball from the rim. If you can get the ball yourself, I realize, you will always have plenty of shots.

I tune in to watch a young black player in the NBA who starred in college at Seattle University and led his team all the way to the NCAA finals before losing to Adolph Rupp and his all-white Kentucky Wildcats. Elgin Baylor would be drafted by the Minneapolis Lakers and, to an even greater degree than his fellow superstars Bill Russell and Wilt Chamberlain, would give me an idea of how basketball could look effortless and beautiful. Elgin taking the rebound and dribbling through traffic is something that I begin doing in my feverish daydreams as I wait three months for that cast to be removed. I feel myself leaping—and taking the rebound and then dribbling downcourt and leaping—rising!—for a layup. I see the movement, reenact it in my mind, and I can't explain to anyone, not Marky, not Freda, not Mom why this excites me but I see it somehow as liberating, the black body moving through white bodies, and the self-sufficiency of the act. For the first time, I have this idea that certain ways of playing basketball are more beautiful than other ways. That there is scoring, putting the ball in the basket, but also the artistry of how that scoring is done. This is a new idea, an idea I have never heard spoken aloud: that some basketball players *look* better than other basketball players because of the way they play.

I want to look better.

But now I can only dream. I can't play.

8.

Finally, we go back to the doctor and he saws off my cast and I cry when I see my right leg: shrunken, pale, scarred.

"It has atrophied," the doctor says. "It's natural."

I can barely walk. With the doctor's assistance, I hobble across the linoleum floor while holding on to the medical bench.

The doctors are pleased by the surgery, proclaiming it a success.

"But I can't walk," I say.

"It takes time. Twelve weeks in a cast, the body now has to adjust."

There is no recovery plan, no physical therapy. Just a follow-up appointment two weeks later for another X-ray.

I grow so tired walking from the doctor's office to the car that Freda has to help me. At home, looking at myself in a mirror, my spindly leg next to my good one, I start to cry.

But Marky won't let me feel any self-pity.

"June, come on, we'll take a walk. I got a dime. Let's go to Miss Pete's, get some Mike and Ikes."

I can't run, I can't jump. All I can do is walk, and climb steps, and Marky walks me back to strength, telling me he needs me because if I'm not on the court then he doesn't get picked for any games.

Marky walks with me until I can run. Then I begin jumping the steps again, two steps, then three, then four, but I don't feel the same spring, the same sense that every jump will be farther than the last. I jump from the swings. I can still land with both feet stuck, but I am reluctant to jump as high as before. I hesitate. I am cautious. Whereas before I never could imagine being hurt, now all I can imagine are the many ways I can injure myself. My knee wobbles when I land, my right leg bows when I come down hard on it.

I had been the fastest kid on the block. I had been proud of that fact, boasted of it to whoever would listen, and now I'm not even fast enough for the pickup games in the park.

Marky prodding me, I limp over to the basketball court and take my place in the line, a captain no more. First pick no more. Archie takes a chance and chooses me and I begin running, but the game doesn't feel the same to me. I am wary, reluctant. I try to imagine myself going up for a ball the way Elgin Baylor does, but I don't have the spring off my right foot so I have to switch and rise from my left.

I think about my playing style, about Elgin Baylor. I do everything with two hands, he does everything with one. But look at my hands. If I hold them up to Archie's, Freda's, even Mom's, mine dwarf theirs. I have big hands, not yet big enough to play with one hand.

Every day I'm playing, I'm getting stronger. And running up and down those steps. I used to be able to jump down all seven steps, but now, with my weak right leg, I'm afraid to take flight, but after just two weeks without the cast, I do it, I jump down, taking off from my left leg, and I turn, and I jump again. The real goal is to rise up, to jump *up* the seven steps, and I couldn't even do that before my injury.

I ride the swings again. I jump. I land. Both legs, firmly planted. Most of the other kids, I notice, don't know how to land. They fall forward, tip over sideways.

When I go back to Dr. Richards, he bends my right knee, twists it, and nods. "Julius, we put a spring in there. You're going to be stronger than ever."

I smile. A spring!

My scar runs up and down my right knee, a pale puff of skin that goes against the grain of the darker flesh.

Dr. Richards smiles. "Your right knee will never be as strong as your left."

"Oh no," I say.

Dr. J

"But you can be just as strong."

I nod. I can be stronger! Jump higher!

At Prospect Elementary, I'm playing on the basketball team, for coach Bill Zaruka. We play in a low-ceilinged gym on eight-foot rims, in a converted coal bin, so even though I'm still just five foot and a few inches, I can time the ball coming off the rim and go up and grab it with two hands. I play effectively, my right knee hardly a hindrance. My teachers and classmates seem to acknowledge that I'm a good athlete, chosen first for most sports, and, just a few months out of my cast, I'm the best high jumper in the school on field day.

9.

In school after lunch one afternoon, they shuffle us into the auditorium and show us *The Jackie Robinson Story*, and I am able to make the connection between what he did and where I am right now. He was the first "Negro" to play major league baseball, which before Jackie was as segregated as South Carolina, with black players and white players in different leagues. And because of Jackie, we now have black players in every professional sport and at most colleges. He becomes our hero, and I tell Archie about going south, about how they have different drinking fountains, bathrooms, about separate but not equal. We are black. For the first time, the burden of that identity settles on us, and we understand that this means the path is a little harder for us, but if Jackie could do it, then so can we.

When we play ball in the park that afternoon, as we do every afternoon, the three best players are Archie, Juanita, and me. My knee is healing. I am strong. I can back my way down close to the basket where I wait for Juanita—perhaps the only child in the playground who thinks about passing before shooting—who can put the ball into my hands in such a way that I am ready to turn and shoot. Nobody else can do what Juanita can: make the game seem simple.

We hold the court all afternoon.

A white man stands behind the fence, watching us. He wears a cloth coat and a wool cap. When we are done and slipping on our jackets, he approaches Archie and me.

"Would you boys like to play for the Salvation Army?"

We've heard of the Sal. It's like an all-star team for kids. Some of the better white athletes at the school play there.

Archie and I both nod. "We have to ask our parents."

"I'm Don, Don Ryan." He holds his hands out. "You're Julius. And Archie."

He says that Andy Hagerty, who manages the park clubhouse, told him there were a couple of promising kids playing in the park. He's been watching us and he thinks we could help the team.

"But the Sal is for white kids," Archie says.

"Not anymore," says Don.

We're going to be the first black kids to play for the Hempstead Salvation Army Team.

Juanita is sliding on her hooded sweatshirt beside us, quiet.

I run home, I jump, and, springing from my left leg, I rise up the seven steps.

I'm excited. I want to tell my mom about the white man,

about how Archie and I are going to play for the Sal. All she has to do is take me down to the Salvation Army after school to tell Don it's all right and then I can practice with—

When I run inside, Mom is sitting at the table, holding a telegram.

"We have to go south," she says. "Your father, he passed."

I go into my room and notice that some of my pencils and pens are messed up. I try to put things in order.

1.

Tonk had been hit by a car, his leg broken and set in a cast like mine. He was living with Uncle Al and then in an apartment in Queens.

According to Uncle Al, he cut the cast off himself before the wound was properly healed. The leg became infected and soon gangrene set in. He said the gangrene caused a heart attack. Did Tonk go to the hospital? Was he alone when he died? Who found him? Nobody tells me. The body has already been shipped south to his family, the Ervings, and we make the long drive down to pay our last respects. When Mom inquires about the will and Tonk's life insurance, she is met with shrugs and silence. He leaves us nothing but a hole. A hole that was already there. A hole where a daddy should have been. He never took me out and taught me how to fish or how to play catch with a couple of gloves and a ball. He never grabbed my hand and walked me through a parking lot or taught me how to ride a bike. He never stood behind me when I was getting bullied so I could say I'm going to tell my dad. I never even knew that's what dads did.

But I feel sorry for him, not for myself. There are so many

kids in the projects who don't even know who their daddy is, so at least I knew mine. And with his passing, I say to Marky, even had Daddy been raising us, he wouldn't be raising us anymore. So his passing isn't anything we should feel sorry for.

Marky frowns and thinks this over. He remembers Tonk even less than I do, since Tonk was gone within months of Marky being born.

"I'm the man of the house," I tell Marky.

"Me, too," Marky says, a cough coming on so that he doubles over.

We're watching television, President Kennedy on the screen, and they are replaying the inspiring words about asking not what our country can do for us.

It's always just us, I tell Marky, always us.

We're growing, we're all growing. Beautiful Freda is almost in high school, a young woman, pale skinned, like Lana Turner in a movie we watch at the Rivoli, *Imitation of Life*, about a black girl who can pass and who starts dating a white boy. Marky has a long chin, thick lips, broad nose, sharp brown eyes, and parted brown hair. He's always observing, watching, and I am already aware of how he looks up to me, but also of how he is different from me. He is not an athlete, and even in his style of dress, he has a more formal manner, preferring leather lace-up shoes to sneakers and wearing his Easter jacket to school whenever Mom will let him. He shuns some of the more physical games we play, the tackle football on the sandlot or the roller hockey that can rip up knees. But despite his sickliness, his wheezing and coughing, he will run out after me when I head to the courts or the football field.

Marky even tags along on the afternoon when Mom takes me to the Hempstead Salvation Army on Atlantic Avenue to meet with Don Ryan, the young man who oversees the Salvation Army sports programs. Archie and his mom, Daisy, join us, too. We pass through the brick chapel and then into the gym, and I look around and then at Marky who smiles because this is a real gym, with shiny wood floors and the Salvation Army shield painted at half-court. The baskets hang from fan-shaped metal backboards and the rims have nets. The ceiling is high enough to shoot an arcing jump shot, not the line drives we have to shoot at Prospect Elementary.

Don, who wears a wool jacket, khakis, and white tennis shoes, explains to Mom that he thinks we'll be good additions to the team sports program. He's old. He's nineteen. He also coaches football and baseball, but basketball is his passion.

"It's not just their size and athleticism," Don says. "It's their character."

And by character he means that he thinks we are mentally tough enough to handle this fraught opportunity of being the first black kids on the team. The Sal charges a twenty-dollar facility and equipment fee, which Don says he'll pay.

It is a real team, with uniforms and a schedule of games all around Long Island. First, we have to make the travel squad, which takes a few practices before it becomes clear that Archie and I are two of the best players out there. The Sal has some good ones: the Conroy boys, tough Irish brothers named Jackie, Terry, Jo-Jo, and Davey, a smooth shooter named Tommy Brethal, and scrappy defenders Craig and Gary Black. Archie and I are about five foot six, so we're among the taller players on the team. The main adjustment is playing according to Don's system. He likes for Archie and me to go down low and sweep the boards, passing the ball out to Terry and Tommy and then running up the floor to rebound on the offensive end. Archie is a better ball handler than I am, so sometimes he catches the ball on the break and gets the layup. I'm still a step slower, recovering from my knee injury, but what I lack in speed I make up for with my ups. I can outjump anyone in that gym, as becomes clear from the first practice. I discover that I have a knack for finding the ball, for predicting from the arc of a shot whether it will hit the front of the eight-foot rim or the back and then going up and getting it as it falls. And even more important, I discover that as long as I can get the ball, gather rebounds, Don will leave me in the game. Every team needs a rebounder. Maybe that's why the white kids accept Archie and me so quickly, because we make them better.

Don whistles if he wants our attention. He uses hand signals to call out plays, holding up a few fingers or touching his nose and then ears like a baseball manager. In practice, we're doing layup drills, jumping drills, passing drills; we're doing the weave. He tells us if he puts both hands to his neck as if choking himself that he's calling a press. The whistle, the hand signals, the set plays, the positions, and the different roles each of us plays on the team appeal to my sense of order. I like to know my role, get down low, establish my position, either take an entry pass and look for my shot or watch Archie or Tommy put it up and then go get that ball. I like the plays being called by the coach, the defensive schemes, the 2–2–1 zones we play, the clean white uniform with the red Salvation Army logo and the number 42 on the back. Don and I immediately form a bond. I may be his most coachable kid, one who rarely puts up an ill-advised shot or loses his temper when not getting passed the ball.

2.

Archie and I walk two miles to the Sal every day after school. We have to bring our progress reports every five weeks for Don's mom to approve. Don told us if his mom saw we weren't making our grades, we couldn't play for the Sal. If I come in there with too many Cs, she holds her glasses out to point at me and says, "Julius, you're spending too much time playing ball. Maybe you need to—"

"Mrs. Ryan, please! *Please!* I'll do better."

"You do that, Julius, you do that."

The twelve best players make the traveling squad, and we travel in two white station wagons with the red shields on the side, Don driving one and Andy Hagerty the other. We ride in those wagons all over Long Island, up to Glen Cove, out to Locust Valley and Huntington, over to Levittown, down to Freeport. We play against elementary schools and boys' clubs and church teams, and few of them offer much competition. The combination of Archie and me, along with the Conroy boys and the Black brothers, overwhelms other elementary school kids. Our offense is the most sophisticated I've ever played in, and for Biddy Basketball—what Don calls our age group—it's disciplined, with Don urging us to move the ball around until we can get it inside to Archie or to me on the wing where I can drive for a layup or pass back out to the Conroys, who are good shooters. Of course, we can't resist hoisting up some bad shots and listening to Don shout at us, "Pass the ball, PASS the ball."

But we are having fun, more fun that I've ever had playing basketball at Prospect Elementary or at Campbell Park. I like the structure of organized ball, the referees and coaches, the score kept on flip cards, and the precise timing of the six-minute quarters, and my team sitting on one side of the gym and the other team sitting on the other. The plays.

And we are very good. Don says we're the best team he's ever coached. He says he's going to schedule some more difficult competition, find us better opponents. Mrs. Ryan comes along to plenty of the games and sits in the stands, knitting while she watches us. My mom, Marky, and Archie's mom, Daisy, come when they can. But mostly it's Don and Andy who drive us, cheer for us, and then take us out to White Castle after the game, buy us a hamburger and a Coke. I love the way those little hamburgers taste after we win, and we win a lot.

My leg is healing. I feel strong. I have my hops back. I can jump twice in the time it takes other kids to go up and down. I can tip the ball to myself and then jump up and get it while other kids are still coming down from their first jump. I believe that every ball in that gym, every shot that doesn't find the bottom of the net, will be mine. It's a fantastic feeling, a sense of confidence about my place in the world. I belong. Here. Under this basket.

I take a rebound, I begin dribbling downcourt, I weave through traffic. I rise. I rise.

I lay the ball in.

The coach calls a time-out.

"Julius," Don tells me. "Pass the ball to the guards. Now sit down on the bench."

Don teaches us about life. He tells us to "win without bragging and lose without crying." He says that even when we feel like showing up another team, about celebrating a good shot, we have to restrain ourselves. Humility, Don preaches, is an underrated virtue. If you're humble in victory, then even your opponents will have to admire you, despite the fact that you just kicked their butts.

We are so good that the gyms we walk into become crowded with people coming to see us, a Biddy Basketball team playing for the Salvation Army. The local newspapers, *Long Island Press* and *Jewish Exponent*, do some write-ups about us, mentioning Julius Erving as among the best players. They add that Julius Erving is expected to attend Hempstead High School.

Don has us playing some games against older kids, against fourteen- and fifteen-year-olds, and we still beat them. We're going over to the Courtsman AA tournament in Queens and playing against teams from all over the city, and Don starts looking to schedule games against teams from Schenectady, Trenton, Newark, Philadelphia. He takes us to NBA double-headers at the Garden, where we watch New York, Philly, Boston, and Baltimore, where I first see Bill Russell and Wilt Chamberlain.

We take the station wagons down to Philly, a three-hour ride, my longest trip away from Mom and Freda and Marky. I wear my blue blazer, my white shirt, brown corduroys, dress shoes. We're playing a tournament in Philly, a few Catholic schools, the local Salvation Army. We're playing two games Saturday and then another two on Sunday, spending the night in a real hotel, the Divine Lorraine, and we're going to see the Liberty Bell, Independence Hall. Don tells our parents it will be an educational as well as athletic experience. Whenever we go on a road trip, Don always tries to add something cultural and makes sure we go to a church on Sunday.

I don't know what it's like to have a real father. I had Tonk, gone too early, but I only saw him a few times in my life. I begin to see Don as kind of like a father. He's tough but fair, and I feel like I can ask him anything, even for help with my homework, which I could never ask my father for. Even about girls, who I am becoming interested in, I can ask Don what he thinks.

Too many young men lose their way because of girls, Don tells us.

3.

The Divine Lorraine in Philadelphia is a monstrous, arched-windowed, dark brick building that hunkers on the street like a big haunted mansion. We've all seen too many horror movies, and each of us is even more terrified when we follow Don into the lobby to check in and the guy behind the desk is this huge black man, he has to be six foot five and weigh 250 pounds and wears the largest shoes we've ever seen.

"Quasimodo," Archie whispers. "The Hunchback!"

He limps around behind the desk, gathering our keys and breathing through his mouth. He glares over at me and nods, his frown frozen.

I'm rooming with Archie up on the fourth floor. We can see out the window, the cars driving by on Broad Street, the clouds rolling in, Philly gray and cold-looking. I unpack my bags, hang my blazer up on a hook, put my clothes in the dresser drawers. Organize my toothbrush, toothpaste, and comb in a nice straight line next to the sink. Archie, who usually rooms with me on the road, shakes his head.

Sometimes he'll mess with my neat little rows, moving the

toothbrush so that it's perpendicular to the toothpaste, and then watch as I get visibly irritated by this and finally can't resist straightening up the rows of toiletries.

"Jule, you got a problem." Archie laughs.

"I just like my things neat," I tell him. "In columns."

We change into our basketball uniforms and sweat jackets and head out to play our game against the local Salvation Army—we're in the middle of our longest winning streak yet, which will get to 47 games, and by now our hosts are assembling all-star teams to try to beat us. It doesn't work.

We come back from the gym, change, shower, and go out to a dinner given by the local Salvation Army—chicken with gravy, some potatoes, spinach—and a few of the other coaches come over and talk to Archie and me, telling us how proud they are of what we're doing.

"You mean winning?" I ask.

Archie looks at me and shakes his head. "They mean because we're black."

"Black's not something you do," I say. "You just are."

When we return to the hotel, Don orders us into bed at eight thirty. We share the bathroom with the Conroy boys in the room next to us.

I'm the last to use the bathroom, and while I'm in there showering, the Conroy boys and Archie pull a trick on me and lock me into the john. I try the door, I knock on it a few times. Archie and the Conroy boys don't answer. They must have fallen asleep.

I'm exhausted as well, from the drive, the two games today, the sightseeing, the dinner. I'll just sit down here on the commode and take a little nap. I fall asleep right there.

While I'm out, Don and Quasimodo come by for the bed

check. Don sees that I'm gone, asks Archie where I am, and Archie says, "I don't know."

Don and Quasimodo go room to room, searching for me. I've always been Coach's most reliable player, and he promised my mother that he would look out for me if I joined the Sal, and now here I am, gone missing in the middle of Philadelphia.

I'm out during all of this. Archie bursts into tears as he confesses that they had locked me in the bathroom.

The bathroom door clicks and I wake up to see Quasimodo's gigantic shoes, these two dark boats on the tile floor, and I look up and this monster is standing there, frowning down at me, this missing boy who was found asleep on the commode.

Don comes in behind him. "Julius? What are you doing here?"

"I fell asleep, Coach."

He shakes his head. "Get in bed, Julius. We have church first thing."

In the morning I put my blazer back on and we head to church, and then we come back, change, and go out on another little tour of Philadelphia, visiting the art museum. We ride in our station wagons back to New York, and when we're crossing the George Washington Bridge, I realize I've forgotten my blazer in the cupboard, where I hung it up after church. Now I'm nervous. Mom is going to kill me. That jacket must have cost $15 from Robert Hall's. It was my Easter jacket. I feel awful; I know how hard my mother works.

After we return, I tell Coach about it, tell him that I no longer have an Easter jacket and we can't afford another one. I tell him that means when I go on road trips, I won't have a jacket to wear to church.

Don arranges with the Divine Lorraine Hotel to have the

jacket sent back to me, and it arrives in a brown paper wrapper with string around it and there is a note that wishes me and the team the best of luck.

"That's nice," I say, showing it to Don.

And he explains it's the night manager, the Quasimodo fellow who checked us into the hotel.

I realize something then, something simple but important: you can't judge people by how they look, the color of their skin, anything. I have to take each person for who they are and believe in them until they let me down.

4.

In the middle of that winning streak, we walk into a gym in Locust Valley when I hear the word "nigger" being shouted. I'm eleven, and this is some grown-up white man shouting "nigger" at me and Archie. "No niggahs allowed in this gym," he is shouting.

Archie and I are the only two black people in the gym. Don looks at me. "Let me handle it."

He walks over to the guy and starts quietly talking to him.

The man shakes his head. "A nigger's a nigger."

"Leave my kids alone," Don says.

Don comes back and leads us into the dressing room. "Some people have problems. Big problems. But I don't want it to affect you. We're a team. A team stands up for each other. Let's do what we came here to do. Just go out and kick their butts."

Dr. J

He takes me and Archie aside. "You guys okay?"

We both nod. "We're ready."

Don leads us back out. At the start of the game, we hear one or two more racist taunts, but after a few minutes, the crowd quiets. I don't let that team get one rebound. I block every shot. Archie steals every pass. We score every time down the court. These poor kids may never want to play basketball again.

Late in the second half, Don keeps holding his hands up to his throat. "Press! Press!"

I look over at him. "Press? It's eighty to twenty, Coach."

He shrugs. Win without boasting.

5.

I still play in Campbell Park in the afternoons and evenings when I'm not at the Sal. And Juanita is still one of the best players there. She's twelve, like me, and has physically developed into a young woman. Now we all notice her chest jiggling as she dribbles. She doesn't go to Prospect Elementary with the rest of us. She's a Catholic school girl, which gives her a certain status in the projects, in that her parents could afford whatever nominal tuition they charged.

After we're done playing, I walk with Juanita back across Beech Street, to our project. She lives on the same floor as me, across the hall. Juanita is so beautiful, with dark hair, oval face, and thick lips, and she is a good ballplayer—which makes her seem even more beautiful to me. She wears these wire-frame glasses and when she's talking to me, she keeps pushing them up higher on her nose.

She wears a T-shirt, jeans, and Converse like the rest of us. And I can feel in her, like I would later feel in my sister, Freda, a certain disappointment already setting in. These are gifted athletes, girls who can hold their own against men in track and field, in basketball, and yet our local schools don't have programs for them to develop as sportswomen. So Juanita, who is better than most boys her age, has no high school sports to look forward to the way we boys do. We talk, at the Sal, on the court at Campbell, about playing for Hempstead, about what Archie and I hope to accomplish as Hempstead Tigers, and all Juanita can do at the park when we talk like this is just sit quietly.

We climb up the stairs, agreeing without speaking to take the steps as slowly as possible, to extend our time together. Finally, we reach our landing, and then our hallway. We can hear echoes from other floors of shouted good-byes and the squeak of sneakers against linoleum as other children make their way home. We stop and look at each other and I kiss Juanita.

My first kiss. And it's with the girl next door.

"You call that a kiss? You're doing it all wrong," says a loud voice behind me. It's James Smith, three years older than I am, one of five siblings of my friend Levi. "That's not how you kiss a girl!"

Now James is a Golden Gloves winner. And since winning the junior boxing championship, he's become even tougher. He walks over, pushes me out of the way, and plants a deep soul kiss—with tongue—on Juanita. It goes on for a while.

"See, that's how you got to do it."

I nod. This wasn't what I had in mind for my first kiss.

6.

At school, I am also becoming intensely aware of the opposite sex. Though I am quiet and shy, my reputation as an athlete is enough to attract some attention from the girls.

There is a girl, Gayle, who I sit behind in homeroom. I don't find her beautiful. But she is nice to me and smiles when she turns around. She sees that I arrange my pencils and pens a certain way in the pencil holder grooved into the desk and smiles.

"You always put them like that?" she says.

I shrug. I don't want to explain to her how I am pleased by order.

We find ourselves walking together after class, and I'm not sure how it happens or why, but she leads me to a closet in the basement of our school and once we are inside, in between the boiler and some sort of storage bin, she pulls down her dress and panties and I pull down my pants and drawers and we begin to rub against each other. We don't do more than that and I don't achieve any sort of climax, we just have this intense friction session that lasts a few minutes until she seems satisfied and pulls up her dress.

I pull up as well and then we are off to class.

At lunch, I go over to where she is sitting, but I have a hard time talking in front of her friends. It is only when we are walking out of the lunch room and we can talk privately that I tell her that I have a good idea. At ten thirty every day, when I'll be in math class and she'll be in home economics, we will both raise our hands and meet together at the same spot.

She shrugs. "Okay."

The next morning, at ten thirty, I raise my hand and tell Mr. Hairston that I have to use the john. I run down the stairs to the basement and open the door and there she is, waiting for me. I can't believe my plan has worked.

We take our pants off and rub. Then, after a few minutes, Gayle decides to stop. We straighten ourselves up and she returns to her class first and I wait a few minutes and then head back.

We meet every day at the same time and in the same place for weeks, and we never kiss each other.

7.

The universe is expanding, they tell us at school, and I am expanding. I can feel the weight of astonishment at what the world might hold for me, at the animals and oceans and stars and planets and people and dreams. At how my own hopes, of leaping, of rising, can become a reality and how other dreams, of growing up, of life, can be shattered. We are suspended in a vibrating web—my mother explains that it is God's love—but that web can snap and leave us falling and falling.

I want to rise.

I can move freely throughout Hempstead, from the Salvation Army, to the movie theaters, to Prospect Elementary, to Campbell Park, a boy's ever-widening gyre of adventure and opportunity, of games and challenges. Archie and Al Williams—a fast little guard who has also joined the Sal—and I wander over to Kennedy or Eisenhower Park and look for games against other kids, often playing with guys a few years older than us. If there's no game going on, then we check out a soccer ball from the park attendant and take turns dunking on eight-foot rims. We dunk in the gym at Prospect Elementary— some guys dunking tennis balls while I dunk a soccer ball. I can palm a soccer ball in my hand already. By the time I'm thirteen, I have hands bigger and fingers longer than some guys six inches taller than I am.

I enjoy pacing my steps off and then running toward the hoop and leaping, soccer ball in my hand as I glide up toward that short basket and then flush the ball through. Dunking is different from jumping. Once you can leap and touch, say, ten feet high on a wall, you can always jump and touch ten feet, but with dunking, just because you did it before doesn't mean you can do it again. There are so many variables, starting with the quality of the jump itself, where you took off from, timing, the grip on the ball, and I'm talking about dunking without defenders trying to stop me. We take turns dunking, Archie and me, and beat up so many soccer balls slamming them through the rim that pretty soon the park attendant won't let us check out any more.

To earn money for basketballs—and new Converse high tops—I take a job as a paperboy with my neighbor Joe Farmer. Joe also has a process, his hair is all steamed and hot combed so that it is flat and he can sweep up the front into a pompadour like Elvis or Little Richard. His hair has gone from black to red. Joe says I should get a process, that everyone's getting a process.

"You should do this paper route with me," Joe says. "We'll both have cool dos riding the truck."

I study his red, oiled coif.

"I don't know about that, Joe," I tell him. "But I'll do the paper route."

He's been delivering papers for a couple of years already and is two years older than I am but he says the fact that I'm underage doesn't matter.

I wake up at four thirty every morning. I put on my galoshes, two pairs of pants, my light coat, *and* my wool coat because it's wintertime and there's "elements outside," that's what Joe says. Rain, sleet, snow: seven days a week we do this route. The manager, Max, comes to pick us up in his Volkswagen van and brings us to the White Castle, where he buys Joe and me each an eight-cent hamburger and a five-cent Coke. He tells us we can't work on empty stomachs. A man needs fuel. He calls us men. I like that. This is his paper route, actually, but he has hired us for $1.50 a day and $3.00 on Sundays. After our fuel, he drives us over to the bus terminal, where we collect the papers, the *New York Times*, the *New York Herald Tribune*, the *Daily News*, the *Daily Mirror*. We gather all the sections, the front page, the sports section, the city section, and then assemble the morning edition of each newspaper sitting beneath that bus station roof, folding them into neat little rectangles and then loading them into the van. Then Joe climbs on one running board and I climb on the other and Max drives up Franklin Avenue from Hempstead to Garden City, taking the turn down residential streets.

"*Times, Tribune, Mirror,*" Max says.

His attendant hands us the papers and I jump off and run up the driveway until I am close enough to toss the paper and land it in the right place. I take pride in how I can fling those papers sidearm, an easy flick of the wrist that sails the *Tribune* up and over a hedge, or curves it around a column, so that it lands right on the welcome mat. I get so good, I can fire off three papers in three quick motions, about four seconds, each landing where the subscriber only has to open his front door to pick it up.

And then my favorite part—running back to the van and jumping back on. I get so good, I can leap back onto the moving van from eight feet away, land, grab the door frame, and Max doesn't even have to slow down.

Max tells me it's easy for me. "You got those big hands, Jule. You were made to be a paperboy!"

But Sundays, man, Sundays are the worst, with those monster newspapers that weigh a few pounds.

I don't mind working, I'm thinking, but I'm not gonna be a paperboy.

By the time we get back home, it's seven a.m., and my mother, brother, and sister are all just waking up. I turn on the TV so it can warm up and Mom comes padding out of her room in her robe and starts cooking us some oatmeal or pancakes and I get dressed. I have a few minutes, so Marky and I watch cartoons or *Our Gang* and then we can eat breakfast. I always bring home a paper for Mom.

I make $12 a week and give my mom $10 and keep $2 for myself, so I can buy Converse and maybe some hair care products.

Marky and I walk the mile and a half to Prospect.

"Can I do the paper route with you, June?" Marky asks.

I tell Marky I don't know. I'm twelve, and you're supposed to be fourteen.

But I don't think Marky can handle the route. It's too cold in the morning, you have to get up in the predawn darkness, and Marky doesn't seem strong enough to handle it.

8.

At school, it's a struggle to stay awake in the warm class-rooms: I've been awake for hours and, with my stomach full and my eyelids drooping, I have to rouse myself by rearranging my pencils and shifting in my seat. I will not let my grades slide. I know Mrs. Ryan won't let me play ball for the Sal if I show up with a column of Cs. So I'm sitting in history class, half-asleep, listening to the teacher, something about the Fugitive Slave Act, the Slave Trade ban in Washington, DC, the Compromise of 1850, when the class is interrupted by the squeal of the Tannoy turning on, followed by a moment of hum, and then our principal telling us that our president, John F. Kennedy, has been assassinated.

We are told that school is canceled for the rest of the day. We're to go home.

I go to the lower school and find Marky and we walk home in silence.

Mom always told us that Kennedy was good for black people; he was on our side. We have a photo of him up on our wall, next to Dr. King, and I always liked the look of him, his toothy smile, his gentle eyes. Dr. King had told blacks to vote for Kennedy, and Mom did, she told us. And Kennedy had sent federal marshals in so that a black man could attend college in Mississippi. He'd also sent in the National Guard. We'd seen that on television.

When I ask Mom what's gonna happen, she just shakes her head, saying, "It's not good for us, June. It's not good for America."

Dr. J 61

9.

I have a step-cousin whom I'll call Theresa, and she is three years older than I am and lives on the second floor of our building. She's always real nice to me and one day I'm over at her house and we're watching TV and she asks me to come into the bedroom with her and she pushes me back down on the bed and pulls her panties off. She tells me to pull down my pants and underwear, and she climbs on top of me and then introduces me to the real deal.

This isn't rubbing. This time I'm inside and I understand what the big fuss is about, why everyone is always talking about this, and it seems to dominate the conversations of all the older guys. I'm confused and a little frightened by this whole experience, by the sight of a woman on top of me and the obvious pleasure she is taking in this and—it ends quickly.

What just happened?

I've been taken advantage of, but I also feel like this has been for my own benefit, like thank God I now know what this is all about.

Theresa often stops me when I'm climbing the steps or if she sees me around the neighborhood to tell me that her parents are going to be out this afternoon and I should stop by. This is my introduction to sex, at age thirteen, before we even cover the subject in school. By the time we do get to sex education, I'm thinking, Okay, I know all about that. But I am lucky, to be active at that age and not have ended up a father way before I was ready.

10.

Prospect School is mixed, we are white and black kids in equal numbers, and we are all expected to participate in the full range of studies, which means I play the cello. And I win the poetry contest reciting by memorizing "If" by Rudyard Kipling. I'm even the lead in a school play.

I've become a student leader.

I've already been chosen by the teachers, by Bill Zaruka, the gym teacher and the principal, to be a captain for Field Day. I'm to lead the Blue Jays, one of four teams. I am the best in the school at the high jump and long jump. I'm the quarterback of the eighth-grade football team (Archie is my go-to receiver) and, of course, I'm the star of our school's basketball team. I play baseball, though I'm not sure I can even hit my weight in batting percentage, as Don tells me any player must do, but at Prospect—and at the Sal—I participate in everything. What is important, however, is that my being chosen captain makes a kind of mathematical sense; it is the only logical outcome of my success in all these sports: the rows and columns are all stacked up just right.

11.

The Hempstead gangs are starting to recruit from around our projects, jumping on several of the basketball players I play with at the park. We're in Imperial Warlord territory, and some afternoons they hang around on the benches outside the

projects, combing their hair, harassing women whose men are too frightened to tell them off. These guys are seventeen, eighteen years old, older even, and some of them were Hempstead Tigers in the past, but none of them were ballplayers, or not so that you ever heard about them. I usually know how to avoid them, taking back ways, going up a stairwell in the rear of the building and then crossing over on the roof if I have to and then going down our stairwell, avoiding the courtyard in the front where the Warlords are holding court. I don't want anything to do with them. They're into drugs. Knocking over parking meters. None of it looks promising to me. After the news agency in charge of my paper route found out I was under fourteen, they fired me. *Newsday* eventually rehired me, but that job also required collecting the subscription money along with doing the deliveries, and I found I was earning much less for doing much more work. I quit that job and was now looking for another, but I was not considering joining the Warlords.

One afternoon I was walking home with Sonny Boy, who I used to help with his homework by tossing mine out the window so he could copy and return it in time for school. Sonny Boy wasn't a great student and he's not known as an athlete as I am. The gangs tend to leave the athletic kids alone. A ballplayer with a rep could get a pass, though not always. But the Warlords were already recruiting Sonny Boy, and when they see us together, the head Warlord—he has a mustache and smokes a filterless cigarette—gives Sonny Boy a big handshake and looks me over.

"Who this?"

"That's Julius," Sonny Boy says.

"He looks like a chicken," says the Warlord. "Chicken chest. Long legs. Big hands. What you do with them big hands?"

I shrug. "Nothin'."

"Needle-dick motherfucker. You got them big hands. How you even gonna jerk off? That must be a sight."

He mimics looking for his penis in his hand. "I can't find it in my palm."

The gang laughs.

I look at Sonny Boy. I'm thinking about running, but a few of the Warlords have taken up positions behind me.

"Now, Sonny Boy, why don't you knock out Chicken Chest? Man, that's what a Warlord would do. Just knock this skinny, bony, big-hand freak the fuck out."

Sonny breathes heavily. He doesn't know what to do. I don't want to fight. I'm not a fighter. I don't fight with anyone. Not even on the court. And I'm not even angry with Sonny Boy. How could I be? I've known him all my life. We played Hot Buttered Peas right here, next to these benches, beside this crazy little Biddy hoop.

"Come on," Sonny says. "Jules is a basketball player."

The head Warlord shrugs. "I don't care if he's Connie Hawkins himself."

Sonny puts up his fists and comes toward me. He launches a weak shot at my shoulder. "Come on."

I get in my best Cassius Clay pose and we start circling each other, launching soft shots against each other's shoulders. We are dancing more than fighting, making sure that we don't inflict any real pain.

"Come on, fight, you chickenshits."

We continue our circling, and by now the Warlords are getting bored.

"Man, Sonny Boy, you're nothing but a pussy if you can't knock out this Chicken Chest."

"You ain't even trying to hit him."

They tell Sonny Boy that he isn't Warlords material. And they chase me home, up the stairs, which I can now leap up in one huge jump, so they don't really have a chance to catch me as I do my usual sprint up to the roof and then down another stairwell and then I'm back home.

12.

Mom has a new man in her life, a sanitation worker named Dan Lindsay, twenty years older than she is. He's a garbage-man, riding trucks for the Department of Sanitation. He used to be Archie's mom's boyfriend, and I'd seen him over at Archie's before he ended up over at our house, sitting at our table, eating Mom's barbecue spare ribs and egg noodles with sauce. He's tall, muscular, always wearing a flat applejack cap, and chomping on a short cigar. His skin is always clean shaven, as if he's been worn smooth from a hard life outdoors, first as a horse trainer, which is what he did down south before he injured his leg, came north, and became a garbageman.

He still walks with a bow in his leg.

When he stays over, he gets up at four a.m., which is earlier even than I ever got up for my paper route. At first, I find it strange having him in the house. I'm the man of the house, but I also realize that Mom enjoys his company. He plays pinochle with her, listens to the same fish sandwich music she likes— Nat King Cole, Ella Fitzgerald—and she is entitled to some happiness of her own.

That summer, Marky, Freda, and I go to Point Lookout, to Jones Beach. We throw our blankets down, run into the ocean, splash around. I learned to swim at Point Lookout. I had no choice after being thrown in the water by older kids. That's how we learned: it was either dog-paddle or drown. We'd been going for years, Freda taking Marky and me. And now that we're older, the three of us still go, only these days she stays sitting on her towel, talking to boys, while Marky and I go clamming or make sand castles. Then I pick up Marky, carry him across the sand, and toss him in the water. He looks terrified, his head bobbing between the swells.

"You got to swim, Marky," I shout.

He nods, looks serious, but then he's paddling, keeping his head above the water.

"Keep paddling, keep breathing." I swim out next to him.

In the summer, Marky's hair turns almost reddish.

"I'm d-d-doing it, June."

"Yeah you are, brother, yeah you are."

Joe would sometimes come with us, and Archie and Al, there'd be a gang of kids all at the beach listening to a transistor radio playing rock and roll—Fats Domino, Chubby Checker, and my favorite, Little Anthony and the Imperials.

I'm on the outside, looking in, oooh, ooh, ooh, ooh, ooh.

Archie and I stand in the breakwater and sometimes talk about our futures together at Hempstead High, about playing JV ball as freshmen next year for coach Ollie Mills and then varsity as sophomores.

Freda is going to be a senior.

"Your sister is fine," Archie says, admiring Freda on her towel.

"Don't be looking at my sister," I warn Archie.

He smiles.

I know Archie would never do anything to anger me, and that includes being disrespectful toward Freda.

And we charge into the water, plunging in and then riding the waves back to the beach.

Later, we play touch football, about a dozen of us, white kids and black kids, and we score hundreds of touchdowns. Marky even scores a few.

We take the bus home from Long Beach, up across Island Park to Rockville Centre where we change for Hempstead. The sun is setting behind us, the early evening light yellow and buttery, warming our necks as the bus makes its rumbling progress. We sleep on the warm seats, our skin sticking to the vinyl, Marky laying his head in Freda's lap, Archie sitting by the window. I'm dreaming of playing ball this fall. We're so happy, I'm not even that worried about making it back after seven p.m. Freda is with us and Mom trusts her.

Mom is waiting for us in the kitchen. She's made a roast, some potatoes. I'm so hungry, I sit down and eat before I shower, with my feet still sandy from the beach.

Usually, Mom would grab me by the ear and lead me to the bathroom if I tried that, but this time, she just sits down, telling us to eat and explaining that she already had her dinner.

"Dan and I are getting married," she says.

And . . .

"We're moving."

Mom explains it in her even, steady voice. She and Dan have seen a place over in Roosevelt, a proper house with three stories. They have made an offer on the property, and they've secured the mortgage.

"Roosevelt!" I say. "That's clear on the other side of the parkway."

She may as well have said we're moving to Canada or China. I'll never see my friends. I'll have to start a new school—I'll never be a Hempstead Tiger!

What about Archie? Al Williams? My Salvation Army teammates? We're supposed to play high school ball together and win our South Shore Division.

Freda also looks forlorn. But I can tell she had seen this coming. She's more observant than I am, a better listener.

And Marky? Marky seems the least upset.

"As long as we're all moving, right? It's not so bad," he says.

But I shake my head. It's awful. Roosevelt? That's on the other side of Uniondale.

That must be three miles away.

I tell Mom I had it all planned out. Playing ball for Hempstead. Being a Tiger.

"Man plans, God laughs," Mom says to me.

13.

We move into the house at 90 Pleasant Avenue. My mom and stepdad paid $6,000, and each of us kids gets a bedroom. I have an insulated attic room with slanted walls so that I can only stand up in the middle of the room. The house is spacious compared to the projects, but I don't know anybody in Roosevelt.

We have a proper living room and dining room with a

console where the nice silver and crystal is neatly stowed, new wooden table beneath a little chandelier, a separate kitchen through a swinging door, and up the stairs is my mom and Mr. Dan's room and Marky's room, and on the top floor is Freda's and mine.

Down the street from our new house is Centennial Park and we're a few blocks from Roosevelt Park. The ballplayers down at Centennial don't know me, and all they talk about is being Rough Riders, that's the name of the Roosevelt team. I wait by the side of the court for a game, keeping quiet, watching the action. It seems like a higher-level pickup game than those down at Campbell Park in Hempstead. For one thing, there aren't any girls playing up here. And it's all brothers. No white guys running in this game.

Still, by now I've come to believe that inside those lines, on a basketball court, there is always a spot for me. By now I am sure of this. From years of playing with Don Ryan at the Sal, and walking into hostile gyms throughout Long Island, I know that the basketball court is the one place where chaos always gives way to order. I try to believe there is an order and logic to life, though by now, with the deaths of Bobby and then my father, with moving from Hempstead, I suspect there is no underlying logic, or none that I can see. There is only the order and structure that I can create, can will into existence, by keeping my room tidy and my clothes neatly folded, and also by finding a basketball court and imposing my will upon that.

I know I can play with these guys the same way I knew I could play for Don. I'm sure I can outrebound most of these guys and get my shot off, but you never know until you play. I ask who's got next, and a well-built kid in a T-shirt, shorts, and Converse says he does.

"Can I run with you?" I ask.

He shrugs.

But when the game ends and five new players take the court, I step in with them and I do my thing, picking up the rebounds, taking off on the break, and finishing with little flips and spins around the hoop. I'm not the tallest guy out there, but nobody can jump higher than I can, and nobody, on any court, anywhere, can beat me to the ball off the rim.

At one point, coming down the court, the kid who told me he had next passes me the ball in the lane, and there are at least two guys clogging up the middle. There's no way around them. I jump, thinking I can get enough clearance to lay the ball in over them, but instead I watch them both spring up and then come down, and I'm still . . . rising. Instead of laying the ball in, my hand turns over, and—

I dunk it. A rim-shaking jam, a skill honed from practicing on eight-foot and nine-foot rims.

The game stops. Guys are whooping and hollering.

"Damn, what's your name?" the kid who passed me the ball asks.

"Julius."

"I'm Leon," he says. "Where did you come from?"

"Hempstead. We just moved in up here."

"I came from Manhattan," Leon says. He's already been here a few months.

There is some grumbling from the players on the court. They've all been playing ball together for years, and just like Archie and Al and my teammates from the Salvation Army were planning to play together at Hempstead High, these guys were planning to play together at Roosevelt High.

Dr. J 71

"This guy ain't taking my spot!" says a little guy named Ronnie. Poor Ronnie doesn't have much game. He's stiff and has an erratic line-drive set shot.

There are a few murmurs from around the court. Ronnie is already sizing me up as a threat.

I shrug. "We'll see."

I like this cat Leon, though he slows the game down by arguing every out-of-bounds and foul call. He comes up with crazy versions of what we all just saw with our own eyes. "I was pushed. So technically, it's not off me, it's a foul on you. So it's skins ball out-of-bounds."

Basketball is how I fit in to my new neighborhood. I meet up with the guys who will be playing for Roosevelt High: there's Leon, Nick Marshall, Ralph Burgess, Robert Mayrant, Lenny Carter, Odelle Cureton. And every day the guys get together at a different park to play, at Roosevelt, Washington, or Centennial. No matter how hot it is, we're out there, usually in the early evening, in a pair of gym shorts and some Converse, playing these ferocious games, pushing each other and fighting to hold the court lest we have to wait for a game in the crazy heat. In the evenings, the older guys come down, grown men finished with their earning day, and we match up with them for some rough games to 11 or 15. But even against the older guys, I am always able to control the boards, gather rebounds. I have to be wary of showing them up too much or they'll try to undercut me.

Some nights this older black man is hanging around by the fence, taking in the action. Leon and the guys nod to him and go over and pay respects and then they tell me, "That's Earl Mosley, the freshman coach."

He was already scouting for his prospective team.

Those of us going into ninth grade are going to play for Mr. Mosley. One evening, he introduces himself.

"Let me see your hands. Hold them up."

I show him my hands. I'm already a men's size 11. It's hard to find gloves that fit me.

"It's nice to meet you, Julius. Now you're coming out for basketball this year?"

I tell him I am.

"Are you a kid who makes his grades, or should I count on you not playing?" Mr. Mosley is also the assistant principal at Roosevelt.

I tell him I make grades. Or my mom will hit me with a strap.

He nods. Only later will I realize that Mr. Mosley shares a similar idea of stern discipline.

14.

I'm in ninth grade and Marky is in sixth. The move is hardest on Freda. She's had to start her senior year in a new school. Instead of feeling comfortable with her old friends and arriving at school every morning to familiar faces, she has to start over, where she doesn't know anybody. I make friends quickly, primarily through basketball and football. I know the guys who play with me at the parks, and my skill at playing ball has paved the way for me socially. Marky is young enough that the change doesn't matter much.

Freda struggles, and after a few months she quits school

and moves in with George Bookhard, a college graduate a few years older than she is. George works at a religious book publishing company, on the business side of the firm. He was a Hempstead Tiger, a good basketball player who used his game to get to college. But despite his success, Mom and all of us are unhappy that Freda is choosing him over her degree.

Mom tells Freda this isn't right, to leave school for an older man. Why can't she wait? Why now? Freda was always so smart, and now she's just throwing—

"I'm pregnant with George's baby. He wants to marry me and I said yes."

"Marky, June, go upstairs," Mom says to us.

We climb the stairs. Marky looks like he's gonna cry.

"Freda's moving out?" he asks.

I nod. "Looks that way."

"Then we'll be only three. Just Mom, you, and me."

"And Mr. Dan," I say.

Marky shrugs and I know what he means. We like Mr. Dan, he's a good man, but he knows that he can't overstep his bounds and get too involved in our family business. Even in this drama over Freda becoming pregnant, Dan just sits there silent, chewing one of his short cigars.

Freda is gone.

15.

I'm lucky to be coached by Mr. Mosley, who takes a liking to me. I respond well to his teaching. He recognizes something in me, some promise or potential that no one else has yet noticed. I've been regarded as a good player, a fine athlete, but Mr. Mosley is the first to see that the combination of my basketball abilities and academic success might be enough to win me a college scholarship.

That's my mother's dream, for me to somehow go to college. Freda was supposed to be the one to go on, but now she's living down the block with George. I know without asking that we don't have the money for college. An athletic scholarship is the only way I'll be able to go.

Mr. Mosley tells me to enroll in the college-preparatory program, which means I'll be taking a full academic load in addition to playing basketball and football. He is always after me about my homework, my grades, and now I do my homework every night as much to please Mr. Mosley as my mom.

To help out and earn some money, I get a job working at a bakery in Freeport, riding my bike over at five thirty a.m., slipping on an apron and a hairnet and filling doughnuts with custard and jelly and shaking on the confectioners' sugar. We prepare the jelly doughnuts, the custard-filled, the old-fashioneds, the eclairs, the long johns. We put the cream into the napoleons, a layer of cream and then a layer of cookie, and I eat a lot of them, taking home pink boxes full of doughnuts. Some mornings, I can barely make it to school because my stomach hurts so much from eating so many sweets. And I get a whole mess of cavities. I am paid $1.20 an hour, and give my mom and stepdad $12 a week and keep the rest so I have some spending money. My mom pays my dentist bills for all those cavities.

I want to look sharp at my new school. They don't allow jeans at Roosevelt High. I take the bus to the Abraham & Straus back down in Hempstead and choose a long wool coat, some

sweaters, dress slacks, leather shoes, and put them on layaway, paying them off with my doughnut money.

But I'm thinking about moving on to some serious suede. That's a look I admire. And around me, among my peers but also in the community, I'm seeing the new styles emerging, the different looks, with a few brothers wearing dashikis or some dressing in the black jacket, white shirt, and black tie of the Nation of Islam. I am stunned when I hear that Malcolm X has been assassinated. I don't understand precisely what he stands for, but I know that I am a Christian, a Baptist, and not a Muslim. I also know that I don't hate white people. Don Ryan and Andy Hagerty are like fathers to me, and those are white men. The Salvation Army program was the best thing that ever happened to me and that was because of Don and Andy and Don's mom. So Malcolm's blanket condemnation of whites as devils does not make sense to me. Huey Newton and the Black Panthers' message of revolution doesn't appeal to me. Even Angela Davis, her fine self, and her message of communism and critical resistance I find alienating.

I prefer order, or to look for order, and all this portends a chaos that I find uncomfortable.

I'm with Dr. King. I hear his message. I'm looking at Coretta Scott King and she could be my mom's sister. Mom is a deaconess in our church, and she preaches love for all. We can't hate whites, she says, any more than we can hate blacks. But also, it's something else, it's a sense I have that this system, as it is currently constructed, might work out for me.

At the basketball courts during that period, we talk about what we are seeing and hearing. When the Watts riots are televised in the summer of 1965, we gather in silence around the RCA in the living room, but very soon the images of smoking neighborhoods and massed police in riot gear spark a conversation that we can no longer put off. I'm confused but also fascinated. I understand, from driving south, from being called nigger on the basketball court, what causes this kind of anger. I can relate to it, but I don't share in that anger. I don't feel the same as those who are setting fire to their own communities.

Some of the guys say we should be joining the Nation of Islam or the Five Percenters or the Panthers. They're talking about going to see Bobby Seale speak in Manhattan. There are meetings we should attend. We shouldn't stand by while our brothers in Watts are dying. Some of the guys—Keith Carpenter, Leon—flirt with militancy, with changing their names and wardrobes and attending rallies. They start reading the Koran.

I'm still reading the Old Testament. No reason to change that I can see. I'm going to school. I want to graduate. Go to college. As far as I'm concerned, that's what I need to be doing. Not starting a revolution.

But unlike some of the other guys, I have an identity: I'm not a Muslim or a Panther. I don't have to be. I'm a basketball player. I'm a son. I'm a brother. Those are my priorities. They are enough, I think; they have to be enough.

16.

The freshman team includes many of the guys I already know from the park. Mr. Mosley is a physical coach, aggressive and tough. He grabs you, pushes you, and practically picks you up to move you to the right place on the floor. He hits you in the

 **Dr. J** 77

chest to get your attention and he'll give you a knuckle sand-wich right in the solar plexus if you get out of line. He'll knock the breath right out of a kid if the kid won't listen.

We have Ralph Burgess at forward, Lenny Carter at point guard, Leon from the playground at the two. I'm playing power forward. We have talent but lack size. Our games are played at four o'clock in the afternoon, in front of nearly empty gyms, before the JV and varsity games. But the freshman games don't count. They aren't covered by the local papers and our own student paper barely mentions us. And a good thing, too, because we are awful, going 2-12. But the basketball coaches at Roosevelt rightly see the freshman team as an entirely developmental program, preparing players to move on to eventually play varsity.

Still, I'm not used to losing. Back in Hempstead we never lost. At the Sal we won 47 straight, and here I am on a basketball team that manages to only win two games?

But Mr. Mosley has taken an interest in me, noticing that I'm still not all the way back from my knee injury and teaching me new leaping drills and leg-strengthening exercises so that I regain my speed. By the time the freshman season ends, Coach tells me they are moving me up to the junior varsity, the only player on the ninth-grade team to move up. I play three JV games that season, coming off the bench to rebound and score, and Mr. Mosley convinces Mr. Wilson, the varsity coach, to let me come up to varsity. Now this never happens, a freshman playing varsity. Years later, it might be more common, but on Long Island in the mid-'60s, you had to put in your time before they let you play with the upperclassmen. But Mr. Wilson puts me in a game, and I drive the baseline, manage to slip past two defenders, start my leap from one side of the hoop, and finish with a neat little reverse flip off the glass. The crowd in the gym loves the shot, and Mr. Mosley later calls me "Little Hawk," saying the move reminds him of Globetrotter and prep legend Connie Hawkins.

I asked him, "Who's that?"

The next day, in the *Newsday* recap of the game, in the box score for the Roosevelt–West Hempstead game it says that "Irving" scored 2 points.

Still, the next season I'm back with the junior varsity.

17.

But my game really takes off on the playgrounds and the parks of Roosevelt; I'm developing a game and a style that is very different from what we are doing inside the gym. I'm dunking backward on eight-foot and nine-foot baskets, able to dunk one-handed with ease on ten-foot rims. I'm jumping over guys ten years older and five inches taller on courts all over town. Some of the dunks are so spectacular that the games almost come to a halt after I throw down.

But I never stop or gloat. I just run back down the court.

Win without boasting.

The game developing on these playgrounds, and all over New York, is more free-flowing and improvisational than the one we play in organized ball. We borrow a little more from what we see Elgin Baylor doing on television. And Mr. Mosley tells me that Connie Hawkins integrated the slam dunk into his game, played the game above the rim, made these soaring leaps and then floated there, as if thinking about how he is

Dr. J

going to finish his move. Indoors, the coaches tell us never to leave the ground without knowing what you are going to do with the ball.

Indoors, the coach always tells me to go up with two hands and secure the rebound, bringing the ball down to chest level before making an outlet pass to a guard.

Out here, I like to pluck the ball with one hand out of the air and hold it up, sometimes flinging it to Leon or Robert streaking downcourt, but often dribbling up court myself and looking for an angle to the basket, a sliver of daylight that will allow me to get to the rim. We seldom set up the offense to the extent our coaches in organized ball like. On the concrete, we are always looking for the fast-break finish. And I begin to leave the pavement unsure of how I will finish the move, with a little finger-roll flourish or, if I can see the opening, with a dunk—or, if the defense has collapsed around me, with a dish to Leon or Ralph.

The game out here is always on the verge of chaos. It threatens to fall apart, both in terms of guys getting into fights or storming off the court and in terms of the individual moves we're making. I'm trying new things constantly, figuring out different ways to get to the rim, trying to fake left, go right, shoot left, dunk lefty, I don't know. I'm making this up as I go along.

Leon tells me that watching me go up for a shot is exciting because he never knows how I'm going to finish or even if I'm going to finish. That's because I don't know. I often have no idea how a move will end or where it will end. That kind of improvisation on the basketball court is a form of expression and I come to see it as a response to what is going on in the world around us, where the politics of race, the turmoil of riots, the drug culture, and rock music are transforming how everyone looks and dresses and acts. Off the court, I'm a conservative kid. I don't mess with drugs. I've seen plenty of guys stoned and I'm not interested in that kind of chaos or disorder.

But I do feel some need to express myself, to rebel, and the only place I can do it is on the basketball court. I like order in the world, and even inside the gym when I'm playing organized ball, I prefer to play in a system, but out here, on the concrete courts, I decide to get a little freaky with my game.

When the games are over at Washington or Roosevelt or Centennial Park, I always try to get one of my friends to stay and play one-on-one or even H-O-R-S-E. Playing one-on-one is like a laboratory for new experiments in scoring. Going up with the ball palmed in my left hand and then switching hands and dunking with my right? Did that in a game of one-on-one. Going up and holding the ball up high in my right hand and finishing with a soft left-hand layup off the glass? Another one-on-one move. A reverse layup that starts on the baseline and finishes as a left-hand jam? That's from H-O-R-S-E.

Leon Saunders, my best friend and fellow teammate, is my regular opponent, and my lifetime record against him must be around 25,546–1. And that one win he secures by his usual method of loudly arguing any call. But Leon stays out there in the darkening evenings at the parks and plays ball with me night after night.

One evening we're at Roosevelt Park and Leon is arguing tirelessly about how a ball he knocked out-of-bounds didn't go off him.

"Here, it went under my arm, and then over my leg," Leon is saying, "like this. And, anyway, you pushed me, and that's

a violation right there. Man, you must have, what, like seven fouls? You should have fouled out."

"Fouled out," I say, "of a one-on-one?"

"At least I should be taking some free throws. Man, here, I'll take two foul shots, and then it should be my ball because that's a technical, actually, because away from the ball like that—"

"Okay, okay," I tell Leon. "Your ball. Man, I should call you the Professor. Everything becomes a lecture with you."

Leon nods. "If I'm the Professor . . . then you're the Doctor."

"Why?"

" 'Cause you got more moves than Dr. Carter has liver pills."

Dr. Carter's Little Liver Pills are a popular patent medicine frequently bought for back pain and other aches.

And from then on, Leon calls me the Doctor.

18.

That summer, I'm working at the doughnut shop and playing summer league ball over at Roosevelt Park. Ray Wilson, the varsity coach at Roosevelt, is watching from behind a chain-link fence. I'm playing inside, putting moves on this big guy who is guarding me, and frustrating him because I keep blocking his shot. He and I get in a little scuffle, shoving each other, and we both pick up technical fouls and I see this big guy sort of grinning at me. I'm furious and I tell him, "Hey, after the game, it's gonna be me and you."

But as soon as we're done, Mr. Wilson comes over and grabs

me and says, "Listen, if you get in a fight on the basketball court, all you're going to do is hurt your team because you are not the type of player who should be an enforcer. Let somebody else do that." He goes on, "I don't want to see you fighting. I don't want to see you running away from a fight, but I don't want to see you looking for a fight because that is not who you are and that is not the best role for you."

He tells me that when I make varsity, he needs me to play smart, not get drawn into stupid technical fouls and dumb fights.

I never forget that.

19.

I'm barely six feet tall and so skinny that Mr. Wilson doesn't move me up to varsity until midway through my sophomore year. The varsity's tallest player, Warren Fleming, is six foot three, and they've got a couple of other guys over six feet, so Mr. Wilson has me riding the bench. Mr. Wilson is a traditionalist anyway, and he believes in starting seniors because they've earned it. This is the prevalent thinking at the time, and while I understand the logic of it—I do like order—I know I can play with these guys and I already have, out on the playgrounds, but Mr. Wilson wants me to wait my turn. Rather than complain, I bide my time.

I've already noticed that some guys who shine on the playground can't make it indoors because they won't play defense or remember plays. They don't have the discipline. One of my gifts is the ability to be a ferocious playground player while also being a steady and reliable indoor player. I'm coachable. I *like* my coaches. Don, Earl, Chuck, and Ray: man, these guys fill that hole where my dad never was. (And poor Marky, I don't know that he has anyone. I have to be that person for Marky.)

Academically, I'm holding my own in the college-prep classes, making my way through algebra, then geometry, advanced English, American history, and while I'm no longer an A student like I was at Prospect Elementary, I am still a solid B student, usually. As an athlete, I have some status at the high school, though I remain as quiet and shy in the school cafeteria as I am sitting on Ray Wilson's bench. Moving to Roosevelt has slowed down my game in one very important area: the ladies.

While in Hempstead I had already gone through a period of having regular sex with Theresa—and shared that awkward first kiss with Juanita—here in Roosevelt I'm starting all over again and I don't know anybody. I mean, I know lots of guys who play basketball, but I don't know any females. Nothing happening in that department. It's just me up on the third floor of our house, getting to know my right hand. It's backward, I know, the way I'm moving down the sexual pyramid from intercourse to masturbation, but I can't help it. I can't even get any dates. I'm too shy to ask any girls out. My manner is too reserved, too quiet. I'm nice, and I try to be well spoken. But that doesn't attract the attention of any of the girls in my class.

It's good fortune, not getting any nooky. Freda's education was ended because of sex, so there is that cautionary tale for me to study. I soon become an uncle, Freda giving birth to her first son, Barry. They're living down the street from us. And

Freda is a great mom, but I still think, Oh, man, she could have done so much. I don't want to be a father before I know what I'm doing.

Mr. Earl Mosley, my freshman coach, is telling me that's right. Girls are trouble.

If you had stayed in Hempstead, Mr. Mosley is saying, you might already have become a father. "That ruins more ball-players than bad knees," he says.

20.

In spring, I step outside and take a deep breath. The air is fresh with the smell of loamy soil and wet pavement and budding trees. The snow has melted, leaving a few icy patches in the shadows, but the basketball courts are dry in the sun. I wear my Converse, my sweatpants with gym shorts underneath, T-shirt and sweatshirt hoodie and wool coat, and I'm waiting for my teammates to pick me up.

Down the street, the sound of a motor, a horn blares. Robert is driving his Rambler and Leon leans out the passenger window, shouting at me. "We making a house call on the Doctor!" Lenny and Ralph are already in the car, their breath making steam when I open the door and tell them to slide over. Smokey Robinson and the Miracles are on the radio, singing "Going to a Go-Go."

We pool our dollars for gas money and toll money. Our crew is going to Rockville Centre, to Baldwin, to Uniondale, to Queens, to Brooklyn, to Harlem, to every court in Long

Island and then New York City to play the best players from the five boroughs and beyond. We've beaten the best in Roosevelt, and now we seek out competition all over the city. After the hard winter, the courts dry off and city kids can be seen making their way to Hillside Park, to Baisley Park, to Jamaica Heights, Prospect Park, West Fourth Street, Thirty-Fourth Street, all the PS schools, Morningside Park, and Mount Morris Park up in Harlem.

Smokey sings, "Well there's a brand-new place I found."

We look for games.

We find games.

All over the city.

We show up anywhere and call next against anyone. Men in jeans and work boots. Stringy kids in shorts and sneakers. White kids. Black kids. Puerto Rican kids. Even a few professional players. Dick Barnett. Hawthorne Wingo.

We even play this kid over at Adelphi University named Bob Beamon. Beamon's already in college, playing ball for the University of Texas at El Paso—UTEP—and he's the national long-jump champ. When we pull up to the gym over there, guys are coming over saying, "Beamon's in there, man, he's dunking on everybody! He's tearing up this gym."

"Julius," Leon says, "you got to let him know whose gym this is!"

We watch for a few minutes, waiting for our game, and Beamon is impressive. But when we finally get on the court, Leon puts up a jump shot that hits the back of the rim, and Beamon goes up to rebound.

I jump up, and rise. Up past Beamon, and I take the ball in my hand and bring it down through the rim.

The whole gym falls on the floor.

Beamon soon decides basketball isn't his game.

I need to test my skill. I need to validate myself, outside of the gym, outside of my community. I am proud of my game, and of my crew, of Ralph and Robert and Lenny and Leon. Can't stop us.

It's like the Salvation Army all over again, only now it's just us. Other teenagers are out there smoking weed or jacking cars, but we're out looking for games. Sometimes we play for a few dollars, but that's risky for us because we barely have enough money for gas to get home. We know how to drive out of Manhattan and avoid the tolls if we have to, but with no gas that means we're walking. And if we lose, then that definitely means no snack money. Still, we're cocky enough to take those bets some of the time.

Most guys in Brooklyn or Manhattan, they don't know we're from Long Island. They figure we're another city crew, so when we beat them and then have to ask for directions back to Long Island, they are shocked and embarrassed. "Man," they say, "you all from Long Island!"

They shake their heads. "We lost to Long Island? DAMN!"

My game travels. I can get to the rim on anyone. On any court. I walk on knowing there are certain things I can do. And out here, when we're barnstorming, a loss means another hour before we get another game. So we are trying our best to win, play smothering defense when we have to. I teach the guys the same hand signals as Don used at the Sal, the two hands up to my neck to indicate we need to press. From playing together so much, we know each other and can run plays if we choose. We bring organization to street ball. We have a rhythm and pace to our game that sets us apart from some of the other guys out here. We're not just running for the sake of running, we are looking for a certain flow and you get that by knowing who is effective in certain spots, where they like the ball, and where you should be on the floor when they have the ball. Within that framework, I like to improvise.

I'm probably the most capable of our five in scoring either off a fast-break or in a half-court situation, but if the inside is too clogged up, then I'll pick out somebody to take a jump shot. We always play inside-out, as opposed to outside-in, the latter of which is far more common in playground games. I'll kick it out to Ralph or Leon or Lenny for a mid-range jumper.

With us, we never come down and just jack it up.

"You don't get it, do you?" Leon asks me when we're sitting down after running the courts for a few hours.

"What?"

"How you're playing," Leon says. "Nobody plays like that. Flying around like that. Snatching rebounds from the air a couple of feet above the rim. Dunking over guys. You're . . . a whirlwind. It's a new way of playing. Man, the Boston Celtics don't play like that. The Knicks don't. Nobody."

And Leon is right, I don't see many guys—or any, really— playing that way.

I start to hear that from opponents, from guys watching us in playgrounds, and can feel it when everyone standing along-side the court starts howling or rolling on the ground—literally rolling around—after a dunk or a one-handed rebound or a pump-fake pass that leads to a fast-break dunk.

We frustrate opponents, and often, when we're getting dunks on the break or from our inside game—Robert is also a fantastic leaper and dunker—then our opponents get either dispirited or angry. We have to be careful when we run into opponents who really can't hang with us on the court.

Those games can degenerate into chaos. Or worse.

I have a keen nose for trouble and, heeding Mr. Wilson's advice, I try to avoid unnecessary confrontation. But sometimes I can't avoid it. There are always guys around basketball courts in New York City looking for trouble, or gangs come around and they might pick on the new guys. And I'm still young enough that even in a situation where it might be more prudent not to park the Rambler and look for a game, we become bored enough or desperate enough that we'll stop at some shady spots if we see a few guys with a basketball.

At one game in the Bronx at Gun Hill Park, we're playing a few locals and the game is getting out of hand and I start making some crazy moves, jumping over guys and throwing down some big dunks. The guys we're playing are starting to get pretty pissed off.

I dunk again.

And again.

We win 15–0.

This chubby guy who'd had a little swagger when we'd started the game, but whom we've been victimizing ruthlessly in the lane, now shakes his head. "Oh, so you're out here embarrassing us, huh?"

"Man," I say, "we're just playing a little basketball."

He pulls a knife out of his pocket. "You want to embarrass me?"

I back away. "No, I'm not trying to embarrass you. Why you pulling a knife on me?"

He's holding the knife up and glaring at me.

That's some bullshit right there. I start backing away.

"That's cool. That's cool. Game over anyway."

I want to go home.

21.

Marky walks with labored breaths. His voice is a gentle hum filled with that soft air so that when he speaks, I lean in to listen. My Marky is a strange figure, with his wool pants, white socks, and dress shoes, his pursed lips, serious expression, brows wrinkled as he makes his way down Pleasant Avenue. He has a curved spine, short torso, small feet so that when he walks it is with an exaggeratedly straight, stiff back, a penguin's march. He tells me he wishes he had big feet like me. How small Marky is, but how he seems to contain all of us, our family, our love, and when I see him go, I have to restrain myself from following after him to make sure he will be safe.

Marky has joined the Civil Air Patrol, now donning blue slacks, his white shirt, his peaked cap as he sets off on his emergency rescue practice sessions. The drills we do in school, the crowding under our desks, closing of windows and blinds in preparation for a nuclear attack—I assume Marky is doing a more sophisticated version of that, preparing medical supplies and canned goods for the eventual Armageddon.

Marky explains that's not actually what they do. They're working on making radio transmitters and how to read navigational charts. It's like being in the Boy Scouts, Marky says, only with more electronics.

"Come with me," Marky urges.

I'm not interested in wearing a uniform.

Marky actually wants to be like me, Mom has told me. He wishes he were tall and strong. He wishes he could jump as high, run as fast. But Marky is smarter than I am, I can already tell. A bookworm, whereas I'm what you might call a lunch-pail scholar. Perhaps because Marky doesn't have the easy confidence of being a good athlete, he has to work a little harder at school, at being liked by his peers for who he is. He is a straight-A student, always reading ahead in his classes, and because of his easygoing manner and gentle personality, he surprises us all by winning his class presidency.

He pays attention. I drift. I dream.

We are in church, kneeling in the pews, my head against my hands and my hands against the hard wood bench backs, and I'm not listening to the sermon. Marky is beside me and suddenly he stands. He shuffles down the pews and then down the center aisle to the front of the church.

"Marky!" I hiss. "Marky, where you goin'?"

He keeps walking.

I listen to the pastor. He's calling congregants up to be baptized.

I stand. I follow.

"Marky? You know what you're doing?"

He kneels. I'm already up at the altar, so I kneel beside him.

Do you believe that there is one God who is father of all, and one Lord Jesus Christ?

Do you believe that Christ died to cover the debt of your sins?

Do you believe that Christ's sacrifice was accepted by

God and that he raised Christ from the dead?

Have you repented of your sins?

And I'm kneeling there beside Marky, and barely listening, watching as Marky mouths the words, his voice soft and his eyes fluttering as he gets the calling.

We bow before God, my little brother and me, the mystery of our connection and the power of our love proof to me that we live in God's universe yet can never comprehend his will.

22.

Roosevelt High has only been around since 1960. Our three-hundred-seat gym only has risers and there are no championship banners hanging from our rafters. We practice in the empty gym, Mr. Wilson walking around us, working on our defensive positioning, knees bent, butt down, chin up, hands away from our sides with palms out. One afternoon, Mr. Wilson comes in and tells us he has something for us out in the trunk of his Chevy. We trot out there, eager, thinking he has our summer league trophies, and he pops the trunk and it's full of red bricks.

"Everybody take two," he says. "I am assigning these bricks to you and before every practice I want you to come out to the court with your bricks and I want you to keep them in your locker all year. These bricks are your life."

What the hell?

We bring our bricks to practice. We do all our drills, our defensive slides, our rotations, our stances, everything with hands up with bricks in them. We run the gym, singing the theme song of *The Beverly Hillbillies*: *Come and listen to a story about a man named Jed, a poor mountaineer, barely kept his family fed* . . . while we do our laps. We run twenty laps a day like that, singing, a brick in each hand.

We divide practice into two categories, brick and non-brick.

One of the players, a skinny guard named Nick Marshall, breaks one of his bricks in half. He comes out to practice with a half a brick in each hand, and gets away with it for a while. Until finally Mr. Wilson notices.

"Where the hell is your brick?"

Nick shrugs. "This is all I got."

Even Mr. Wilson had to start laughing at that.

23.

My last name starts with an E, and sitting right behind me in homeroom is Grace Fenton, an F. Sitting near Grace feels like sitting near a movie star. I steal glances. I wonder what she is thinking. Her thought processes are as mysterious to me—and as powerful-seeming—as the interior of the atom. The way she swishes her hair, the curve of her sweater, the lilt in her voice as she answers, "Present," the soft rub of her feet against the floor, the smell of soap and vanilla that seems to waft from her.

This mystery, of confusion and crush and proto-love and lust all barely contained in this school, in my person, in my

Dr. J

trousers, is derailing. I am on a track when it comes to basketball, to sports. I am moving forward in an orderly, steady manner. The game is pleasing and logical, returning to me what I put into it. Yet here is this lovely female, and I am as unequipped to play with her as I would be if Lew Alcindor stepped onto the court against me. My precocious introduction to the wonders of sex and, um, genital rubbing did nothing to prepare me for the actual games of love. And my first kiss, with Juanita, hasn't been replicated since. I haven't been intimate with another female since my deflowering lessons administered via Theresa. Now I'm a half-foot taller, the best athlete in the school, and popular enough that the deacon at my church asks me to come up and say a few words to the congregation, but I can't find a single word for Grace.

The pressure builds. I feel her behind me every morning, this force urging me to turn around, sucking in my attention, sweeping me away. If this distraction were in algebra instead of homeroom, I would be lost.

I sharpen my pencils. I organize them in their pouch. I straighten my notes and then straighten my binders.

Today, I will speak with her.

I turn.

She is beautiful and high toned like Freda. Her skin shimmers like brass. Her eyes are pleasingly ovoid with wisps of an inverted V-shaped brow above each. I can't look her full in the face, to see beyond the gloss of her actually being Grace Fenton.

Her smell: there is something at once buffeting and deeply private about it, as if I have uncovered a secret.

She smiles. But what is she thinking? Her thoughts, and the potential for the disapproval they contain, frighten me.

"Man," Leon tells me when I ask what I should do, "just *ask* her. Everyone knows you."

I want to take Grace Fenton to the ball, the underclassmen's version of the prom.

He tells me I am underestimating my own popularity, my own stature.

"Everybody knows you!" Leon says. "Man, you can operate on the court, but you got no game out here."

After homeroom one morning, I slip into her wake.

"Um, Grace, my name is Julius—"

"I know your name!"

I want to flee.

"Grace," I begin again. "My name is Julius Erving and—well—"

"Do you want to go to the ball together?" she says. "I mean, is that what you are asking?"

Suddenly, she is embarrassed, shy at having inadvertently asked me before I have actually asked her.

"Okay," I say.

The night of the ball, I wear my best suit and walk over to pick her up. We are so shy, we don't manage to say more than hellos and good-byes and, again, I am almost too frightened to look at her. We manage to dance to two slow songs and then I walk her home. I don't even kiss her.

I have no swagger.

When I get home, my stepfather, Dan, is sitting up in the dining room, smoking one of his short, black cigars.

He tells me that Marky is in the hospital. He had a real bad asthma attack, couldn't breathe, was turning blue. Even with his medicine, his inhaler, he couldn't catch his breath. Mom called an ambulance to take him over to Mercy Hos-

Dr. J 95

pital and he'll spend the night there. Mr. Dan says he'll take me over.

Marky is in a four-bed ward. Across from him is an old Chinese man who seems to be talking in his sleep. Mom and Freda sit beside Marky as Marky sips juice from a plastic cup.

He turns as I walk in. He smiles.

"Marky, my man!" I say, trying to be cheerful. "How you doing?"

I turn to Mom. "How is he?"

Mom shrugs, taking Marky's hand. "Doc don't know."

I know that Marky lately has had some new problems. He complains that his joints ache. And he's been developing strange skin rashes if he goes out in the sun too long. But he's never been hospitalized before, or not overnight, anyway.

"Maybe it's just the allergies," I say, repeating our common suspicion.

"June!" Marky says, smiling. "How was the ball?"

I want to tell him it was strange, uncomfortable, that Grace Fenton remains unfathomable and mysterious, that I assume this will be the start of a lifetime of tongue-tiedness and confusion and fear around the opposite sex, but I know that's not what Marky wants to hear. Marky wants to live through me a little, to participate in those parts of life he can't have because of his health, his weakness, without me. So I oblige him.

"It was fantastic. Everything I wanted. And Grace, well, um, Grace really seems to like me."

Mom and Freda both look at me, as if unsure of what they just heard, because it is so unlike me to boast.

But I tell Marky what I think he wants to hear.

24.

The only person in Long Island who can stop me from scoring 25 points a game is Ray Wilson. Coach Wilson is such a traditionalist, he believes in playing his seniors. We're a small, skinny team. Our front line averages about six foot two and our backcourt about five foot ten, and after five games Mr. Wilson breaks down and realizes that he has to start me and give me serious minutes. While the offense doesn't run through me, I average double figures almost entirely on putbacks.

Under Mr. Wilson's guidance, I work on my defense, on establishing position, on the team game. During warm-ups, in the layup line, I'll throw down some dunks, but in the game, we never dunk. I remember when we played JV ball and one of the varsity players, Joe Scott, attempted a dunk during a game and clanged it off the back of the rim. Coach Wilson pulled him out and sat him on the bench the rest of the half.

I use all the crafty layups I've developed on the playground and in one-on-one games, so on fast breaks I like to take off from about the foul line and then finish with a little finger roll or a spinning bank off the glass. I've noticed I have an ability to use a wider portion of the backboard than some of my peers. Because of the size of my hands and the spin I can get on the ball when flipping it up, I can bank it off the backboard well outside the rectangle above the rim with enough English to get it to drop. I see the basket almost as a pocket on the pool table. If someone is between me and the basket, that's like a billiard ball blocking me from shooting straight into the pocket, so I can either go around them, or else just shoot around them,

Dr. J

using the ball's own rotation to bank it off the glass from an improbable angle.

I rise. I am the team's leading rebounder, averaging over 12 a game.

I can't explain it, but even teammates can see that I seem to know where the ball is going before the ball goes there. I can watch a shot making its way to the rim and predict the trajectory of its carom. I can outjump anyone on that court. With my long arms I can outreach anyone. With my huge hands I only need to get my fingers on the ball to control it. And with my second jump being so fast, I can come down with the ball.

It's a gift, one I spend ten thousand hours giving to myself.

I do jumping drills, rim touching drills, backboard touching drills. I'm out in Centennial Park by myself after even the one-on-one games are finished and Leon has gone home, doing an hour of jumping, touching the rim with my left hand, coming down, and jumping again, touching the rim again with my left, and repeating that ten times. Then I do a squat, gather myself, jump up, and do the same thing with my right hand. After ten right-hand touches, I squat and then jump up and touch the rim with both hands. The tenth touch I grab the rim with both hands and hang there. That's when I rest, on the rim, and then I drop and do it all again.

The idea is to perfectly land after each jump on exactly the same spot because that allows me to spring back up faster since my weight is already evenly distributed. That's hard to do and requires practice, but it's what gives me that fast second hop and third hop. I do that, ten times lefty, ten times righty, ten times both hands, and then I do another set of ten, and then another, and then another, until I do it perfectly, landing on the same spot, hitting the same part of the rim. If I'm all over the place or falling or gathering myself before each jump, then I stop and start over from one.

I like perfection and order in my drills.

I also jump for distance. I start at the half-court line and run toward the basket and take off, my goal being to hit a spot on the backboard above the rim. At first, I'm taking off from the dotted line, and I keep moving it farther and farther out, my goal being to take off from the foul line. Momentum converts height to distance. My ability to rise translates to flight. I can take off a dozen feet from the hoop; with enough vertical lift, I soar through the lane. I can hit that same spot on the backboard ten out of ten times.

Then I do little hook shots. Right hand, left hand, right hand, left hand, let the ball hit the ground, get a rhythm going, make fifty in a row. Then change it up, fake left, shoot right, fake right, shoot left, make fifty in a row. If I miss, start over. I believe I should never miss a layup or hook shot from inside ten feet. (I am amazed at how many of my teammates, and guys I play with and against in playgrounds around New York City, can't make ten layups in a row with alternating hands.)

I do these drills so often and with such consistency that when I do get the ball in the lane during a game, either indoors or on the playground, I can look at the ground, at the paint, and know exactly where I am on the court and can put the ball up with my eyes closed and get the kiss of the glass or the swish through the rim. It becomes automatic for me.

I sacrifice more. I practice more. I drill more. I rise.

Some of the other guys want to experiment with beer, with weed. Maybe they need girlfriend time. And by not doing any of that, I give myself so many advantages. And the work shows.

Mr. Wilson notices, compliments me on how my left hand has developed, on how I can do everything with my left or my right, so that late in the game, when other players are getting tired and going toward their dominant hands, you can't force me one way or the other on the court, you can't assume I'm going to finish with one hand or the other. I've become, as my friend Leon puts it, "an amphibian."

My junior year at Roosevelt I grow another two inches, so I'm six foot two by the end of the season. We go 13 and 4, making the county playoffs but losing in the first round. I win the Most Improved Player award in Nassau County as I average 18 points a game and 15 rebounds. They don't keep track of blocks, but I probably would have led South Shore Division 4 in that as well.

In a game against a South Shore rival, all these hours of drills contribute to this moment: I go up for a missed shot, tip the ball, then go back up and grab it with one hand, holding the ball over my head. Lenny and Odelle are both covered, so I take the ball myself, dribbling easily up court, weaving past my man, and then taking off from just inside the foul line, looking for an angle to spin the ball off the glass. I go up, I'm rising, I see my path to the basket. It will be a little layin, but my hand is so far above the rim that instead of a layup, I turn my hand over and dunk it.

In a game. Indoors.

I didn't mean to.

Our crowd is hollering, stamping their feet on the bleachers. Our bench is all standing, slapping fives. The refs are even looking at each other.

I don't stop to celebrate. Win without boasting.

As I'm running down the court, I look over at Mr. Wilson,

expecting him to pull me out of the game. He pretends not to see me, and he leaves me in.

My hand just turned over. And it never stops turning over after that.

25.

At night, the gym doors are open and yellow light cascades down from the cage-protected fixtures and reflects off the varnished floors and spills from the gym onto the pavement outside where the last of the straggling students and teachers make their way from campus.

Practice is over. Mr. Wilson keeps the gym open for us. He tosses the ball off the backboard two feet above the rim and tells me to go get it.

I fly across the lane to get it, snatching it from the air.

"Shout when you get that ball, boy!"

Another toss up.

Another leap.

I rise.

"Ah!"

"Boy, get freaky. Get mad. That's your ball. Shout. Shout!"

I rise.

"Aaaah!"

He throws it up again.

"AAAAH!"

For the first time, Mr. Wilson and Mr. Mosley both tell me this is my ticket. That my game can take me to college. That I have a gift, and if I continue to do well in school, then I will be the first in my family to go to a four-year college, to get a degree.

"You want that?" Mr. Wilson asks.

I nod.

"Then get it."

He tosses the ball up again.

I rise.

"AAAAAAAAAAAAH!"

26.

In the summer I ride my bike, a five-speed English racer (skinny wheels, gears on the crossbar, curled handlebars) down Seaman Avenue to Goldie Blum's jewelry store in a little mall in Rockville Centre. I breathe in the exhaust of trucks and cars, of families on their way to the beach or beating the traffic back to Manhattan. I have a job this summer, as I do every year, and I ride the six miles to work on my bicycle, the knees of my bowed legs pistoning so high that they hit my elbows.

I'm a curious sight, I know, this big boy on this tiny bicycle. Head down, pedaling forward: this is what my life feels like.

There is a war in Vietnam. There are riots on the streets of Newark. There are those who tell me that I need to make a choice. That the black man in America has been oppressed. That what is needed is nothing less than a revolution, a new society, or, even more confusing, that we need to return to Africa, to rediscover our culture and ourselves. And, man, some brothers are telling me I need to say if I'm with the Man, or against him.

The Man?

I don't know who that is. I don't see the world in those stark terms. And I listen to Mr. Wilson, to Mr. Mosley. I have a chance to make it to college, to make something of myself, and that is through this system that some of these brothers want to burn down.

I put my head down. I pedal.

Even the music is changing. There's Otis Redding, maybe the greatest R & B singer of the '60s, but there's also the funk of James Brown and the rock of Jimi Hendrix. Never mind the Beatles, who everybody, black and white, is listening to. Up in my room, sometimes, I'll sit in my cushioned chair, listening to James Brown on my eight-track player singing "Fever" and "Good Rockin' Tonight," and I'll feel connected to what is going on, to the turmoil and strife and the desire to fight to change all that—by any means necessary, even—but I'm also self-aware enough to know that isn't me. I'm not a fighter.

I put my head down. I ride.

I park and lock my bike in the parking lot and go up the stairs to the store and then down an interior stairwell to a shipping area where I pack and ship jewelry. Goldie Blum is a kind, middle-aged Jewish lady who sells trinkets and gifts. Her mail-order business is composed almost entirely of out-of-state buyers looking to avoid paying New York taxes on their modest necklaces and bracelets. We carefully set the jewelry in the small, plush boxes with the Goldie logo on the satin inside of the top, and then seal those boxes in slightly larger shipping boxes. We have a Monarch labeling machine that requires we sort through the built-in case for letters and numbers and our own postage machine, the first I've ever seen, and we spend an entire six hours, from ten till four, assembling these little packages for shipping to Altoona, Pennsylvania, and Decatur, Indiana, gold, silver, and diamonds in plain brown boxes, an entire week's salary, sometimes, or even a month, packed and shipped. At the end of the day, we load the boxes onto a hand trolley and roll them over to the post office.

It's subterranean work, and for the six hours that Junior Poulsan and I are down there, the only sunlight we see is when we're biking in or making a run to the post office. We're getting $12 a day but something doesn't seem right about this.

I've been working since I was twelve, and it's taken me a while, but I've now realized what I'm not going to do for the rest of my life. I'm not going to punch a clock. That's not going to be me. Leon and some of the other brothers are talking about how they are going to avoid this life of drudgery. I don't mind work; Mom taught me I have to earn my own way. What I mind is the sameness of the tasks and days, the repetition, the way time spent working unfurls as slowly as catsup pouring from a cold, stuck bottle. The idea is a little bit alien to me, as I have been taught to be humble, but I think, I realize, I am above this. I am. Better than this. Even while I am doing this, packing those bracelets into their little boxes, I am somehow floating above myself and thinking, No, this isn't you. You are meant for something else.

And, pedaling back along Seaman Avenue, I feel the world around me, the possibilities, the opportunities, the subtle shifting and rearranging that my gift with a basketball will make possible. I am, I think in a moment of giddy fantasy, an artist, like James Brown, like Otis, like Jimi even. Only my song, my art, is basketball.

It will set me free from this life of being a wage slave. I don't think it will make me rich, but it will get me to college. I am determined.

I will rise.

27.

In exchange for a one-week stay at the Shamrock Basketball Camp at Schroon Lake in upstate New York, I wash dishes and pour bug juice for prep basketball players. It is a good exercise in humility, and perhaps Ray Wilson and Earl Mosley came up with this as a lesson for me. Wash the dishes of players who don't belong on the same court as me, who don't offer much competition in the few scrimmages in which I participate in exchange for the week's $50. But the real prize comes in the competition. Wayne Embry, a forward with the Boston Celtics, instructs at the camp, and he drills the other campers during the day, but at night a select few players join the counselors and instructors—and kitchen boys—and some serious games begin. The kids who I'm serving during the day are now sitting and watching. Wayne has recruited some Boston Celtics teammates to come up, as well as a half-dozen college players and some of the top prep players in the country. And those games under the lights are some of the best competition I've faced, and the first time I'm playing night after night against NBA-level competition.

I'm still able to play my game, getting up and over the six-foot-eight Embry to grab my one-handed rebounds, and throwing it down over kids who have won college scholarships. Some of these guys I don't even recognize, but Wayne is looking at me and nodding because I am apparently confirming what he has already told some of his Boston Celtics peers: Julius can play.

One afternoon, Hawthorne Wingo from the Knicks comes up and he's working out and he asks Wayne if there's anyone around who can give him a run.

Wayne tells him there's a kid around who's not too bad.

"A kid?" Hawthorne is skeptical. "I said *a run*."

"He's pretty good," Embry says. He sends one of the campers up to the kitchen to get me.

I come down, in my T-shirt, shorts, and sneakers. "What's up?"

Wayne asks me if I want to play one-on-one against Hawthorne Wingo.

I shrug. "Sounds good."

He gives me outs, I dribble, once, twice. Hawthorne is sort of sizing me up, seeing what kind of game I have. He's giving me the 17-footer. I drain it.

I take the ball back out. Now Hawthorne is up on me, doing a little hand-check, his way of telling me he's not going to give me anything.

I dribble and hold the ball up over my head and behind and take off from a step inside the foul line. He's running with me and manages to get his hand between me and the basket, but I power through it for a hard dunk.

Hawthorne is shaking his head. "Damn!"

Wayne is smiling, nodding. "Told you he could play."

28.

Coach Ray Wilson is also my guidance counselor. He's helping me work through the recruiting process that starts my junior year but accelerates the next summer. College coaches become a regular sight in the stands for the last high school season, Louie Carnesecca from St. John's, Lou Rossini from

NYU, Jimmy Valvano from Rutgers, Paul Lynner from Hofstra, coaches from Manhattan, Niagara, from plenty of other schools in the mid-Atlantic region. I'm six foot three now and in many ways blessed to have grown at my own leisurely pace. I never have one of those crazy three- or four-inch spurts that some guys have when they're fourteen or fifteen that causes their size to outpace their coordination. At every stage of my growth, I retained my shooting touch, my deadeye passing, and natural ballhandling. I don't have an awkward phase.

Now Mr. Wilson is telling me a full ride is a real possibility. I've got the grades—I'm a B student taking college-prep classes—and in the spring of junior year when I sat for the Scholastic Aptitude Tests I scored close to 1,000, which puts me well over the threshold for college eligibility.

"You got options," Mr. Wilson is telling me.

He keeps a separate office for his guidance counseling duties, a small room on the administration corridor that he shares with another counselor. There are guidebooks and pamphlets scattered around, and he does a great job not just with me but with the rest of the team, many of whom will go on to four-year colleges, even if they don't get athletic scholarships.

Mr. Wilson tells me he's getting letters from schools as far off as Iowa and Illinois.

Iowa? I'm thinking that's too far.

"I wanna stay close to Marky and my mom," I tell him.

Mr. Wilson nods.

"You should still take a few trips, see a few campuses. See what feels right. This is college, man. You only go to college once."

Mr. Wilson played his college ball at Boston University. "Think about the whole experience," he's telling me, "not just the sports."

I like that. The whole experience. I have been thinking about that, imagining a bucolic campus, trees, lakes, lawns, old classical-style buildings. I picture myself, the student-athlete, learning about business in between basketball practices.

I tell Mr. Wilson my plan: to use my basketball to get a college scholarship so that I can secure a business degree. I want to go into business for myself. I need to make sure I don't end up a wage slave, working in some mailroom or bakery the rest of my life.

"Solid plan," Mr. Wilson agrees. "Let's have a great season, and you keep up the grades, and we can put that plan into effect."

29.

The first meeting of senior season, Mr. Wilson calls all the guys to take a knee before the first practice.

"I want you to understand what we're doing out here," Mr. Wilson says. "It's like growing up on a farm, you gotta work if you want to meet your goals, you gotta till the soil, you gotta sow the fields, you gotta harvest the grain, and if you're lucky, you possess a horse to which you might hitch your plow. Man, that horse makes plowing that field a lot easier, that horse makes getting in that harvest a lot faster."

He looks around the gym and then at me.

"Well, we got a horse and that horse is Julius Erving. And we are going to hitch our plow to him and he is going to take us to a championship."

The guys all nod. No one even seems surprised by this assertion.

It may be the first time a coach has told my team, point-blank, that I am now the alpha dog.

As Mr. Wilson tells me later when we talk, "You're a leader, Julius, that's how it's gonna be, and you need to get used to that. Not just on the court. But in life."

I do end up leading the team in most statistical categories, averaging over 25 points and 17 rebounds. But more important, we go 17–2, losing to Long Beach and again when we go back to play my old teammates Al Williams and Archie Rogers from the Sal, who are now starting for Hempstead High. We go down to their gym where I had once dreamed of playing high school ball, and they take us apart, beating us by 20. We don't have an answer for Al, who can break us down on the dribble and also pass out to hit open shooters.

When they come to play us in our gym, I am hungry for revenge. The game is tied after the third quarter at 57. It's close all the way through the fourth until we pull away to win by 8. I score 22 and collect 17 boards. Al scores 27. Our students come rushing out of the stands after the game and I find Al and Archie and give them each a big hug. Both Hempstead and Roosevelt are going to the playoffs, so we may play them again.

Al and Archie and I had great times at the Sal, and that's a bond we will always share. Al is such a fine athlete, a sleek point guard and the quarterback of the Hempstead football team. He is being recruited and offered scholarships by dozens of schools all over the country, powerhouses like North Carolina and Michigan. Man, he's going to be a star and sometimes, even now, I think about what if, you know? What if Al and I played high school ball together?

Dr. J

No one would stop us.

And it seems like nothing is going to stop Al.

But during his senior year, he comes to a school dance and he's drunk, so intoxicated that school officials eject him from the dance and then expel him. They don't suspend him, they actually kick him out of Hempstead High School. When the colleges hear about it, he loses every single scholarship offer. Just like that, he goes from a future-can't-miss prospect to . . . nobody.

One strike and he's out.

When I hear about that, I realize how careful I have to be. For a young black athlete, there is no safety net. One mistake and I can lose everything, no matter how talented I may be as a basketball player.

Mr. Wilson, Mr. Mosley, and Mr. McIlwain all reinforce this, reminding me that the world is waiting for a young black athlete to screw up. By then we've heard of Connie Hawkins, of how one of the greatest players in the history of New York City basketball has been robbed of a college and pro career because of a bogus point-shaving scandal, despite never being arrested or indicted for anything. He is now playing ball in Pittsburgh in this new league called the American Basketball Association where they use—get this—a red, white, and blue basketball.

Al is heartbroken, but he doesn't give up, transferring to another school to get his degree. He ends up playing ball at Laurinburg Institute, a two-year college in North Carolina.

One Division I coach, Frank Layden, decides to take a chance on Al Williams, despite his tarnished reputation, and offers him a scholarship to Niagara College after Al's sophomore season. Al leads the team in assists, following another pretty smooth point guard named Calvin Murphy. Al will end leading the 1972 team that went all the way to the NIT Championship game, losing to a Len Elmore–led Maryland team.

Archie and I go back to Campbell Park. He was also a captain of Field Day at Prospect Elementary, but he goes down a very different road than I do. First of all, he's more of a football player than a basketball player, and he goes to the State University of New York at Cortland but drops out after a semester. I don't judge his life, but I know it is a difficult one, as he will become addicted to heroin and then get arrested and imprisoned multiple times for assault and robbery, spending much of his life behind bars.

In my mind's eye, we are still two boys playing for the Sal, with Don standing on the sideline holding his hands up to his neck.

Press. Press.

It could go either way, I realize early on.

30.

There is little risk that I will be knocked off course as Al was. But like any young man, I am intensely attracted to members of the opposite sex and starting to need some relief in that area. Hempstead and Theresa are a long time ago, and I haven't been intimate with another woman since. My shyness is partially to blame, but there is also my single-minded focus, at least during basketball season, which between high school ball, all-star tournaments, summer leagues, and barnstorming around the city lasts pretty much all year. No girl is getting my basketball time.

My desire springs up, in English class, in trigonometry, on my way to practice. I feel a sense of longing, combined with worry about what that longing might produce. I know how desire and sex can lead to the one mistake that could prevent me from going on to college. A teen pregnancy, as I have seen firsthand with my sister, Freda, forces you to abandon your dreams. I'm not ready for that. What saves me? My shyness, of course, but there are also those angels looking out for me.

Though Roosevelt is primarily known as a football power, the success of our team and my own individual play have garnered me renown as a basketball player. For the first time, athletics gains me traction with the female portion of the student population. And I can sense that with a little more effort, I might be able to make some serious time with the faster girls in our school.

Robert, one of our forwards and the owner of the red Rambler that takes us on our barnstorming trips, is a little more successful with the ladies. He's made it a point to show us how the seats in the Rambler can be made to lie flat, like a bed. One afternoon, we have about forty-five minutes before practice, and Robert has convinced two cheerleaders to join us out in the parking lot, Robert and his girl in the front, while I'm sitting with mine in the back.

It's a cool November day. Fast-moving gray-white clouds dapple the sky and occasional gusts of ocean wind blow through the parking lot, leaves and cigarette butts and gum wrappers dragging along the pavement, making a light scraping noise as they go.

Robert switches on the radio, the Fifth Dimension singing "Up, Up and Away," and pretty soon Robert is making out with his girl and I'm engaged in an intense tongue-kissing session with mine. The windows are fogging up, and we may need to adjust these seats. This is a hot situation, and there is potential out here, where nobody can see us. We've got forty-five minutes before practice . . .

"JULIUS? BOBBY?"

Who is that?

We see a tweed-sleeved arm rubbing the outside window, trying to clear away the fog. "JULIUS?"

Oh, no.

It's Ray Wilson, our coach.

"Don't unlock the door," Robert says. "Whatever you do, don't."

"JULIUS? TOO MUCH KISSING LEADS TO BABIES."

He's shouting in the middle of the parking lot.

"YOU HEAR ME? BAAAABIES. YOU GONNA HAVE BABIES!"

Coach is definitely killing the mood.

"OPEN THIS DOOR."

I can't say no to Coach. I unlock the door.

"They got to get out of this car, Julius, right now. You can't take no chances, Julius."

He stands there, arms folded across his chest.

I turn to my girl. "You got to go. Coach says so."

31.

Mr. Wilson is right. Because even without messing around with any women, I manage to get pulled into a pregnancy scandal. One morning Vice Principal Lester Gaither calls me

into his office and tells me that a classmate of mine is pregnant and she has said that I am the father.

"That's impossible," I say.

"She is quite sure," Vice Principal Gaither insists.

"Well, it's either someone else or maybe this is an Immaculate Conception situation, because that's the only way this happened." I'm thinking, Man, I'm going to college. I've taken my SATs. I'm passing my classes. I got coaches coming to see me and talking to me and my mom about colleges, and now this?

No. No way.

Not a chance.

"We need to talk to your parents," he says.

"Look," I tell him. "This is simply not possible. I haven't had relations with ANYBODY. Do you understand? NO ONE."

The way I said it seems to back Vice Principal Gaither off a little. He realizes he may have given too much credence to the girl's story.

I never hear about the issue again. But it makes me realize how close I am to blowing everything, how tight my game has to be. One mistake, and instead of going off to college I might be stuck living in Roosevelt and working at the jewelry store for the rest of my life.

32.

We are the top seed in the postseason Nassau County basketball tournament, and we beat West Hempstead by 40 in the first round. Our second-round game is in Freeport, Long Island, a neutral site, against Elmont Memorial, a predominantly white school. They're a smaller, less athletic team than we are, as I can see from pregame warm-ups, and I'm a little surprised they've made it this far. This feels like our time.

Three buses rolled out from Roosevelt High, bringing our fired-up student body, who also sense this could be the year we finally get a banner for our gym. On campus, I feel the love from my fellow students and I feel motivated by the opportunity to give something back to my school. I think about Bobby, and how my cousins are living down south in their segregated communities, and I realize how lucky I am to be going to a school that is so racially diverse. I'm friends with black kids and white kids and they all come out to support the Rough Riders.

The slide-out wooden risers with their clackety iron undercarriages are all extended accordion-like, and our students are hooting and cheering during our layup drills. Our powder-blue-and-gold warm-ups catch the shimmering light so that as I go up to dunk the ball, I am like a patch of sunny sky somehow trapped indoors. My leaps—my search for freedom.

Yet from the opening tip, there is something wrong. The officials begin making questionable calls. Our other forward, George Green, has this move where he does a little hop when he catches the ball. He does his hop, he catches—it's simultaneous—and then he either passes or shoots or puts it down for a dribble. It's legal, and he's been doing it all year and he's never been called for a violation. But this ref calls it the first time George touches the ball.

"Traveling. Number 4."

What? That ain't no travel. Ref, come on.

You can hear our guys murmuring and the ref puts his whistle in his mouth, as if to call a technical on us.

Dr. J 115

I look over at the ref, a bald guy with a mustache and a chest puffed out like a rooster. He looks at me as if to say, What are you going to do about it?

Mr. Wilson is clapping. "Don't worry about it. Focus. Focus."

But the next time down the court, when George's man swings over to double-team me and I pass the ball to George, he is called for traveling again.

"What the—?" George bounces the ball hard off the floor.

I grab him and pull him downcourt.

"Don't worry about it."

But every time we touch the ball, something like that happens, strange traveling calls, and when we complain, technical fouls. Still, somehow, we manage to pull ahead by a couple of points.

Then the ref calls a foul. Saying it's on Number 4: George Green. But George isn't even under the basket. He is slowly making his way up court and is still on the half-court line.

Our crowd is by now agitated, murmurs of protest giving way to loud catcalls and boos and questions about the referee's integrity. "You making money betting on Elmont?"

George is standing near half-court, fuming. "What? Are you crazy? Who's paying you?"

The ref T's him up. That's his second. "You're out of here."

By now our fans are seething. And George's own family is verging on hysteria, with his mother screaming at the ref, "Shame on you. Shame!"

And then his cousin, Glen, comes running out of the stands and takes a swing at the referee, who ducks but goes down when Glen tackles him. By now, there are about a dozen spectators on the court.

Glen and the ref are separated; the court is finally cleared.

Clockwise from top

1. Me, my cousin Ricardo, and my sister, Alexis, around 1954. **2.** My mother, Callie, in 1946. 3. *Left to right*: Alexis, my brother, Marvin, my cousins Ricardo and Charles, and me, 1958. 4. Marvin in 1967. **5.** My nephew Barry, my cousins Charles and Janice, and Marvin in 1968.

Clockwise from top

1. My high school basketball portrait in 1968.
2. These guys hadn't seen the likes of me.
(University of Massachusetts–Amherst)   **3.** I had to bide
my time to play varsity. (UMass/Getty)
4. Representing the United States in Estonia for
the Olympic Development team.

Ripping the ball down on my way up with the Virginia Squires. (The Virginian-Pilot)

Bottom

Jamming one over my future Nets teammate Billy "the Whopper" Paultz. (John D. Hanlong/Getty/Sports Illustrated)

Clockwise from top

1., 2. At home and on the sidelines with my two loves, Turquoise and my Afro, in 1975. **3.** In 1968, my sister, Alexis, and her children, Barry and Keith, lived with me in Virginia and made my house a home.

Clockwise from top

1. A rare photo of me during the forgotten 1972 preseason, when I played with Pistol Pete and the Hawks. **2.** Dunking over Nuggets player Dan Issel. (Manny Millan/Getty/Sports Illustrated) **3.** Cracking up with Wendell Ladner (with crutches) in 1974. (New York Daily News/Getty) **4.** That's me in the front row between Paultz and Larry "Kat" Keenan in our first post-championship team photo. (Larry Berman/BermanSports.com) **5.** This is what celebrating an ABA title in 1974 looked like. (New York Daily News/Getty)

I always admired the style of Walt "Clyde" Frazier (*bottom*), and here, at the 1974 New York versus New York game, he admired mine.

(Ron Koch/Getty/NBA)

Somehow, the game starts up again. Elmont is awarded another pair of technical free throws. We are now off our game, and we end up losing by 3 points, 62–59.

Soon our fans are fighting with Elmont students out in the parking lot. Some of our students start vandalizing Elmont cars. When the Elmont team tries to get away, they surround the bus and start rocking it back and forth, vowing to tip it over. The Elmont team looks terrified, and in newspapers the next day, they call it "the melee."

We're in our locker room, furious, and we can hear the chaos outside. When a *Newsday* reporter comes in and tells us there's a brawl going on, a few of us, and especially George, want to join in and get revenge. But Mr Wilson, who is standing with his jacket hanging over his shoulder, tells us to stop, wait, that we should think about what we are doing and the risks we are taking.

"You know, you go through life and everything is not going to be fair, but you just got to hang in there, hold your head up high, realize all you can do is the best you can do and not let the results, even the ones that seem unfair, define you. You men are better than this." He looks at me. "Nothing is promised to us. But we keep moving forward. Some of us are going to keep playing ball. For some of us, this might be the last basketball game of our lives. But all of us are moving on. We are going to go upstairs and get on our bus and act with dignity and pride and show that no matter what, we will keep going."

It's one of Mr. Wilson's finest hours. Who knows what would have happened if I had gone back upstairs, gotten involved in the melee, maybe helped to tip over a bus and injure a bunch of kids. I might have lost everything.

Later, Mr. Wilson will tell me that he thinks our being the best

Dr. J

black team left in the playoffs may have had something to do with the way the game was called. But he wouldn't let me get involved in postgame violence that could have damaged my prospects.

33.

In part because of my winning the Most Outstanding Player award for Nassau County my senior season, the college recruiting has picked up in intensity. I'm an easy target for recruiters because my grades are solid and my SAT scores guarantee I'll be eligible. Since the beginning of senior year, I've had college coaches come and sit in our living room, talking to my mom and Mr. Dan about what they have to offer. No one comes over more than Louie Carnesecca from St. John's. He sits with my mom and sips tea and tells her about St. John's. Mom always reiterates that her main concern is my education. She wants me to become the first in our line to get a four-year degree.

"Julius is a smart boy," she says. "Don't think of him only as a ballplayer."

Louie nods, agrees, adjusts his glasses. He visits moms all over the country and sits and charms them and he tells my mom that he will personally guarantee that I get an education.

"Julius will be my son," Louie says. "Do you hear me, Mrs. Lindsay? My son!"

I sit quietly, sip my tea, watch, and nod.

One evening he picks me up in his Cadillac, and sitting in the passenger seat is Willis Reed, all-star center for the Knicks and a friend of Louie's. They take me to a steak house, the first

I've ever been to. I don't know what to order so I order the same thing as Louie.

"Man, Julius, Louie is a great coach." Willis lives in Queens, not far from Louie.

"I know that," I say.

"And a great guy," Willis says.

"I know that, too."

They bring us steak, baked potato, creamed spinach, sour cream. I don't know what to do with the sour cream. Do I put it on the steak? I'm watching Willis and he puts it on his potatoes. So I copy him. And there is this brown sauce?

"What do I do with the sauce?" I ask Louie.

He looks at me and smiles. He's always wearing these cardigan sweaters and a checked shirt—that's like his signature look. He tells me the sauce is for the steak.

"Try it, Julius, you'll like it."

So I'm looking around the table, watching these guys, to see what goes with what. Every recruiting dinner is like that. The first time I go to a restaurant with proper place settings, the different forks and spoons, I don't know what to do with them. This time coach Jack Leaman of the University of Massachusetts shows me to start from the outside, with the salad fork, and then move in.

I fly out to Ames, Iowa, with a Connecticut player named Bob Nash. The place is literally in the middle of cornfields and I'm thinking this isn't really what I have in mind for my college experience. They have one of the few black students at Iowa State show us around and he even takes us to a Temptations concert in Des Moines, definitely a highlight of that trip. I am thinking if Nash and I both come here, then this will really put the program on the map. But I can't see spending the next

Dr. J 119

four years in the middle of a cornfield. And Nash, he's telling me about Hawaii. It's beautiful out there, he says, palm trees, ocean, and it's warm. Man, Ames, Iowa, is cold.

Nash ends up playing for Hawaii before his eight-year NBA career with Detroit and Kansas City.

For me, Hawaii is too far away. I'm recruited primarily by northeastern and Atlantic schools. The national powers, UCLA, North Carolina, Kentucky, they seem to have never heard of me. It becomes a familiar pattern: the powers that be underestimating me.

I narrow my choices down to two: St. John's and Louie or UMass and Jack Leaman.

Now, UMass may have become a front-runner because Mr. Wilson and Mr. Leaman played together at Boston University, but what really convinces me is a campus visit that fall. I have always envisioned myself on a mall among ivy-covered buildings, immaculate paths through kept lawns, all the clichés of campus life that have come to represent for me a kind of escape. If I can find myself on those paths, in those buildings, then I will have ascended, risen, to join a certain class of American society, the educated class. This is what my mother has wished for me all along, whether it be St. John's or the University of Massachusetts, and what I desire, too. But I want it to look and feel the way it is supposed to feel, and that means a proper campus with proper-looking buildings and dormitories.

The appeal of St. John's is its proximity to Mom, and to Marky, who has lately been more sickly than usual. If I'm over in Queens, in the next county, I'll be so close to home, it will be as if I never left. Louie stresses that.

"Family, Julius, how can you leave your family?" He's telling us how I'll be playing at Madison Square Garden. About the prep stars who are also coming to St. John's: Sonny Dove, Joe Depre, Mel Davis, Billy Paultz (all future NBA players).

But St. John's is a commuter college, with the athletes living in these rented apartments that, while pleasant enough, don't really make for a campus life. I see myself as more than an athlete. I'm actually going to try to be a student. I want a real campus.

There is another issue about Coach Carnesecca and St. John's that troubles me. Louie plays a more conservative, half-court-focused offense where the guards handle the ball the majority of the time. Louie likes to keep games in the 40s and 50s. I'm not sure I can thrive in that offense. Jack's offense is more open; the ball moves more freely. He likes to get out on the break, look for easy transition hoops. I don't verbalize this at the time, but it is a feeling I have about which system will allow me to bring my playground game indoors. Also, because of Mr. Wilson's relationship with Jack, I feel comfortable that between them, they will make sure that I get a chance to succeed.

But it's that visit to UMass that does it for me. Driving up Highway 91, coming through those mountains, then seeing the different colleges, Science, Liberal Arts, the Old Chapel, Memorial Hall, the campus pond: it just looks like how I imagine a college should look. It is orderly, neat, everything where it should be. There is the Boyden Athletic Center, where there are a half-dozen indoor practice courts, and then the Curry Hicks Cage, that old four-thousand-seat gym that gets louder than the Garden. And academically, UMass's business program is among the best on the East Coast, just a notch below the Ivy League. That's a meaningful degree that would forever lift me out of the jewelry store mailroom.

"You have to make the decision," Mom tells me. "I'm not gonna make it for you. Whatever you do, I'll stand by you."

Mr. Wilson tells me the same thing, but after getting in his pitch for Jack Leaman and UMass.

My mind is made up, and I tell my mom and Marky, who are disappointed I'll be out of state but say they understand my choice. I call Louie and tell him, and I break down while we're talking and for the first time in a long, long time, I start crying.

"You're a good kid, Julius, and a fine player," Louie is telling me. "I wish you nothing but the best."

I know what I'm crying about: this means I'll be leaving home, leaving Mom and Marky—and Freda and my nephews, Keith and Barry, and Mr. Dan—in just a few months.

34.

Some of my classmates are talking about the draft, about the injustice of the war in Vietnam, about how they can avoid going to fight. We have friends from previous classes who have already been drafted and stationed in foreign countries. Some of my friends, like Leon, believe the African-American has no obligation to serve a country that has exploited him, from slavery all the way up through the discrimination that we are still experiencing. He echoes Muhammad Ali in his insistence that he has no beef with the Vietcong. I'm torn by this issue. Nonviolence, as preached by Dr. Martin Luther King, would seem to argue against taking up arms, even on behalf of one's country. Yet I also believe that the United States of America, for all its flaws, is the land of opportunity. Look at the opportunity I am being given: a full scholarship to a great university, a chance to get an education.

Even Leon, who has been offered an academic scholarship to UMass, is benefiting from what is right about the United States.

We're red-blooded Americans, my mom tells me, we're patriotic. "But this war," she says, "this war doesn't make sense."

But my father served in Korea. I have uncles who have been in the service. And while that doesn't appeal to me, I believe that if I am drafted, I will go. Of course, I already know I'm going to college, so that puts it off for a few years.

This represents a larger idea, however. I am firmly in the camp of those who believe in the American dream. I'm not flag waving or crying at the sight of a parade, but America, in my view, works. It is a force for good. It is the greatest nation. And if I work to the best of my abilities, then I will be rewarded.

And I like order, neatness. The protests and burning of draft cards and renouncing of citizenship, it all seems messy and unorganized. I shy from chaos.

Leon accuses me, "You're going to end up working for the Man."

I disagree. "I want to work for myself. That's all."

But all around us, this debate, over who we are, over the kind of society we want to live in, over the nature of that society and our relative freedom within it, has become suddenly vital and real. What is our obligation? How can we force change? And what, exactly, is the athlete's responsibility in all this? Do we have a special role? We hear that Lew Alcindor, the greatest New York City basketball player of them all, has not only changed his name to Kareem Abdul-Jabbar, but that he will also be boycotting the 1968 Olympics, refusing to play for his country. Muhammad Ali was stripped of his championship for refusing to serve in the Army. Soon, in Mexico City, Tommie Smith and John Carlos will both medal in the 200-meter dash and, on the podium, raise their fists in the black power salute. We all watch this and some of my teammates and classmates are thrilled by this show of defiance, but I am troubled. It is actually shameful to me that they are escorted from the podium.

I love America. I'm buying the American dream.

We should solve our problems through negotiation, arbitration, mediation. Not with a raised fist. What does that solve?

These times will challenge that dream, however, as each assassination and protest and evening news clip of napalmed villages causes me to wonder at what price this dream is protected.

The world is upside down, yet we have made progress. The Civil Rights Act passed in 1964. It's illegal to discriminate. So there are programs in place that address the most grievous of our issues. Yet Leon and others are demanding restitution. They want to blow up the system, and I'm not buying that. They talk about the midnight plane to Africa. I'm not getting on that plane.

They want to destroy the system.

I am a product of that system.

Yet my views are tested; my belief in that system will be challenged on a warm April morning.

35.

The spring air moves with the first flies and gnats hatching from the dark, wet places in the shadows of our school. The holly tree branches are still heavy with moisture, the boughs barely swaying under the footfalls of squirrels still skinny from the long winter. Sun pours down on me, on us, on graduating seventeen- and eighteen-year-olds who can sense the potential and promise—and the anxiety—of impending freedom. I appreciate the beauty of the world, of our little suburb, and I have eased into the warm familiarity of my peers, of boys and girls (now young men and young women) I've spent four years with and who I know by sight and name and temperament and personality. The surety of my lope, the familiarity of my smile, the confidence that any greeting I extend will be returned, and as warmly, I move through the halls of Roosevelt High as pleased and content as a child surveying his stamp collection. Why does this ever have to end?

Yet our teachers interrupt us, in calculus, in trig, in humanities, in French, they are stopped short, this time by a message sent from the principal through the school by runners, and a school full of graduating seniors now is told that Dr. Martin Luther King Jr. has been assassinated in Memphis.

The man who spoke for me, who embodied the beliefs that allowed me to be me, who espoused nonviolence. He has been taken by a rifle shot?

It is inconceivable to me.

A dark mood settles over the school. Many of the white students immediately gather their books and depart. The black students are stunned, slumped over at our desks. For the first time, I understand that urge to rage, to exact revenge, and momentarily I think about seeking out someone, anyone, a white face perhaps, to punish for this awful crime. It is a flicker of emotion rather than a thought, and one I instantly dismiss as wrong and inappropriate, for my white classmates have as little to do with this as my black peers. This is a crime against all of us, white and black, Ray Wilson tells me when I find him

Dr. J

in the guidance counseling office to talk about what has happened to our world.

We don't harbor anger, nor do we seek revenge. We must do the best we can, that's all. But as Mr. Wilson is telling me this, he, too, appears heartbroken, his eyes sagging, his cheeks fluttering, his lips parting and closing as he seeks the words. He gives me a handshake and reminds me that I have to stay on track, not let this change my thinking, my plan.

I walk the main hall and then out the double-door entrance to the school. Ahead of me, her form silhouetted in shadow, walks Stephanie Cardone, a cheerleader and our class valedictorian, a white girl with whom I am friendly. We are in homeroom together and I know Stephanie to be a quiet girl, a good student. She is carrying a half-dozen books held in both arms against her blue-sweatered chest. Now in the last semester of my senior year, and in no contention for valedictorian, I am carrying just one textbook. It doesn't even occur to me that Steph is white and I am black, but as I am out the door and my eyes adjust to the sunlight, I see Stephanie surrounded by seven black kids. They are from the middle school, eighth and ninth graders. The classes behind ours, I know, are 90 percent black, as more and more white children are being pulled from the public schools or white parents are moving from our suburb to whiter ones farther out on Long Island. My class, and the one just below mine, will be the last racially balanced classes at Roosevelt High.

But these kids are sneering. They are enraged by the news of Dr. King's murder, and like many young men that day, they seek to exact revenge arbitrarily, on any white person they see. Their faces surprise me in how they are contorted with malevolence and disgust. And for Stephanie, of all people, who

I know to be a good, gentle person, and very liberal as well. I'm taken aback by the anger I see in these boys. It is similar in its hatred and disdain to what we have seen in southern white sheriffs and Klansmen on the evening news.

These boys want to harm somebody.

"Honky bitch," a boy says.

"Fuckin' white bitch."

They are spitting at her, and perhaps too young to understand the implications of a gang of males surrounding a female, and I am not sure I can comprehend all the villainous nuances of this scene. I drop my books and push aside the boys.

I am unafraid.

The boys size me up. They know who I am.

"That's Julius Erving," one of the boys says.

"Don't care," says one, the tallest, perhaps the bravest, perhaps the angriest.

"Leave her alone," I say. "Go find trouble somewhere else. You're not gonna mess with her."

What could I really do against them? But the boys seem suddenly unsure. What had been a menacing pack shot through with the adrenaline of rage and bitterness is now suddenly softened by their doubt. Not about the righteousness of their cause but by their fear of *me*.

They shrink. They retreat. "Let's go over to Baldwin and beat up some kids over there."

Stephanie and I collect her books. She smiles at me.

"Will you walk me home, Julius?"

I nod. "Of course."

And on that cursed day, perhaps the darkest day of my high school career, certainly one of our darkest moments as a nation, we—a black boy and a white girl—walk home together. She tells me about looking forward to college, how bad she wants to go and study business. I'm going to college, I tell her. I want to study business, too.

"I didn't want to get beat up today," Stephanie tells me. "I have homework to do and I'm, I mean, we're all getting ready to graduate."

"We. That's right."

This is our hope, as a nation, I think, that two kids—the little black boys and little white girls of Dr. King's speech—can just walk together, and share their dreams, and in sharing somehow give strength and validity to each other's dreams. Teachers, our parents, Ray Wilson, Earl Mosley, Don Ryan, they keep telling us we are America's future. Adults repeat the sentiment so much it becomes a platitude, as meaningless as a car advertising jingle, but now, at this moment, as Stephanie thanks me for walking her home, it becomes real.

1.

In the summer heat, we pack up the car, my two suit-cases and eight-track player fitting neatly in the capacious Oldsmobile trunk, the heavy door swinging shut with a creak and a thunk, and Marky climbs in the back and Mom and I sit up front for the long drive on the Southern State Parkway to the Whitestone Bridge to I-95 to 91 all the way up to Amherst. It's a cloudy morning and as we pass through sudden rain showers, we roll up the windows and then roll them back down when it's dry again.

"June," Marky asks, "you excited?"

Of course I'm excited.

Mom looks at me and smiles. "He's nervous! That's what he is."

But I can also see in her stern expression, the way she leans into the wheel, that she is also concerned, perhaps even holding back tears. I think she must be feeling both pride at my going to college and sadness at my leaving home.

Freda and Mr. Dan and my nephews, Barry and Keith—Freda has two sons now—said their good-byes at the house.

The team said their good-byes the night before, after a game at Roosevelt Park. And Leon will be meeting me up on campus.

"June," Marky asks, "can I have your records?"

"You can borrow them, Marky."

When we finally arrive at Hills North, the athletic dorm just down Pleasant Street from the campus pond, I move my suitcases up into my dorm room where my mom makes my bed for me and puts away my clothes in the careful, precise, sharply folded manner that I like. Marky points out that we live on Pleasant Avenue in Roosevelt. "That's quite a coincidence."

I tell him that we're on Thatcher, off Pleasant, but still, I can see that Marky finds the parallel reassuring.

Mom insists that I show her the athletic dining hall where I'll be having my meals. And when we return we meet my new roommate, a fellow I'll call Tim, a stocky, bearded white guy from rural Massachusetts who is standing straight up in the middle of the room.

He's begun to unpack since we've been gone, and I notice on his desk an array of hunting knives, shining in the fluorescent white light of our dorm room.

"I'm Julius," I say, also introducing him to my mother and brother.

He nods, shakes our hands, and goes back to unpacking.

Mom looks at the knives, obviously concerned.

"I'm fine, Mom. Now you got a long drive home."

As a scholarship athlete, I arrive on campus a few days before most of my fellow incoming freshmen. I'm to meet with my tutors and get familiar with the athletic facilities and my new environment. With practice every day and a full academic course load, Jack Leaman and my freshman coach, Pete Broaca, want us to become familiar with the campus and our new routines.

I feel for the first time how alone I am. Leon hasn't arrived on campus yet. We have another friend on her way to UMass, Coach Wilson's daughter Carmen. But for now, I am alone, and as I walk down a brick path between lawns, I search the faces of my incoming classmates and the upperclassmen, those who are already on campus and those who perhaps never left for the summer, and I notice that, for this evening, at least, there are no other black faces, or Hispanic or Asian for that matter. I knew there were just 125 black students in the incoming 4,000-plus-student freshman class, but I hadn't considered what that would actually feel like.

Hempstead and Roosevelt were both integrated communities, with whites and blacks in equal measure. Now, I realize, going on to a big state school like UMass means going into, to some degree, the white world. I feel I am prepared but I am also, for the first time, intimidated. We have a telephone in our room, and when I get back, I plan to call Coach Wilson, just to check in, tell him I've arrived.

My roommate, Tim, has unpacked even more knives, and spring traps and snares.

"What are you going to do with all those knives?" I ask.

He smiles. "I'll show you. We're gonna have some fun."

"What do you mean?"

I've never seen these kinds of traps before, they're like mousetraps only larger, and the snares are made of some kind of synthetic material, the white nylon-like rope looking like little bones against the wood veneer of the desk.

Tim grew up on a farm in the vicinity of North Adams, and like me he is the first in his family to go to college.

I explain where I'm from, Roosevelt, Long Island, and I try to describe my suburban upbringing. I tell him that I feel like I

grew up somewhere between the city and the country. We had trees, and a lake over in Roosevelt Park, and in the summer, of course, there was the beach.

Tim nods, thinking over what I'm telling him.

"Did you have indoor plumbing?" he asks.

I don't know what that means. "You mean a bathroom?"

He nods.

"Well, yeah, of course."

Tim shakes his head. "Then you're city folks."

He goes back to work looking over his nooses and snares.

I think about calling Coach Wilson but then decide to go out for a walk instead.

2.

Every morning, before the heat makes the gym stifling, I go over to the Boyden Building, where I shoot a few hundred jump shots, foul shots, and layups and then do my leaping drills and finally, after about two hours, I'll take off my shirt and count out my steps and then throw down a few dunks. By the time I'm finished, it's so hot that I'm drinking about a gallon of water from the fountain and then lying back on one of the benches. I meet a few of my future teammates over at Boyden, and after my workouts, we'll play some two-on-two or three-on-three or even get a pickup game going with other students. There's a couple of freshman five-foot-ten shooters named Mike Pagliara and John Betancourt, both white kids, and a six-foot-five forward named Rick Vogeley. Among the upperclassmen working out at Boyden that late summer are Ken Mathias, our tallest player at six foot six, and the senior captain, Ray Ellerbrook. I'd met Betancourt and Pagliara before, when I came up to visit the campus, but both of them size me up.

"Julius, man, you've grown," they tell me.

They're not the first to point that out. I played my senior year at six foot three, and right now I'm just an inch and a half shorter than Mathias.

My first taste of college-level ball comes at Boyden, during these summer pickup games, which introduces us to our teammates and establishes a basketball pecking order. Most of us, having been the best players at our respective high schools, don't trust another player unless he's staring down a layup. This is especially true of Betancourt and Pagliara, two gunners who always think they're open, and every time I get an offensive rebound, they are looking at me, wiggling their fingers and nodding with their eyes wide. The basket always looks gigantic to them.

But very soon, my teammates, especially the guards, recognize that if they get me the ball in my spots, on the left baseline or down low, then I will not only shoot a very high percentage shot, but if I miss, there is a good chance I will get a rebound and if I don't put that back up, I will kick it out for an open jumper.

After a few mornings of workouts and then afternoons of pickup ball, I arrive at the gym to find about sixty people sitting up in the bleachers. I'd noticed small crowds coming to watch me work out, but this is the first time I realize that these crowds are growing, and they don't stay to watch the pickup games, they come to watch me dunk the ball. Because of Lew Alcindor's dominance at UCLA, the NCAA has made the slam

Dr. J

dunk illegal in college games, but that doesn't mean we can't do it during warm-ups or practices. Just like back home, the dunk remains the ultimate crowd-pleasing shot. I showboat a little for my new classmates, throwing in some reverses and then rock-the-cradles and make sure they will leave talking about this new player they've seen over at Boyden.

Betancourt and I quickly become friends. He's from Westwood, New Jersey, which I tell him must be the middle of nowhere because I've never barnstormed a game out there. But I like John, and those first few weeks of school we start to hang out, and he takes me to a few fraternity parties. He and Pagliara have decided to pledge a frat, and they are urging me to join them as Kappa Alphas.

My new roommate, Tim, is turning out to be a difficult guy to get comfortable with. He's almost always in the room, except for a few hours just before dawn when he slips out with some of his strange trapping gear. I've never met anyone like him, but then, besides my cousins down in South Carolina, I don't know too many people who grew up on a farm. Maybe he's used to getting up before sunup to milk cows or something, so it's just a habit he can't shake.

I join Betancourt and Pags at a few frat parties. The music at these parties is always good: they play some Motown, some Aretha Franklin, and plenty of Beatles. While I don't share in the alcohol, I do enjoy the camaraderie with my teammates and their friends. Being a highly recruited athlete does make it easier to slide into a social life on campus, and plenty of the fraternities make it clear they would like me to rush. The Kappas have a reputation as the frat for jocks, and John and Pags have already decided to pledge. They tell me again that I should join, that Rick Vogeley is also pledging.

"Come on," John is telling me. "You join a frat and you have people looking out for you."

I don't need anyone looking out for me.

There is something about the pledging process that turns me off. I don't like the ritual humiliation, the paddling, the secret vows, and it seems that the social life of a fraternity revolves around drinking. Also, I would have to give up a lot of my personal life if I join a fraternity. I tell the brothers I'm not rushing and head back to my dorm.

When I get back, I find that Tim is seated at his desk, wearing thick gloves and carefully scrutinizing what appear to be little brown mittens.

I look closer and realize they are dead chipmunks. He has laid them out on a cutting board. This is what he's been doing every morning, going out to trap chipmunks.

He looks up at me, a strange smile on his face.

"Julius, would you like to cut the head off?"

"What?"

He nods. "Here, watch."

And he takes one of his large hunting knives, turns the chipmunk over, and adjusts it on the board, sort of probing the animal with the point of the knife. When he has found the spot he is looking for, he presses down with the handle, and the animal's neck is cut with a crunching noise that reminds me of a knuckle cracking.

He slides the head to the edge of the board and then pulls over another chipmunk and gets to work severing that head.

I'm terrified. "Why are you doing that to chipmunks?"

He nods. "I have some squirrels, too."

After that, I feel like I'm stuck between this crazy animal vivisectionist and the endless keg parties of fraternity row. And

Dr. J

I don't want either. I just want a place where I can sleep without listening to the arteries and spinal columns of small mammals being severed.

3.

Finally, after a few nights of this, I go see Jack Leaman and tell him that they have me in a room with a madman.

I explain what Tim has been doing.

Coach Leaman shakes his head. "He does what?"

I tell him again.

Coach sits back behind his desk. "This is a first."

I tell Jack that he has to either get me a new roommate or give me a single, because I can't live with Tim.

"Let me see what I can do."

Jack arranges for Tim to be moved to another floor, to a single of his own. I stay in our room, which gives me among the most spacious singles in the dorm. Now, I'm thinking, *now* I can enjoy college life.

I sign up for a full schedule: psych, soc, English 101, History 101, mathematics. I don't have to declare a major yet but I'm taking all the prerequisites for a business major.

Freshmen aren't allowed to play varsity basketball, so instead of playing for Jack Leaman, I'm playing for Pete Broaca, our freshman coach. A medium-height, well-built man with slicked-back black hair, he seems to have a complete lack of empathy for his charges. He runs our practices as if determined to break us and make us quit school and surrender our scholarships to tougher kids who are more worthy of playing for UMass.

He has this one drill where we all stand on the baseline and he rolls the ball out, and two of us are supposed to sprint and fight for the ball. It's like going after a fumble on the football field, only on a hardwood basketball court. Broaca rolls the ball out and I dive for it and I get it first, but when I come up, my right hand doesn't feel right. I can't bend my thumb or squeeze my fist with any strength.

"Coach, my hand is killing me."

"You're soft, Erving," Broaca says. "Now get back in line."

After practice I go to see the trainer who sends me to get an X-ray. The doctor comes back and tells me I have a fractured thumb. He sets it in a cast and says I'm done practicing for a few weeks.

When I show the cast to Broaca in his office, he shakes his head.

"Candy ass," he mutters.

So I miss the last few weeks of practice recovering from my injury. I have nothing to do but work on my left-handed dribbling and shooting. I develop as many lefty moves around the basket as I have right-handed moves, and I am able to tip and then control the ball entirely with my left hand, which will allow me to keep another player off me with the right. I also spend that time working on my running and leaping. And I have to make sure I know the plays, which I do by studying them on my own.

For all of Broaca's complaining about my supposed gold-bricking, once my cast is off and the season begins, he has me playing more minutes than anyone else. As usual, it is my re-bounding that keeps me on the floor. Because I'm more of an "amphibian" than I was before, a two-handed player who can use either hand to tip a ball or block a shot, I'm more effective at pulling down rebounds. I find that even though we're in college, and the competition is supposed to be tougher than back in Roosevelt, I'm still able to exert my will upon the game.

For me, that means getting offensive rebounds and putbacks, and making low post moves that start between the left elbow and baseline. From there, I have plenty of options, almost all of them bad for my opponents. I can face up, jab step, and then surge toward the daylight, where I jump over a shorter opponent, or fake the defender so he leaves his feet, and I can go under him and lay it off the glass. I feel like if I can see the glass pane of the backboard, then I can find the right combination of angle and English to bank the ball into the hoop.

Broaca, once he's done trying to break us, turns out to be serious about developing us for the varsity team, and he urges me to improve my jump shot, to extend my range so that my 15-footer becomes more of a weapon. In practice, he has me shoot thousands of jumpers from the left elbow, from the left baseline, telling me that if teams give me that shot, and I can't make it, then they will be imposing their will upon me.

I won't let that happen.

We start the freshman season burning through our conference schedule, easily beating Yankee Conference foes Vermont, Rhode Island, Maine, Connecticut, and New Hampshire, and also handling out-of-conference teams like Rider, Boston University, and Syracuse. Ironically, our toughest game is against a nearby prep school, Rockwood Academy, where players who need to make up some academic credits do a sort of thirteenth grade before going on to a four-year program. Among their players is a pair of highly touted, future All-Americans named

Henry Wilmore and Ron Rutledge. Wilmore will go on to play for Michigan where he will average nearly 24 points a game for the next three seasons. Rutledge will star at St. John's.

Wilmore is from New York City, a Manhattan boy, and is already a playground legend. We've been hearing of each other for years. So this is like a game from Harlem somehow airlifted to the Curry Hicks Cage. It's the only time all season that we'll find ourselves behind at halftime. Wilmore's got the kind of all-around game that Broaca is urging me to develop. He's a big, beefy player, about six foot three, with a sweet shot that he can create off the dribble or on a catch and shoot. And he can battle inside for rebounds. He has these broad shoulders that are boxing me out. I'm still skinny, though not as much of a chicken-chest as I was back in Roosevelt, and so Wilmore is succeeding in pushing me off the block. He scores double figures in the first half, and at halftime Broaca lays into us, giving us the evil stare. Every aspect of our game, he tells us, is the pits.

He fixes his gaze on center Tommy Austin, who at six foot eight is our tallest player. "You're letting a guy six foot three push you around. Tommy, you're getting PUSHED AROUND."

Broaca is a hands-on coach who is not shy about getting in our faces or jabbing a finger into our chests. "You need to wake up, Tommy!"

Then he does something I've never seen before. Broaca turns red, his forehead pulsing, and he comes over to where Tommy is standing and grabs him with two hands by the front of his jersey and starts pushing him back so that Tommy actually falls into his locker, his legs and arms sticking out. "Candy ass!"

Dr. J

Then he storms out of the locker room.

We go out and light up Rockwood in the second half. I finish with over 20 points and 20 rebounds. I figure if I can play with Wilmore, and impose my will on his team, then I should be okay when we move up to varsity. Our freshman squad goes 17-0.

At home, we often play in front of a few thousand spectators before the varsity game tips off. After our game, a bunch of us freshmen come back out to watch the varsity play. The funny thing is, I notice the stands usually empty out in the interim.

I'm sitting with John Betancourt when I point this out to him.

"Strange how the students seem to like freshman ball more than varsity," I say.

John looks at me and laughs. "They only come out to watch us because of you, Julius."

4.

UMass is certainly more challenging academically than athletically. Coach Leaman has made available a room in the athletic department where I meet with graduate student tutors who are helping me adjust to college-level work. I understand most of the material, but I find that we are required to prove our knowledge to a degree that I've never had to before. Writing college papers is a very different proposition than high school homework. I realize that though I took college-prep courses at Roosevelt, I'm not as well prepared as the kids who come from better high schools or private schools. They have already been trained to function in this setting, the ways to organize and structure an essay or a précis. I've never even heard of a précis. There is a kind of code, I realize, of how to talk and write. In college, we are expected to show up already knowing this code. But for those of us from more modest backgrounds, these codes are mysterious. Even the diction of the academic paper is new to me. It's one of the greatest adjustments black college athletes have to make; we almost have to relearn how to speak and write. It is an intimidating and often overlooked part of the journey, and we know of too many cases where an athlete can't make that transition.

I struggle, first with accepting that my own diction and style will not work in a college course, and then with adapting to what is required of me. When I show my work to my tutors, they tell me that perhaps there is a better way to say what I want to say. They explain that it doesn't sound, well, collegiate.

"But do you understand what I'm writing?"

Yes, they do, but they explain that sometimes, in college, you use different vocabulary, longer sentences.

"This looks all right to me," I say.

My tutors proofread my work, rewriting some paragraphs to show me how they think I should write it. I tell them that I think my way is also correct.

They point out that this is about getting a good grade, staying eligible, remaining on track to graduate. Correct doesn't enter into it.

"Look," an English tutor tells me, "the best you're going to get is a C. I'm going to change this, and you are going to get an A or a B. Isn't that better?"

All right, that's an okay deal.

Dr. J

This is how things are done in college. This is the form.

I like form. I like order. Okay, that makes sense. Grammar is a kind of order; it is making sense of language, putting words in their proper places so that they line up and meaning can be extracted. It should be efficient, I think; it should be clear.

Soon, I'm writing my own papers and my English tutor is barely changing any of them.

I relearn how to write. I also change my speaking style, trying to differentiate my Ds and Th's, seeking to speak the King's English. If speaking less colloquially and writing grammatically mean getting my degree and going into business, then that's what I will do.

Not every black student on campus struggles with this adjustment. Sitting in front of me in sociology class is a pretty black girl who already speaks properly. There aren't many black faces on campus, so we naturally strike up a conversation. She's Natalie, and her father is Nat King Cole. Natalie Cole went to prep school in New England, so she already knows how to write college papers. While I find Natalie a very polished and attractive classmate, there is no sexual spark between us and, despite her charms, we never become more than friends.

But freshman year of college is where my cold streak, which has lasted five years since Theresa took my virginity back in Hempstead, finally ends. As a popular athlete, I'm a fairly prominent freshman on campus, and for the first time in my life, I am encountering females who are aggressively coming on to me. Maybe it's the era, the late '60s, the Age of Aquarius and all that, or maybe it's that I'm more poised and confident, grown-up—though I still don't really have to shave more than once every week or so. I have a telephone in my dorm room, and I begin getting calls from female voices, saying things like,

"You don't know me, but I know you. I've been watching you, checking you out around campus."

"Who is this?"

The girl will tell me that she will be wearing a red blouse, jeans, and cowboy boots and standing at a certain spot in the student union in thirty minutes. If I like what I see, then we can take it back to my dorm room.

This is the first time I ever participate in the so-called sexual revolution, and while I don't know this yet, these are my first groupies: women who want to have sex with me not for who I am but for *what* I am. Even exchange students. And I have to say, this is fun. It's the first time I'm intimate with different races, different cultures. I have so many women calling me that I can't meet all of them.

Some of my teammates plead with me, "Man, just tell them to come over. If you don't like them, one of us will."

5.

I'm a comical sight, so cold in the biting Massachusetts winter that I wear a leather jacket under my wool overcoat. I've never shivered so much as I do in the Amherst valley that first winter. While the campus tucked in beneath the white drifts is beautiful, the brick buildings beckon from the snow like cakes in a bakery display case. The trees are heavy with ice. The students are puffy in black and brown wool, trailing scarves in slashes of red and green, half-submerged as they make their way down icy paths. I find the cold to be almost unbearable. Winter is an

Dr. J   145

imposition I hadn't quite prepared for, the days even shorter than back in Long Island, the dawn's dark persisting in the gaps between the lamplight so that my classmates become invisible as we walk to our first classes. So I bundle up, sometimes wearing every jacket and scarf I own until I resemble a frozen hobo. If there were a trash-can fire on my way to stats, I would stop and hold my hands over the flame.

The gym, of course, is warm, and the training room blessedly tropical, the usual mix of steam and sweat making a welcome refuge from the horrors of winter. I would hide out at Boyden all semester if I could, avoiding classes, hibernating in puffs of steam atop soft white towels beneath a comfortable swaddling of athletic tape and ace bandages, my feet dangling in swirling hot water. One such evening, after practice in the Cage, as I am preparing for a warming whirlpool soak, I walk in and find another black man already in the tub, sprawled out, legs fully extended, one foot elevated up and out of the bath. He has his head back, is reading a newspaper in one hand, and has an unlit cigar in his mouth.

I stop. That looks like Bill Cosby.

Damn, *that is* Bill Cosby!

Cosby is one of my idols. Along with Bill Russell and Dr. King, he's one of those guys whom I've viewed as role models.

"What are you doing in my whirlpool?" I ask.

He laughs. He explains he's hurt his foot and takes the water as a kind of therapy. He's up in Amherst as part of his stand-up tour.

"You playing ball up here?" Cosby asks.

I nod.

"What's your name?"

"Erving," I say. "I'm Julius Erving."

"Erving? Erving? Never heard of you."

"Man," I say, "I've heard of you."

I ask him for his autograph. What else can I do? He signs a UMass basketball schedule. I tell him my brother Marky will never believe that I met Bill Cosby.

6.

The campus emerges from the winter, the ice retreating, giving way to mud that shoots forth from the grass and the buds that promise spring—and blessed warmth. As perhaps the best-known black student, I am again under pressure to join one of the school's political movements. Eventually, there will be a student strike protesting the war in Vietnam that will shut down the campus. Leon, my old friend from Roosevelt, is active in the drive to establish an African-American studies program, the first in the United States. He's a rabble-rouser, and he's always talking to me about throwing my weight behind our causes.

It's 1969. A decade of upheaval has almost passed, with violent riots, three world-changing assassinations, and the passage of the Civil Rights and Voting Rights Acts, and I know that Leon is right to be involved. (Leon actually changes his name to Kwaku.) But I'm not going along with his taking over college administration buildings and chaining himself to doors.

I am constantly besieged, almost every time I go to the student union, by a brother in a black suit and skinny tie named Sadiq.

"As-Salaam-Alaikum," he says.

I nod.

"Have you given any thought to the teachings of the Prophet Muhammad?"

I tell him I have. I remind him that I'm a Christian, a Baptist.

"Have you read your Koran?" he asks.

I have a lot of patience for people, and I always take a few minutes to stop and hear Sadiq out. But it becomes an almost comical refrain. Every time I step out of my dorm, here is Sadiq.

"As-Salaam-Alaikum. It is time for you to let Allah into your life."

I return home for spring break. This is an exalted time, where I can pick up again with old high school friends, and even date a few of my former classmates. Either I've changed or the world has changed, because suddenly girls who had seemed inaccessible to me are paying me plenty of attention. Sharon, a senior cheerleader at Roosevelt High whom I had previously considered out of my league, and I strike up a friendship and that spring we become intimate and she even takes me to her senior prom.

My uncle Al, one of the strong male role models in my life, fixes up a blue 1962 Chevy for me, restoring it so that it runs great, with one hiccup: every time I make a sharp left turn the horn sounds. With my new wheels, I feel a sense of freedom and Sharon and I settle into a friends-with-benefits arrangement. I'm catching up with my barnstorming guys, even playing a few games at the old courts, my mood dampened only by the fact that Marky is back in the hospital, this time because his lungs are acting up and the doctors are worried about his weak heart. He's over at Mercy Hospital in Hempstead, and when I go to see him, to show him Bill Cosby's autograph, he seems happy to see me but also a little delirious.

"Angels are coming, June," he is saying. "Angels."

He complains about how his joints ache, how his muscles feel as if they're tearing. I've never seen him in this much pain.

He's lost so much weight and his skin is drawn around his face. He's still only sixteen, but looks much older than his years, and I want to lift him from this hospital bed and take him with me, to load him into my new blue Chevy and introduce him to women, to my friends, to the world. There is a great injustice in this, in one brother, me, getting the gifts of size, of height and strength and speed, of the ability to leap, of the opportunity to rise, while Marky has been shortchanged. He's smaller, he's got bum lungs, he's sickly.

But Marky always comes back, I tell myself.

Mom's scared. Freda is telling everyone not to worry. For as long as we've had a little brother, she says, he's recovered.

"Marky is strong," Freda says. "He's got a strong soul. You'll see."

Marky always comes back.

I believe.

7.

I'm back on campus just a few hours when Mom calls and tells me I have to come back.

"The doctor is saying that Marky isn't gonna make it," she says.

"What do you mean?"

Dr. J

Mom is silent. I hear her fragile breathing. "Just come home, June."

I drive back down, pushing hard on the accelerator but also believing, as Freda does, that the doctors are wrong, that Marky always comes back. He may be weak. He may need a month or two, but he'll come back. He'll show them.

I make the trip in just two hours, but when I pull into the driveway of the house on Pleasant and then come in through the back screen door, there's Mom and Mr. Dan and Freda and my nephews and neighbors and everyone in the house is crying.

He didn't make it, they're telling me.

"Make it where?"

"Oh, June," Mom says, hugging me. "Marky passed."

This doesn't make any sense. Marky is younger than I am. This is . . . this is out of order. The order should be Freda, then me, then Marky. How can Marky be the first to die? And he's only sixteen.

"Can't be," I'm telling them. "He's, he's just—"

But I stop myself. They're telling me that my little brother, my Marky, who followed me and played with me and who was my best friend and who was one of the four, that Marky is dead.

I start crying.

"Where is he?"

Mom tells me he's still at the hospital.

She's asked for an autopsy, to find out what happened, how a sixteen-year-old could have been taken from us. It turns out Marky suffered from a severe, undiagnosed case of lupus erythematosus, the autoimmune disorder that affects the skin, joints, kidneys, and brain and causes almost unbearable pain.

Oh, my heart, all our hearts, break again at the thought of how much Marky must have suffered throughout his life.

I stay home until the funeral, where Marky is buried in a family plot my mother has purchased for us over in Rockville Centre.

I'm in shock the rest of that semester, thinking about the last time I saw Marky and he talked about angels coming to get him, about Marky's wooden casket being lowered into his grave, about my mom and Freda and me crying as we said good-bye. I never stop seeing Marky in my dreams. Even when I'm walking across campus I see him, out of the corner of my eye, strolling alongside me, with his briefcase, his suit jacket, his warm smile, his reddish hair, his unique understanding of me, his forgiveness of me, his love for me. It's like he's always with me.

But I'm reminded, again, of our mortality, yet another sign that life is but a brief interlude between the great mysteries of where the soul begins and ends. I don't pretend to understand or to dwell particularly much on the transformative nature of the soul, but I am convinced the souls of Marky, and of my father, and of my cousin Bobby, and so many more who will be taken before their time, are still with me.

Their souls are the winds that blow me upward. They are part of my rise.

8.

That summer, as my family staggers without Marky, I return to a home where the absence of his inimitable sound, of his

wheezing, his coughing, his long stride down the hall, is a kind of dreadful silence where Marky should be.

Of course, I have to work to supplement my scholarship money, so Freda gets me a job delivering encyclopedias and educational books. She and another girl are the sales staff. They go door-to-door throughout Brooklyn and Manhattan selling these books, which is the easy part of the job because they aren't collecting any money. They just offer these encyclopedias and educational books that help kids learn math or history for a trial period. The customer doesn't pay anything. All he does is fill out an order form. And if the customer doesn't like the books, they promise, they don't have to accept them when the delivery boy arrives with the first volumes.

Freda and her partner, both young, pretty girls, secure an awful lot of orders.

Now, my job is to show up a week later with the second volume of the encyclopedia or textbook and get the customer to sign a contract and agree to a payment plan. There is a monthly payment, a weekly payment, and a daily payment, and I'm the one who actually has to close the sale, to collect the money. Plenty of folks, maybe 25 percent of the orders, don't even let me in the door. They were happy to talk to the pretty girls, but now that this big black brother has arrived, they want nothing to do with our book business.

I spend hours negotiating and haggling over these books and the price, pointing out that the cost of the encyclopedia is just pennies a day. How can they deny their family the benefits of the wisdom and knowledge contained in these volumes? Think of the advantage their son—do you have a son? a smart, promising daughter?—think of the advantage your daughter will have in school if she has access to this kind of information at home!

My pay is based heavily on commission, and the way the business is structured, I receive a good percentage of each sale I close. Once the contract is signed, I get a few dollars every week straight into my pocket. Some weeks, I am making $400, which is more than I've ever earned before. I'm going to return to campus with a sharp new wardrobe.

But even after work, I don't want to go home. The quiet, of a too-big house and just my mom and Mr. Dan now living there, and the space itself are reminders of who we are missing. Mom can't bring herself to clean out Marky's room, and when I go in there, I break down all over again.

I play ball every night at the park. Weekends and some evenings, I'm barnstorming again with Leon, Lenny, Tommy, Ralph, and Robert, and we're looking for games all over, in Queens, Brooklyn, Manhattan, Harlem, and by now plenty of the ballplayers have heard of, and want to test themselves against, me.

But there is only one guy I want to test myself against: Lew Alcindor.

The man I believe is the greatest basketball player in history has just completed his senior year at UCLA and been drafted by the Milwaukee Bucks of the NBA. One Saturday afternoon, my guys and I go looking for him at Riis Park in Queens, on the beach, where he supposedly plays ball and hangs out. We pull up in Robert's Rambler and we see a few games in progress on the courts, but I don't see anyone over, say, six foot five.

"Where's the seven-footer?" I ask some guys waiting for a game. "Where's he at?"

They point down toward the beach, and we see this long, long brother in a yellow dashiki and sandals, sitting on a beach chair, reading a book. He's not playing basketball today.

I walk over to him. "Hey, man, I'm Julius."

He's reading Eldridge Cleaver's *Soul on Ice*.

He nods, lifts up his sunglasses, extends his hand.

I feel like I'm meeting the president.

He smiles. "So Julius has come."

He's heard of me.

"You're not playing ball today?" I ask.

He shakes his head. He has nothing to prove—to me or anyone.

Then we both do something strange, as if even though we won't be playing ball, we need to measure ourselves against each other somehow. We hold up our hands and press them palm to palm. Mine are larger.

9.

When I return to campus, I run into Pete Broaca, who is goose-stepping his way over to Boyden. "Julius! You must have grown three inches!"

Since the end of the freshman season, not only have I grown taller, my arms seem to have gotten longer, so that my reach resembles that of a pterodactyl. In practice, I find myself improvising in a manner that I know my coaches don't like. (Ray Wilson has come up to UMass to join Jack's staff as an assistant.) There are numerous instances where I'll do something on the court like, say, throw a bounce pass from one baseline over the half-court line to the far foul line to hit a teammate in stride for an easy layup, and the coaches will be shouting at me, "Julius, who the hell throws a stupid pass like that?"

But that was the angle: the picket of defenders was cutting off the outlet and I saw a way to get the ball through them by bouncing it.

In one practice, we are learning how to defeat the 2-2-1 zone defense. My shooting guard, John Betancourt, and I have worked out this move where I run the baseline behind the zone, he throws it up, and I grab it and lay it in. So we do this in practice and Coach Leaman stops it and yells, "No, no, NO, ya'll can do that on the playground, but not in here."

He throws me a long pass. "You have to work to defeat the zone." Pass, pass, pick, cut, get a guy open, boom. Catch them sleeping, weak side, strong side. You gotta work! "It takes twenty seconds to defeat a zone."

My play with Betancourt had taken about one second.

"I never wanna see you guys do that again!" And Coach blows the whistle to resume practice.

Perhaps I have known this for a while, but now I can articulate it to myself: I see the game differently than other players, than even my coaches. I am capable of doing things that they have never seen before and so don't know how to coach. Jack Leaman wants to run most of the offense through his captain, Ray Ellerbrook. Ray has a nice shot and is a steady player, but it is clear to everyone on the team from my first varsity game against Providence in which I pull down 28 rebounds and score 27 points, that whether Coach is running plays through me or not, I'm going to handle the ball more than anyone else because I can simply go up and get the ball. My additional height has made me as dominant a rebounder as this conference has ever seen, and there are plenty of plays where I can't resist putting the ball down and taking it coast to coast. My coaches have stopped even complaining about the shots I take, about my leaving the ground before I've decided to shoot or pass, because Jack and Ray have seen enough to trust that I'm operating at a different level than they are used to.

And besides, now that I'm wearing the white uniform with red piping and MASSACHUSETTS spelled out over the number 32, I definitely feel a little more swagger in my game.

That's not to say I'm a difficult player or moody or hard to coach. I'm a listener, I'm a disciplined practice player, and I'm a shut-down defender who never misses his rotations. That's why Jack puts up with my freelancing on offense: because he knows he can count on me in practice, in the games, and during the last five minutes. I shoot the highest percentage on the team, and lead the conference in scoring and rebounding, averaging 25.7 points and 20.9 boards a game, the highest single-season rebounding average in school history—and second in the nation to Artis Gilmore of Jacksonville, who averages 22.2.

We go 18-7 overall and 8-2 in our conference, good enough for an National Invitational Tournament bid where our first-round opponent is Marquette University, coached by Al McGuire and led by a New York City legend I've played against, Dean "the Dream" Meminger. Marquette had won 26 and lost only 3 and actually turned down a bid to the NCAA tournament to play in the NIT, McGuire deciding he would rather play in New York than Fort Worth, where the NCAA committee had seeded Marquette. The game is back at Madison Square Garden, and I love playing in front of my friends and family, though for a half-second, I'm haunted when I think I see Marky in the stands.

McGuire has Marquette playing a ball-control style, down tempo game. In the first half, we take the lead in the low-scoring battle, and I'm the leading scorer and rebounder.

McGuire has never seen me before, and he's shouting at his bench, "Who is that? Who is thirty-two?"

Meminger tells him, "That's Julius."

"Who the hell is Julius?"

"He's for real. He's got serious playground credentials."

But the second half, McGuire uses a Brooklyn boy named Ric Cobb to get me in foul trouble. I score 18 and grab 14 rebounds but it isn't enough: Marquette beats us by 13. They would go on to defeat St. John's in the finals to win the NIT Championship.

Our season is over.

10.

I don't dare tell anyone this, but I find college basketball a little easier than I expected. The only thing difficult is resisting the urge to dunk. The academic work is actually more daunting for me, but by my sophomore year, I've developed good study habits and I'm on track for a degree in management that will propel me into my career in business.

My social life is also thriving, as I meet a pretty girl named Carol, whose father is the head of the geology department. She's tall and fair skinned with a pleasing, oval face and beautiful, straight hair. We meet in class and I ask her to go to the student union for a soda. Our conversation flows naturally; there are none of the awkward silences that I experience with so many women. She invites me over to dinner with her parents, who live in a house in Amherst. This is a long way from the groupie-ish situation that I fell into my freshman year. With Carol, we don't even mess around until I've met the parents a few times. I just see her . . . differently.

She's always well dressed, with a sort of neat, tidy appearance that I find reassuring. But she carries herself in such a classic, dignified manner that even in sweats and sneakers she has this authority about her. We relate on so many levels: we both worked our way through high school, Carol picking tobacco in western Massachusetts during the summers. We share that intense work ethic and that deep belief in family. I cry when I tell her about Marky. She takes me with her to Bible study classes.

One afternoon, we drive the blue Chevy over to Amherst High School and spread out a blanket on a field behind the campus, the sun setting over the pumpkin and tobacco fields, casting us in orange glow. Carol has packed us a picnic of chicken and salad and we drink soda and watch the sunset. She is leaning into me when a red-breasted finch starts flying close circles around us, chirping as it swoops and then comes down and lands right on Carol's leg, just sort of walking around and tweeting. It feels as if the vibe we are putting out is so soothing and gentle and loving that it actually draws in small creatures.

I've never felt this way before.

I am realizing something about myself, about how I view women at this point in my life. Perhaps it is a product of the impersonal manner in which I was introduced to sex, but I divide women into two categories. There are those who I consider relationship material, who I view as good girls, and then there are those who I see more as objects, as bad girls. I know that's simplistic and even offensive to many women, and that among the so-called good girls there are plenty of bad people and vice versa, but I am mired in that kind of patriarchal thinking on the subject and it will take years for me to break out of it. My struggle to respect women and to see them all as God's creatures is one of the ways I've had to rise above my own circumstances and perhaps the cultural norms of when and where I was raised.

So while the rest of my teammates indulge in frat parties and some heavy beer drinking and plenty of my college classmates are smoking marijuana, I'm bitten hard by the love bug. Up until that time, I've been drunk once in my life, at a high school graduation party when I took a few pulls of whiskey and immediately realized I couldn't drive home and walked back to my house. Why would anyone intentionally do that to themselves, I think, to decide to lose control in that way? To leave the house in a car and then to have to walk home without it? It just seems so . . . out of order. I mean, if I'm going to do something, it has to make sense, to be constructive, to help me get to where I want to go. I really don't understand the desire among my peers to get into an altered state. At campus parties, I find the whole furtive rolling of joints, the sucking on a roach, the slit-eyed glaze of a stoned face, to be very uncool. First of all, it's illegal, so it's something you have to hide, and I don't want to hide anything from my parents, from the law, from authorities. And it just looks ridiculous to me, the balling up of a stash in your socks or whatever. I just don't understand the appeal of it.

At parties, while other students are getting drunk or high, Carol and I are like our own universe, sober, yes, but intoxicated on our love. One night, we're over at Kappa house with some of the guys on the team, and there's a keg in the back and a little dance floor in front and they're spinning some slower jams on the hi-fi, and Carol and I are dancing to Smokey Robinson,

clinging to each other on that dance floor, and it's another of a thousand moments like that finch landing on Carol's leg. We feel that we have tapped into such a powerful force—our nineteen-year-old desire and affection—that the terrible events of our world, the assassinations of Dr. King and Bobby Kennedy, of the horrors recently reported about My Lai, of the murders at Kent State, of the riots that tear apart black communities throughout the country, even of losing Marky, and Bobby, and Tonk, that this simple goodness of the two of us in love can protect us from evil.

11.

Coach Leaman becomes my greatest advocate. The 1970 NCAA All-American team includes Pete Maravich, Bob Lanier, Dan Issel, and Calvin Murphy, a pretty good lineup right there. The second team has Austin Carr, Charlie Scott, and Sidney Wicks. With the exception of Lanier, who had led St. Bonaventure to the Final Four that season, these are guys from big-name programs. Leaman believes that I'm as talented as any of them, and my going unrecognized nationally is due to playing in the lightly regarded Yankee Conference.

This is made clear to me when I'm not invited to the Olympic development program.

The intention of the Olympic Development Program, as it's called, is to groom a dozen players in preparation for the 1972 Munich Olympics. The United States had finished in fifth place at the 1970 World Basketball Championships in Ljubljana, Yugoslavia, a sturdy team that included a high school senior named Bill Walton. That team would beat the USSR but would lose to Italy, Brazil, and home team Yugoslavia. The plan now is to assemble the best forty players in the country, ten from each of four regions, and then bring them out to Colorado Springs, Colorado, to scrimmage against each other over the course of a three-week camp to see which twelve should make the Olympic development team that will tour Europe playing national teams.

Johnny Bach, the head coach at Penn State, is one of four coaches running the program and Coach Leaman and Bach are close, so Leaman keeps calling him and telling him he's crazy to leave me off the program. Finally, Bach relents and allows me to be listed as one of four alternates. "If anyone gets hurt, he can come out to Colorado."

So early that summer, as I'm all set to work at Roosevelt Park as the manager, I get a call from Jack telling me I'm to fly out to Colorado Springs and join the Olympic Development Camp at Air Force University.

For the first time, I'm on a team with the most famous young ballplayers in America. There's Tom McMillen from Maryland, Joby Wright from Indiana, Cyril Baptiste from Creighton, Paul Westphal from USC, and my old recruiting buddy Bob Nash from Hawaii. I get there a week after most of the guys, who have been learning Coach Bach's systems and getting familiar with the style of play and dimensions of the international game—slightly wider lanes in a slightly narrower court. I adapt quickly to the new setting, and from the first scrimmage, I am able to impose my will, to get to my spots, control the boards, and find angles to the basket. Once again, it is my rebounding that forces Coach Bach to keep me on the floor. McMillen is six eleven, Baptiste is six ten, Wright is six nine, and I'm outrebounding all of them.

They teach you to always box your man out so that he can't go up and get the ball. My style is to always check where my man is, and as long he's not in position to get the ball, then I go up and get it. It's a slightly unconventional approach because instead of focusing on blocking out, I'm sort of leaving my man early to get the ball. And if I'm timing my jumps correctly, I can take rebounds away from other guys who are in the area because I can get up higher and faster than they can.

But the biggest difference between the college game and the international game?

Dunking is allowed.

I rise.

Bach stops me after practice one day. "How are you doing, Julius?"

I shrug. "I'm doing my thing, Coach."

He laughs. "Well, just keep going and getting the ball and there is no way we are going to leave you at home. No way."

That becomes my plan. I will snatch more rebounds, collect more loose balls, and get my team more possessions than any other player there.

Pretty soon, it becomes clear that I'm one of the top players at the Olympic Development Camp. I mean, the players can feel it and the coaches can see it and while I don't have that perspective, I do know that my contribution is clear and measurable. When we watch film of our scrimmages, I notice I'm rising up out of the pack in the lane to grab more balls than any other player, and my outlets are crisp and efficient, and I'm blocking shots. I'm clearly not the best shooter on the team, but that doesn't matter—we've got plenty of guys who are willing to hoist the ball. Maybe our best offensive threat is Paul West-phal, who has such a smooth game, great handles, flashy, and can dunk with both hands.

In the evenings, after practice and showering, we play cards in these lounges that connect the dorms. (I'm rooming with James Brown from Dartmouth.) During the card games, some of the guys start talking about their plans for the future. And a few of the guys, Joby Wright, Ricky Sobers from UNLV (he's originally from the Bronx), and others start talking about how big a bonus they are going to demand.

Bonus? What are they talking about?

Wright is saying he's going to ask for $50,000 so he can buy a Corvette. Other guys are saying they're going to get more.

I'm silent, just listening, but I realize they are talking about playing professional basketball. Because there are two rival leagues, the ABA and NBA, for the first time college players have some leverage and don't have to sign with the NBA team that drafts them. Rookie salaries have been going up, and these guys are talking about how much money they are going to get when they turn pro.

Pro? Are they serious?

They are.

Now I'm thinking, If Wright and Sobers and Westphal are talking about playing pro ball, and I'm outrebounding and out-scoring these guys, then that means . . . I should be thinking about playing pro basketball.

I had never thought that was possible before. I mean, pros were Bill Russell and Wilt Chamberlain and Jerry West, the Lakers and Celtics and Knicks. I'm a kid from Long Island who plays in the Yankee Conference. My whole plan is to get a business degree.

Nobody from UMass has ever played in the NBA.

12.

When they announce the final twelve spots, there are six white players and six black players and I don't think that's a coincidence. I know they weren't expecting me to be on the team because when they present us with our blue team blazers, with USA on the chest, for the team photo, the sleeves on my jacket barely reach my elbow. I guess I'm taking the place of a shorter player.

So instead of working at Roosevelt Park, handing out basketballs and roller skates, I'm going to be flying to Europe on a Pan Am flight to play basketball in Finland, Poland, and the Soviet Union. For almost all of us, this will be our first trip abroad, and the coaches have impressed upon us that we are ambassadors for our country. I take that seriously. I like the mission. We are basketball players for our country, and this is the middle of the Cold War, and these countries, at least Poland and Russia, are Communist states that represent a stark contrast to the freedoms of the USA. Mom is so excited for me. Freda and her kids come over to say good-bye, Barry and Keith giving me big hugs.

"Juliuth is going to Europes," says Barry.

Barry is a good little ballplayer himself. I pick up both my nephews. Man, I'm thinking before Mom and Mr. Dan drive me to JFK, I'm gonna miss America.

We fly on a Pan Am charter to Moscow. Most of the guys have cameras and many of us are keeping diaries as well. We're staying at the Cosmos Hotel and the first night they host a special dinner where we meet the Russian national team, who we will be playing in a series of games throughout the Soviet

Union. These are men in their twenties and early thirties, big, stocky, tough guys, Army officers, many of whom, like Sergei Belov and Modestas Paulauskas, would win gold at the Munich Olympics two years later. At the welcome dinner, held in the hotel ballroom, the Russians lay out a big banquet, with crab, salmon, and caviar—at least we recognize those dishes—but there are plenty of other foods that most of us are reluctant to try. And the main beverage, as we discover, is vodka. The Russian players are guzzling it down. We are sticking to soda and water. I'm looking at these guys, with their mustaches and muscles, and I'm thinking: these guys look serious.

"Na zdorovie!" they keep shouting, and draining another shot. *To your health!*

I've never seen anyone drink that much alcohol.

It certainly doesn't seem to affect them on the court.

We tour the Kremlin, visit the famous onion-domed Orthodox cathedrals, and spend some time window shopping at the GUM department store. But despite the attempts of our Russian hosts to show their country in a positive light, the guys and I can feel that there is something dour and downbeat about this culture. We see long breadlines everywhere. And there are women working construction, digging ditches. "Man, they got ladies over there with a *jackhammer!*" Even worse, it's a culture without rock and roll. In the stores, they play marching band music. Every once in a while, when we are walking around on the streets, some kids will sidle up to us and say, "American, yes? Beatles? Rolling Stones?"

I'll nod. I don't know what they want.

And our interpreter will come over and run the kids off.

"What do they want?" I ask.

"They want your music," he will say.

I think about how we take it for granted that we can go

down to the Sam Goody's and buy whatever album we want. For these kids, that music must sound like freedom. At night, when I'm sitting in my room with James Brown, he'll put a Sly and the Family Stone eight-track on his tape deck and I'll think it sounds just beautiful.

> *Dance to the music*
> *Dance to the music*

That sounds like freedom right there.

We play the Russian national team three times, in Moscow, Kiev, and Tallinn, and we lose in very tight contests. They are the toughest opponents any of us have ever faced. That we hold our own against these physical, grown men is amazing, but we don't feel that's any consolation for losing as representatives of our country. These guys are tested veterans, and they play with a machine-like efficiency and execute no matter how we play them. Excelling at every aspect of the game, they play crisp zone defenses and every player on the team can shoot. And they have arms as thick as my legs.

This is a road trip beyond any I've ever been on. The courts are different, irregular, with more divots than the old Boston Garden, and the officiating is unfamiliar. Louis Nelson from Missouri is one of our best defenders. He's a little guard who sort of wiggles his butt as he gets down low on defense. When he's guarding the inbounds passer, he puts his hand up in the passer's face to block his line of sight. Whenever he does this, the officials come over and tell him to stop.

"Why?" Louis asks. "It's legal."

"Discourteous," he is told.

I play well against the Russians, pulling down over 10 rebounds a game and scoring double figures, most of my points coming on dunks over the big Russian centers. Only we can't beat these grizzled Russians.

When we sit down for a meal after the game, our interpreters bring in *Pravda* and the other Russian papers. There's a photo of me and in the story they talk about the good fight the Americans put up and single me out: "American Erving is doing things on the basketball court that we've never seen before . . ." They say I'm doing things with "spin" and "elevation" that nobody in Russia has ever even tried.

I leave the Soviet Union thinking I wouldn't mind another shot at these guys in the 1972 Games.

We go on to Poland and Finland, again playing against veterans of Olympic and international competitions. For the rest of the tour, we only lose one more game, finishing 10-4. My teammates vote me the Most Valuable Player of the tour.

After our last game in Helsinki, we walk around the city, which seems like a different planet after Poland and Russia. In Poland, they don't even have proper toilet paper, just this white stuff that comes apart in your hand. And the food: they are serving us these stews and we're finding bits of meat that don't really look like any part of the cow that I'm used to eating. The whole Scandinavian feel, the beautiful blond women, the way everyone is so well dressed, the stores stocked with consumer items, even record stores with the latest Beatles and Stones albums, not to mention Ike and Tina Turner, Isaac Hayes, and Marvin Gaye: it feels great after the dingy and dusty Moscow and Warsaw streets. Because it's still summer, it's always light, the day going to dusk and then right back to dawn, so that we never feel like sleeping. Finland feels like a burst of Technicolor after the gray of the Eastern bloc.

Still, after a month of traveling, when we finally land back

in New York, at JFK, I actually kneel and kiss the American tarmac. The USA, with all its problems, still seems like the place to be. Here I've been to three very different countries, including the great Cold War rival Russia, and none of them compare to America.

Mom and Mr. Dan pick me up at the airport. For a heart-rending flicker, I expect to see Marky. I'm about to ask where he is when I remember. Of course.

13.

As an upperclassman, I have every reason to add a little swagger to my step. Not only have I returned from a tour of Europe with the US national team, I'm also now the acknowledged leader on a basketball squad that should win the Yankee Conference and secure an NCAA tournament birth. And if you consider the level of competition I played with and dominated over the summer, it's not inconceivable that All-American recognition could be coming my way.

I move out of the athletic dorm and over to Orchard Hill. My goal since arriving on campus has been to be a student-athlete, not just an athlete. I am fulfilling my goals as the latter, but I want to work on being a better student. Living in the athletic dorm over at Hills North, I felt stereotyped as a jock, something I am sensitive about. I want my peers to see me as a serious fellow student.

I'm eager to live with my friends, and many of the African-American students on campus, over at Orchard Hill. And it helps that Orchard Hill is closer to Amherst, where my girlfriend, Carol, lives with her family. Our relationship is serious and exclusive, and has withstood the test of our many weeks apart this summer. (We'd only been allowed one phone call back to the US each week during the tour, and I always called my mom's house.) The separation has convinced us both that we want to be together. We spend every minute that I'm free, outside of practice and studying, in each other's company.

My priority remains getting a business degree, but I've concluded that a degree in marketing is unlikely because of my epic struggles with statistics. I take stats and I'm sitting there and thinking, "Are they serious?"

For the first time, I feel that a subject is beyond my abilities. It seems like the kids in that class who can grasp and follow the material showed up with a basic understanding already. And then there are the rest of us who will never figure out what is going on around the summation and gamma distribution symbols.

I have met my academic match in stats.

I am never passing this class.

I declare myself a management major.

14.

Coach Leaman won't let us skip practice. So, as soon as I shower, I run over to Bowker Auditorium to try to catch the last few minutes of Bill Russell's lecture. For me, seeing and hearing Bill Russell is like seeing Abraham Lincoln or Dr. King; he's one of the truly great Americans, a living legend to us black students. I've already read his book *Go Up for Glory*: he didn't receive a single recruiting letter or visit when he was at McClymonds High School in Oakland, California, yet he went on to become, in my opinion, the best all-around player in the history of basketball. Just last year, as the player-coach of the Celtics in his last season, he led Boston to their ninth championship while averaging over 19 rebounds a game. I relate to his story, and admire in him what I have yet to accomplish. Like Russell, I feel like I have to earn my success. I wasn't recruited by the big-name schools, I wasn't selected to the Olympic development trials but was instead invited as an alternate. If you go back even farther than that, playing for the Salvation Army as the first black player or moving to Roosevelt High before I began high school, I've always come in through the back door.

Russell does everything on the court. He blocks shots, he rebounds, he starts the offense with a great outlet pass, and he can score when the team needs it. But his game isn't about stats. With Russell, the only stat that matters is wins.

And like Russell, I like to think that my game, and my ability to impose my will on opponents, speaks for me. But more than that, it's all that Russell represents beyond basketball. He urges young black men to use their minds, to get their education. He reminds us that it's not good enough for us to be good enough. We have to be exceptional.

But tonight, because of practice, I'm too late. The crowd is already filing out.

There he is, near the side exit, standing in his black suit and skinny tie, nodding as he talks to some of my classmates.

I approach him, extending my hand, introducing myself.

"I'm Julius Erving."

He looks at me and does a double take. "You're Irving?"

I nod.

"I've been reading in the *Globe* about this Jewish guy at UMass who is getting all these points and rebounds."

They've been misspelling my name in the *Boston Globe* for a while now, and Russell, who reads the papers every day despite his famously testy relationship with the press, has assumed that UMass has an athletic Jewish guard named Julius Irving.

"I've never seen a guy named Irving that looks like you," Russell says.

Then he does something I never expected. "Let's get a cup of coffee," he says.

So we head over to the student union, where we take a booth and for the next two hours, it's just the two of us. I mean, William F. Russell and me: a nobody from Hempstead, Long Island. Russell is here for our Distinguished Lecturer series. On our walk over to the student center, he had been admiring our campus. I tell him that this campus is why I came here. I love it. I love the whole college experience.

"And there are so many new buildings," I tell him.

He nods, sips his coffee.

"What's the most important building on campus?" he asks.

Hmmm. "The gym? Yeah, the gym."

"Wrong," Russell says. "It's the library."

I walked right into that one.

He tells me that what is being given to me here in college is more than the opportunity to play ball. It's also access to the knowledge in that library. "What is in that building, the books that are now at your disposal, will impact you for the rest of your life."

Dr. J

He pauses, squinting at me. "Impact you more than anything you do on the basketball court."

Hearing this kind of wisdom from a professor or coach is one thing, but hearing it from the greatest basketball player in the world is completely different. While I was already intent on being a student-athlete, now I am sure that I want to keep learning, to keep growing. I don't want to be just another jock.

Russell lays out his whole story, how he was raised by his dad, grew up in Tennessee before moving to Oakland, all the way to present-day Boston, which he tells me he's leaving because of the racism and discrimination he still feels in that city. He'll never go back, he says. He stays with me until midnight, despite the fact that he has to drive ninety miles home.

I walk him to his car. I shake his hand and feel that I have made a new lifelong friend.

15.

Coach Leaman names me cocaptain of the varsity team my junior year, along with Ken Mathias, and by the time the season begins on December 1, 1970, I've grown another half inch so I'm now six foot six, my full height, though I'm still narrow-chested with what Carol reminds me is a skinny butt. We start the season winning 12 straight games. I'm averaging nearly 30 points a game and against St. Michael's I pull down 30 rebounds, which is a new school record. At the end of January, Providence finally beats us by a point when I have an off night.

Despite the loss, I feel a certain serenity about our team and my game. I have realized, at least at this level of competition, there is only one person who can stop me from scoring 30 a night and that is my coach, Jack Leaman, who takes me out whenever we're blowing out opponents. Against Iona, Vermont, Boston College, Connecticut, there are plenty of games where I have a shot at breaking the school scoring record of 41 set by Billy Tindall a couple of years ago, but Coach always removes me for the last several minutes. It's not my style to complain about being pulled from the game, but after it happens a few times, I start to wonder about Coach's motivations.

On my birthday in February the Syracuse Orangemen come down to Amherst. The Orangemen are a huge team, with two six-foot-ten big men, but I'm just killing them, somehow finding space in the lane and laying it in or just jumping up and over their guys. I'm having a great game, going for 36 points and 32 rebounds, and we still have a good three minutes left to play. It's a night, in other words, where I am imposing my will on the game, taking it over. (Little do I know that Bob Costas, a Syracuse broadcast journalism major, is in the stands.) I'm thinking, Okay, that's it, the record is mine tonight.

But Coach Leaman takes me out. "You're done for the day." What?

I take a seat on the bench. Later, I ask Coach Leaman why he removed me. I was going for the record, man.

"I want you to have something to play for in your senior year."

Like I said, Leaman is the only person in New England who can stop me from scoring.

But those 32 rebounds remain the single-game UMass record to this day.

Our next game is down in New York, at Madison Square

Garden. We beat George Washington, and I score 35 and collect 17 rebounds.

We finish the regular season 23-3, going 10-0 in our conference. I set school records for scoring and rebounding, averaging 26.9 points and 19.5 rebounds, both marks that have never been broken. Despite our success, however, we miss out on the NCAA tournament and have to settle for another NIT bid, again drawing the eventual champion, this time North Carolina, in the first round. Featuring guard George Karl and forward Bill Chamberlain from Long Island Lutheran High School, the Tar Heels take us apart. I foul out early in the second half and they pull away, beating us by 40.

It's disappointing when I learn that I haven't even made the NCAA's All-American team, losing out to Ken Durrett, Johnny Neumann, Howard Porter, John Roche, and Curtis Rowe. Now I respect all of those guys, have even run in the playgrounds with a few of them, but I know I can play with anyone in college basketball at this point.

At least the coaches make me a third-team All-American and the UPI wire service also puts me on their All-American team. But still, how much better can we as a team play than going 23-3 and unbeaten in our conference? What do we have to do to get invited to the NCAA tournament?

I keep my doubts to myself.

Win without boasting, lose without crying.

Coach Leaman tells me that we will do whatever it takes to improve. In addition to Al Skinner, a slick point guard who I remember from Malverne High in Long Island, he tells me he's got another kid coming up from Oyster Bay, New York. In fact, would I mind showing him around? His name is Rick Pitino.

16.

There are students smoking joints by the campus pond. Sure sign of spring. I am making my way past the chapel, then down Hicks Way to Boyden. The college, especially when it warms up during the spring, when I can shed a layer or two of outerwear, really feels like home to me now, and as I walk down the path, among the birch and maple trees, many of my fellow students nod toward me or say hello, reinforcing my sense of belonging. I feel that next year will be better. But also, I feel the very first flashes of a kind of sadness that this has to end, that this experience, the campus life I had sought, is fleeting. And I feel so lucky that I have been given this opportunity.

When I get to Boyden, Ray Wilson pulls me aside and says he feels obligated to tell me something.

A sports agent has gotten in touch with him and wants to speak with me.

"About what?" I ask.

"About turning pro."

17.

I haven't really been following the rivalry between the ABA and the NBA. Before attending the Olympic development program, I didn't think about turning pro at all. My plan was, and still is, to be the first in my family to get that bachelor's degree.

Yet since the ABA was founded in 1967, a succession of top

basketball players has joined the new league. Established pros like Rick Barry and Billy Cunningham have jumped to the upstart league. New York playground legend Connie Hawkins was the league's first MVP. More relevant to me, however, is the fact that college players have been leaving school early to sign with ABA franchises, and earning hundreds of thousands of dollars in the process. Spencer Haywood left the University of Detroit after his sophomore year and signed with the Denver Rockets of the ABA for $450,000. Ralph Simpson left Michigan last year and signed with the Rockets for $750,000. Dan Issel, Rick Mount, and Charlie Scott are among the college stars who have signed or will soon be signing with the ABA, and these are all contracts paying at least $100,000 a year. George McGinnis of Indiana University has recently signed a $200,000 contract with the Pacers—and he's only a sophomore. The rivalry between the two leagues is driving up salaries. And these ABA clubs are paying a premium for young talent. The NBA, on the other hand, is still underpaying young stars, giving UCLA guard Henry Bibby just $25,000 for his first year. The only guys who get seriously paid over in the NBA are big men. A couple of seasons ago, Wilt Chamberlain made news when he signed for $100,000 a year and then Russell literally one-upped him when he signed for $100,001.

"Ray, you think I should talk to this agent?" I ask Coach Wilson.

"It can't hurt, Julius," Ray says. "It's worth taking a look at. At least hear what he has to say."

The agent I speak with is named Steve Arnold, and he explains to me that the leagues will soon be merging, eliminating the competition for players and driving salaries back down to Bibby levels for all of us.

He says he believes the Virginia Squires of the ABA would be interested in making an offer for my services.

I've never heard of a Squire. "What's a Squire?"

"It's like the Virginia version of a Minuteman," he says.

Steve stresses that this merger is imminent, perhaps a few months away. By the time I graduate with my class and am drafted by an NBA team, there might be only one league and I will have to take whatever I can get. I have leverage as long as there are two leagues.

When I hang up, I talk to Mr. Wilson and ask him what he thinks. "At least hear what they have to offer," he says.

I tell Carol about it, and we both agree that it doesn't make sense to leave college with only one year left. A degree, after all, will last forever.

I drive back to Roosevelt in the blue Chevy for spring break. I meet in New York City with Steve Arnold, who has slicked-back hair and wears a sharp suit. He's very persuasive and he starts to intimate how much money may be involved here. It's much, much more than I had previously imagined.

I go straight to visit my old freshman coach at Roosevelt, Mr. Mosley. When I recount the conversation with the agent, he says he's going to make a few calls and get back to me.

I'm at home the next morning when I hear a knock at the front door and my mom answers and shouts upstairs, "June, Coach Mosley is here."

Mr. Mosley has decided we need to go see Louie Carnesecca, who is now coach of the New York Nets, in their offices over near Island Gardens, where the team plays. Mr. Mosley thinks if I do leave school, then I should at least explore playing locally with Louie and the New York Nets. I drive us over in the Chevy, the horn honking every time I turn left, and we

Dr. J

park in this little parking lot next to a run-down office building. We go upstairs to see Louie in the Nets office suite. It's two rooms at the end of the hall, a receptionist behind a desk and Louie in the office behind her.

Mr. Mosley tells me to wait here. I take a seat, pick up a copy of *Sport* magazine, smile at the receptionist, and wonder at the wisdom of joining the ABA. This office doesn't really seem any nicer than Coach Leaman's back at UMass. Mr. Mosley and Coach Carnesecca stay inside for a while, but when Mr. Mosley comes out he tells me we're going.

"What happened?" I ask.

"Louie would love to have you play for the Nets. He called Roy Boe (the owner of the Nets) who told him he won't sign underclassmen. He thinks you should stay in school. That's the best thing for you."

I nod, start the car. "He's probably right, right?"

Mr. Mosley nods. "Louie would have signed you today, Julius, if it were his decision."

"Well, I'm staying in school," I tell Mr. Mosley.

But Steve Arnold is talking to Mr. Wilson, who is also back on Long Island. Arnold says we should come down to Philadelphia, meet with the representatives from the Virginia Squires, at least entertain their offer. It won't cost us anything and who knows, maybe something will come of it. I tell Mr. Wilson I'm 100 percent against leaving school, but we might as well hear them out, maybe learn something that I can use later, when I do finally graduate.

Before we go down, Mr. Wilson puts me in touch with Bob Woolf, who represents John Havlicek, Carl Yastrzemski, and Jim Plunkett, among other notable athletes. I tell Woolf what I'm doing. He tells me to call him during the negotiations if I need to. But I assure him, this is just an exploratory mission. I'm not going to sign anything.

Mr. Wilson and I take an early-morning train down. We don't tell anyone, not even Coach Leaman, where we are going. Meeting us at the Airport Motel in Philadelphia are Johnny Kerr, the Squires' general manager, Al Bianchi, their coach, and Arnold. I like Bianchi immediately. He's a Long Island guy, and a former guard-forward for the Syracuse Nats and Philadelphia 76ers. He has a big smile that splits his round face like a wedge taken out of an orange, thick glasses, and brown hair combed over his receding hairline. Kerr is another basketball legend and former teammate of Bianchi's. I remember Red Kerr, as he is known, from his career with the Knicks. He's a big man, about six foot nine, and has a rectangular face with a square jaw. Both men are wearing jackets with turtle-necks beneath them.

Al and Johnny have taken a suite at the motel. We meet in the sitting room, with room service coffee on the table. Al and Johnny both shake my hand and I can see them carefully checking the size of my hands and then nodding at each other, as if I have confirmed something they've heard before. Red is taller than I am, but my hands are much larger than his. "Man, look at your hands," he says.

Red makes a similar pitch to what Arnold has been telling me: the leagues are going to merge, giving players less leverage.

"If I stay in school," I tell them, "I could be a first-round draft pick."

Red counters by asking: "What if you get hurt? A career-ending injury, you break an ankle, leg, whatever? Then it's all over, off the table. Nobody will draft you."

They talk about the Squires, who were originally the

Oakland Oaks before moving to Washington, DC, for a season and now play in Virginia.

Arnold keeps looking at me and nodding, emphasizing the points Red is making.

Then they start talking about money, a lot of money. They are offering over $400,000 for a four-year contract, but the payout will be deferred over twenty years. At this point I realize that I wouldn't be in this room, with an agent and the general manager and coach of a professional basketball team, if I am not seriously interested in playing professional basketball. The offer of the money makes it all suddenly very real.

Ray and I decide to get a couple of rooms and stay over in Philadelphia for the night.

As we're talking, it becomes clear there are two different sums involved here. There is the actual annual salary, and then there is deferred money. The big numbers we've been reading about in the newspapers are the gross payment, including salary and deferred payments. What the ABA has been doing to make the contracts seem larger is including deferred payments that are actually annuities that will pay out over twenty or so years. When University of Cincinnati forward Jim Ard signed with the Nets for, supposedly, $1.4 million, the actual cash was $250,000 over four years. The rest was to be paid in annuities into which the Nets would invest a few thousand dollars a year that would start paying Ard decades later. So his annual salary was more like $60,000.

I'm no financial genius, but I know the difference between cash now and the promise of cash later. I excuse myself from the meeting and go into the bedroom, shutting the door behind me to call Bob Woolf and lay out the situation. He agrees with me: cash now is our goal.

He tells me to put him on with Red Kerr.

He tells Red that he is advising me to stay in school because I'll be a first-round draft choice.

"Then why is Julius here?" Red asks.

Woolf tells Red that the offer isn't even close to enough to make him advise me to leave school. "This kid has the Olympics coming up, the Pan-American games. I can't tell him in good faith to go pro."

The negotiations continue all afternoon and evening. Wilson, Arnold, Bianchi, Kerr, and I sit around that table, our jackets off, room service hamburgers and french fries and congealing ketchup on white plates spread out before us. And that evening, the owner of the Squires, Earl Foreman, arrives. Foreman had basically taken over the Oakland Oaks from singer Pat Boone two years earlier by assuming Boone's debts. Despite the Oaks winning the ABA Championship in 1969, Foreman immediately moved them. (This was the second year in a row the ABA champion moved after winning the title. Connie Hawkins's Pittsburgh Pipers had moved to Minnesota after winning the title the year before. Then they moved back to Pittsburgh the next year. The ABA, I am discovering, is an interesting league.) Foreman's team played in Washington, DC, for a year as the Washington Caps—while remaining in the ABA's Western Division, which meant the longest road trips in the league—before moving to Virginia and the Eastern Division. Their biggest star had been Rick Barry, who Foreman sold to the New York Nets for cash, but they have second-year guard Charlie Scott, a New York City legend who is coming off a Rookie of the Year season averaging 27.1 points a game.

Foreman shows up wearing a blue suit and a striped tie.

Dr. J 181

He's smiling and eager and now it seems like the negotiations really have momentum. He gets on the phone with Woolf and they kick around some more numbers while Arnold is talking to me, telling me that the latest offer, $500,000 for four years, is better even than George McGinnis has gotten. "And George went to Indiana!"

I get up and call my mom to tell her what is going on.

"Oh June, I don't know. But that is so much money!"

My mom and Mr. Dan make less than $15,000 a year. I mean, we are already talking about more money than I ever dreamed of making. And for playing ball!

I tell her I won't do anything without calling her first.

I call Carol and fill her in.

"This is exciting, Julius! But if you turn pro, what about us?" she says. "This is Julius, my college boyfriend, and you're talking about playing pro basketball? For the . . . Virginia who?"

She's never heard of the Virginia Squires.

I tell her that we'll be fine, we'll stay together no matter what.

Ray is calling Jack Leaman and now telling him what is going on, warning him that I may leave school.

Earl Foreman is agreeing to the $500,000 over four years, but he wants a twenty-year payout.

No, I'm not interested in that.

"Now, Julius—" Arnold says.

"Call Bob," I tell Ray.

I explain to Bob that I need more money up front, shorter payout. Earl gets on the phone with Bob.

By now we've had two dozen room-service hamburgers on that coffee table, drunk about six pots of coffee, and Earl is smoking cigar after cigar. I'm sitting on the sofa, listening to Bianchi and Kerr talk about what a great fit I will be on the Squires, with Charlie Scott, with Fatty Taylor, big man Jim Eakins, the power forward Neil Johnson.

Finally, Earl comes back in.

"Five hundred thousand dollars, $125,000 a year for four years, paid over seven years."

Now I get up and call Bob back.

He says it's the best we can do.

I tell everyone in the room that I'm going to sleep on it. Earl is having his secretary down in Norfolk, Virginia, draft a contract and she'll be here in the morning with it.

The next morning, I call Mom and talk it over with her. I tell her I'm thinking about signing.

"June, promise me one thing."

"What is it?"

"You're an adult and you have to make a decision you can live with. But promise me you'll finish school."

"I promise."

I'm going pro. I sign. (Mom, Marky, Tonk, Bobby, you are all with me. We rise together.) They give me my first payment, $10,000 in cash, right there.

It turns out Al, Red, and Earl Foreman have never even seen me play. They've only seen one grainy film of me in the NIT against North Carolina, the game I fouled out of, maybe my worst varsity game. Arnold has seen me play a couple of times and he has managed to convince these guys that I'm worth every penny.

On the train back to New York, Ray and I sit next to each other in the row of three seats, both staring forward. I'm thinking, What have I done? I'm moving to Virginia? To play in the

Dr. J

ABA? When I go back to campus for the last few months of my junior year, that will be the end of my college experience, the end of being a student-athlete. I'm just going to be a . . . jock. I never wanted to be a jock.

My only regret, and it hits me riding in that train back to New York, is that I will never get to play in the Olympics, to represent my country, and maybe even make a difference for the United States in the 1972 Munich Games.

18.

I take over my mom and Mr. Dan's mortgage, I give Freda some money for her kids, and I head back up to Amherst, where I drive my old blue Chevy over to a Lincoln-Mercury dealer with my friends Al Skinner, Leon Saunders, Herman Curtis, and Alonzo Somerville. I'm going to trade in the Chevy for a new car. I like the look of the Mercury Cougar, and when I take it out for a test drive, I'm thinking it's a done deal. But the guys are all crowded in and they are saying, "Man, it's kind of tight back here." The Cougar is a coupe, and they are saying I should look at something a little roomier, maybe a Lincoln.

Never bring your friends when you're going to buy a car.

When we're back on the lot, the dealer shows me the new Lincoln Mark III, a coupe with a grill like a set of chrome shark teeth. This car is a beast: blue on blue, with a 460-cubic-inch V8, eight-track player, power everything, and plenty of space in the back for my friends. Man, now that I've driven the Mark, I can't go back to the Cougar, so I make a deal to trade in the Chevy and pay another $5,000 plus some financing so that I can leave that day in the Mark. Driving back to campus through those two-lane Northampton roads, my Afro—I'm starting to get a little freaky with my hair—almost but not quite brushing the padded top, I feel like I've made it. All my dreams, my hard work, it was all for a reason. This is the fruit of my labor, the Mark an obvious symbol of my success, but there is also an accompanying feeling, this sense of flight, of rising, of this opportunity. There was never a schedule, or even really a plan. I just kept working and playing and staying focused, kept my life in its neat columns and rows, and now look, I get to drive around in the Mark with a contract to play ball for $125,000 a year. I'm on my way, Marky, I'm on my way.

Not necessarily academically, however, as my grades slip my final term. I finish my three years at UMass just 30 credits shy of my degree, and I plan on going to summer school as well, so I'll pick up a few more.

My promise to Mom I intend to keep.

19.

So that summer, I spend the weekdays up in Amherst with Carol and attend classes. Every Friday I drive back to Harlem in the Mark. Because I'm no longer protecting my college eligibility, I can for the first time play in the Rucker Pro League. A schoolyard player I've run with named Dave Brownbill sets me up with Pete Vecsey, a sportswriter for the *Daily News* who's the player-coach of the Westsiders (sometimes known as the

Daily News All-Stars). Brownbill and another New York City player, Ollie Taylor, have sold Vecsey on me, and by the time I meet with him he tells me he has saved me a spot. But when I ask for a paycheck, he tells me that's not how the Rucker League works. You play on what he calls the World's Greatest Outdoor Arena for love of the game and to test yourself against the best.

Rucker, at that time, is comprised of playground legends and NBA and ABA all-stars, all competing in free-flowing games where, if the contest is good enough, the timekeepers will shut down the clock just to keep it going. I'm intrigued, and since I'm about to play pro ball, I need to know how I measure up against the best players in the world, and most of them are right here every Saturday and Sunday, playing for one of the dozen teams in the league. We have my future teammate Charlie Scott, Billy Paultz from St. John's, Walt Szczerbiak, New York Knick Hawthorne Wingo, so we're loaded with professional talent, and Vecsey isn't even sure how many minutes I'll be able to play. Clyde Frazier is playing in the Rucker League, along with Nate "the Skate" Archibald, Willis Reed, Pee Wee Kirkland, and Earl Monroe. I can't wait to test my game against these legends.

On my first possession of our first game, against the Cincinnati Kings, their star Sid Catlett and two defenders converge on me as I dribble the ball along the baseline, take off from the left side of the basket, and slam down a reverse dunk. Man, it's great to be playing in a league where I can dunk the ball.

After college, playing up in Rucker Park is like a release. Finally, there are no coaches or rules to stop me from playing to the best of my abilities on the court. I'm discovering that some of my playground moves, the dunks and spins and finger rolls, will not only work against this professional-level competition, they are actually more effective than some of the methodical zone-busting, outside-in, pass-and-cut offensive moves that my coaches taught me back at UMass. And equally important, the fans *love* the game when I take it higher, up above the rim.

Because when you're balling, really balling, up at Rucker, you feel like a straight-up rock star. I pull up in the Mark, throw it into park, don't even have to lock it because no one dares mess with it, and when I walk in through the chain-link gate, I'm going through a herd of people and the crowd is just parting and I can hear the murmurings of recognition. "Julius. Julius. Juliussssss." There are people reaching out and touching me, putting a hand on my shoulder—"not the hair," I have to tell them—because, I have given them something they can't buy. These are people who are going to the Garden during the season to watch the Knicks. And they come up here every weekend to get a taste of something even better, often with Knicks all-stars playing up here as well. At this point, the Knicks may be the best team in the NBA, but what fans are getting up at Rucker is something more beautiful, sponta-neous, improvisational, it's jazz versus classical. Plucky Morris is doing his rap over the PA, introducing me like I'm a heavy-weight champ, making up nicknames for me, "Little Hawk" and "Black Moses" and "Houdini" before I finally tell him, "Yo, man, just call me the Doctor."

"The Doctor is *in*," Plucky shrieks. "He's gonna be opera-tin'. He's gonna be *dissecting* brothas."

And the crowd is hyperventilating. Women fanning them-selves. Guys whipping their T-shirts around. The bleachers are packed. There are people leaning out the windows of the buildings along Eighth Avenue, up in trees, lined up on the

Dr. J

roofs, sitting on top of the chain-link fence, even standing along the viaduct leading to the 155th Street Bridge. And there are always some beautiful women in attendance up at the park, and these are women dressing to be seen. Somehow, the word has gotten out and Braniff and Pan Am stewardesses are making it to the park whenever they have a layover in New York City, and some of these fine ladies let it be known that they are available. I take up with a fine female, one of the Braniff stewardesses, my Rucker girlfriend. I'm still in a committed relationship with Carol and living up in Amherst during the week, so this is my first taste of the temptations of big-time basketball.

There is this intense emotional connection I feel with that audience. They seem to know that they are witnessing an emergence. They are discovering me at the moment when I am discovering myself as a pro. I mean, think about this, this black community, they don't have very much. This is their outlet, this park, and this experience. And if you're not here, in this park, then you don't see it. These games are not televised; they are played once and the only highlight or replay is the story you tell your brothers who weren't there.

I feel like a gladiator walking through that crowd. My Afro is flaring; it's adding a good four inches to my height. I'm skinny and long and ropey and strong as a lion; in fact, one brother describes me as looking like a "lion on stilts." And my game, I don't know why, but once I'm playing at Rucker, it's like the chains are coming off. Even though I'm on asphalt instead of wood, I'm running faster and rising higher and playing with a creativity and imagination that I never dared back in college.

At one point, Pete Vecsey and I are sitting on the bench after a game and Pete is shaking his head and he looks at me and says, "You know what, Jules? When you're playing, and you make a sweet move, somehow, you give the people a taste of what it's like to be you. They feel like they're making the move just by watching you."

I nod. I know it's a compliment. And, coming from Vecsey, who's a pretty good player himself with a silky mid-range shot, it must be high praise. But I don't know what he's talking about.

The games are so pure. I'm not worrying about the coach taking me out if I make a bad decision or don't make an outlet pass. I can go coast to coast if I want, whenever I want. But in this league, if you throw it down on your man, he is going to come right back at you. No respite. You make a shot, then you know you're going to have to make a great defensive play because your man is going to be looking to get even. It's back and forth that way, games going to 162–160, and every crowd-pleasing move my opponent makes just motivates me to come up with something even bolder.

In part because the games are not televised, some of our exploits are exaggerated and certain matchups get blown out of proportion with each retelling. There are some legendary games, among them a game against Milbank, a playground squad that includes the man who is supposed to be the best playground player of them all: Joe "the Destroyer" Hammond. My teammates are telling me, "Man, *the Destroyer is gonna show up.*"

I'm like, "Who's the Destroyer?"

Charlie Scott fills me in. Joe is six foot three and has the reputation of being the best one-on-one basketball player in the city, which basically means the world. He never played high school ball, was drafted by the Los Angeles Lakers of the NBA and New York Nets of the ABA in 1971, and refused to

Dr. J 189

go pro because that would mean taking a pay cut from his lucrative career as a heroin and marijuana dealer. He claims that
when the Lakers made their offer of $50,000 a year, he already
had $200,000 in cash stashed in his apartment.

Before the game, I'm sitting on a bench with Charlie and
I can hear people in the crowd sort of getting excited and
pointing to a limousine that has pulled up on the other side
of Eighth Avenue. The limo door swings open and out comes
the Destroyer, and I'm thinking, Okay, so that's the guy who
everyone is talking about, in a full suit.

"They gonna go crazy," says Charlie.

Later, we would hear that he was shooting craps in a social
club. He slips out of his suit and dress shoes to reveal a tank top and
basketball shorts, and then bows to the four corners of the court,
saying, "I'm here, man, THE DESTROYER BE HERE!"

Charlie stands up. "Yeah? Bring him on in here then!"

Milbank has plenty of hoops legends on the court—in addition to Joe they have Pee Wee Kirkland and Ric "the Elevator
Man" Cobb. Our transition game is killing Milbank, as we're
getting clean breakaways and Ollie Taylor and I are putting
down some huge dunks. I head fake the Elevator Man and finish
with a two-hand dunk to put us up double digits. "The Doctor
is operating," Plucky shrieks, "and the patient is . . . dying."

Charlie is the main guy on our team, the ABA Rookie of
the Year, college All-American at North Carolina. And he's a
two-guard, so Joe is his responsibility. It's still Charlie's team.

I'm matched up against Herman "Helicopter" Knowings.
Charlie is guarding Joe. The two are calling each other out all
afternoon, and Charlie is getting the better of him. We win
the game in triple overtime—and with those timekeepers, that
means the game could have lasted two hours—but it is never a

contest between me and Joe. Still, I do throw down my usual complement of dunks on Milbank and a few over Joe. And he plays well, but no way he scores 55 points against me, the way some people will later go around saying. (The only guy who ever could ever have scored 55 points on me is Bernard King, and he could drop 55 on *anybody*.)

Joe didn't drop 55 on Charlie, either.

That's some bullshit.

20.

Proving myself at Rucker means never backing down. I'm the new kid, with the big rep and the half-million-dollar pro contract. There are plenty of pros. But you also get guys who are trying to break heads out there, because they're outside of the pros and trying to get in by making a reputation for themselves. Every player guarding me is thinking if he can shut me down, then maybe he is in line for a $500K deal. I'm just trying to break a sweat, I'm not looking to bust anyone up. However, I do have something to prove. I'm the eager upstart rookie. After a few weekends up at Rucker, I start to develop a rep because I'm scoring pretty much at will. The focus on our team is Charlie, he's the star, so I'm able to get free and I start to get pretty freaky with my dunks, doing baseline and reverse dunks, rock-the-cradle jams, and I'm out running on the break so much, I'm taking off from the foul line, or just a step or two inside, and Ka-chunk, the ball hits the back of the rim or my hand hits the front and it just goes down. In games against pros, guys like Jo Jo White or Tiny Archibald, I notice are sort of moving at three-quarters speed, getting to their spots, taking their shots, but they are pacing themselves. This is the off-season after all, and they don't have anything to prove. I eventually realize that. You gotta give them a show, but you don't have to give them the whole show because nobody is paying to get in here.

I learn that from Clyde Frazier, with whom I form a friendship that summer. He's playing some ball up at Rucker, and he's so talented he can go at three-quarters speed and still control the game. He takes me under his wing a little, bringing me downtown to his tailor where I have a few suits made, slightly less flamboyant versions of some of the extreme styles that Clyde favors. He also introduces me to his agent, Irwin Weiner, who also handles pros Willis Reed and Fatty Taylor. At this point, I'm already frustrated with Bob Woolf, who is never in when I call. (I found out later he was in Europe that summer.) And Steve Arnold, who had acted as my agent, was also working with the Squires, so the way I see it, he's more like a double agent. I like Irwin, and Clyde has already told him I'm killing guys up at Rucker.

Irwin is a high school dropout turned garment union negotiator. He's short, with curly red hair, and he's always talking around a cigar in the corner of his mouth. He and Clyde share a taste for big diamonds.

Irwin says we may be able to make a move after this season because of the conflict-of-interest issue around Arnold. But the most important thing is that I go out and have a great rookie season. "Don't get hurt up there at the Rucker," Irwin says. "They're not paying you. It's not real."

But sometimes, it suddenly gets real, like *real*-real. Tom

Hoover is a six-foot-nine backup center who has played for the Knicks and Nets and wouldn't mind another shot at the pros. He's got a reputation for cutting down guys when they drive through the lane, throwing a lot of hip and elbow. When I take off in the lane, he just pulls me down by the shoulder and then stands over me. "Don't be coming in here with that weak stuff."

I nod. I get back up. "Okay, so that's how it is."

When we're running downcourt I tell Charlie, "Get me the ball in the post. I want to go back at him."

I'm standing facing the basket between the left elbow and the foul line when Charlie hits me with an easy pass. I palm the ball and hold it back behind me, jab stepping with my left foot, then I dribble once, beat my man, take a step, and lift off from my right foot. Hoover is waiting for me in the lane, looking to knock me over again. He goes up, his right hand up over the front of the rim, his left reaching out to grab me. I rise up over his extended hand and rear back and throw it down through his right hand, the ball smashing his fingers so hard against the rim that there is a wet cracking sound like pulling apart a roast chicken. As the ball goes through the hoop, the crowd doesn't let out its usual roar, as if they know that something is wrong. Hoover is standing there, holding his hand, this big, sad giant with a pained grimace on his face. He leaves the game. I'm not sure he'll ever play at Rucker again.

It's payback, but I feel terrible about it. I did it intentionally because I was angry, but it doesn't feel good to hurt a person.

There are other Rucker dunks that are memorable but for more whimsical reasons. On one dunk, I take the ball at the baseline and elevate. I don't know how high I am, but I feel like I am within inches of the top of the backboard, and so I throw it down with such force that the ball hits the blacktop and then bounces back up, kisses the backboard, and then goes through the basket again. Everyone is like, "Four-point play! Four-point play!" It's because there is no net on the basket, and the trajectory somehow is just right. That's one of those plays that has guys coming onto the court and pretending to faint.

Carol happens to be there that day, and I can look over and see her smiling, but I can also see that she is taking all this in, that this is a new scene, so different from UMass and the Curry Hicks Cage. I was a big man on campus, sure, but a pretty girl like Carol didn't have too much to be jealous of on a college campus. Here, she is observing a different breed of girl, the type who hang around arenas like birds of prey—chickenhead basketball hawks, basically.

Afterward, when we're driving back to Long Island in the Mark, Carol is asking me what I think of those women who are there.

"Who are all those girls?"

I tell her I don't know.

But I can see that she realizes something new: now that I have gone pro, and despite the promise we have made to be faithful to each other, we are playing in a whole different league.

21.

I drive the Mark down to Petersburg, Virginia, for the Virginia Squires rookie training camp and tryouts. This is supposed to be a two-day camp where Al Bianchi and Johnny Kerr can watch the drafted rookies in action—the Squires had taken Willie Sojourner, a center out of Weber State, and Dana Pagett, a point guard out of USC. I'm technically a free agent signing, but the three of us already have contracts, so we know we're on the team. The rest of the guys invited to the camp, however, are a mix of players who lack the speed to be pros and big, burly, athletic thugs who are probably heading over to a professional wrestling tryout as soon as this camp is over. Willie is a big man, so he doesn't mind being out there banging, and Dana is a point guard who is probably the twelfth man on the roster. But I'm a high-wire act so when I'm out there, I'm getting swarmed by these six-foot-eight guys who are free agents trying to get a spot and they figure the fastest way to do that is to take out my ankles and knees so that my place on the roster opens up. They've got nothing to lose.

Not that this motley collection can stop me, but I am getting banged around, and Bianchi and Kerr aren't taking me out. It's because they've never seen me play before. So Bianchi is sitting there on the bench in this dinky Petersburg gym and his jaw is sort of hanging open and he's squinting, as if trying to figure out if what he's seeing is real. At one point, Kerr rushes outside somewhere to find a pay phone to call Earl Foreman, he's so excited. I'm doing everything—running, dunking, blocking shots, grabbing rebounds—and getting knocked down every other trip down the court. Welcome to pro basketball.

Finally, Bob Travaglini, the team trainer, who we call Chopper, goes over to Al and says, "If you don't take Julius out, he's gonna get hurt."

Bianchi comes to his senses.

Chopper comes over to where I'm sitting on the bench.

"You know, those guys out there are trying to hurt you, so I'm gonna keep you over here on the side."

Chopper and I become real close.

In fact, after a few days in rookie camp, Chopper says we need to come up with a new nickname for me. Because there's already one Doctor—Dr. Mason, the team physician. So guys keep saying Doc, and both Dr. Mason and I respond. "This ain't gonna work," says Chopper, who frequently needs to address both of us.

"I'm callin' him Dr. M," says Chopper. "And you . . ."

He looks me over, nods, and smiles. "You're gonna be Dr. J, so everybody knows who's who."

22.

The Squires are what's known as a regional team. NBA franchises have one hometown and home arena—the Philadelphia 76ers, say, playing at the Spectrum or the Boston Celtics at the Garden. However, some ABA owners have the strange idea of giving a franchise a regional base instead of one home city. For example, there is a team in our division known simply as the Floridians. That's how they appear in the newspapers, not the Miami Floridians or Tampa Floridians but just the Floridians. They play all over Florida: a few games in Jacksonville, Tampa, West Palm Beach, and Miami, where they play in a converted aircraft hangar. I don't pretend to be an expert at basketball attendance, but even a former undergraduate marketing major such as myself can see that this may not be the best way to build up a loyal fan base.

The Virginia Squires take this same approach, playing in Roanoke, Richmond, Hampton Roads, and Norfolk. We play most of our games in Norfolk, and that's where the Squires' training facility and offices are located. I decide to rent a house on the water in Virginia Beach, just down Route 264 from Norfolk and the Norfolk Scope, the eleven-thousand-seat, brand-new arena we consider our real home court.

I'm not alone. Freda is having a hard time. She and George have split. She never got her high school degree, and she's been working in low-wage, go-nowhere jobs. It's like Mom always told us growing up, if you don't go to college, all that hard work just earns you another day of hard work. (Freda is trapped in the jewelry store basement of life.) I tell her she and the boys can come down and live with me in Virginia Beach. It's warm here, Freda, I remind her. We're sunbirds.

So Freda and her two sons move down. And a good buddy of mine from UMass, Herman Curtis, rolls shotgun with me, sort of as my driver and personal assistant but really so I have a friend with me in Virginia. My first house, a suburban A-frame house on Honeytree Lane, has a sunken living room with a fireplace, two bedrooms on the first floor, and two bedrooms upstairs including my master suite, which is quiet and secluded at the end of a secluded hall. I'm still a kid, just twenty-one, so as much as I enjoy having my own house, I need to have a woman's touch, and Freda does the cooking and cleaning, making the chicken and greens like Mom made, and having her young boys, Barry and Keith, around gives the place a real family feeling.

Our practice facility is at the Norfolk Jewish Community Center. They have a regulation court, so every morning, a half-dozen of the tallest brothers Norfolk has ever seen walk past the old men and ladies playing pinochle and take to the court to play some ball. And we've got some serious hair going. My Afro is starting to take on some epic swell. In college I never let it get more than an inch or so from my scalp, but now, after Rucker and coming into the pros, I just let my freak flag fly, growing it out to three inches on top, which makes me seem even taller.

This is the beginning of my Afro as part of my image, when fans come to see the wind pushing back my do as I'm skying toward the basket. Over the years, Darnell Hillman of the Indiana Pacers and I will vie for the biggest Afro in the ABA, with Darnell actually beating me out. He has this technique, which he shares with me when the Pacers come down to Virginia, where he takes an angel cake cutter, and after he's washed his hair, while he's blow-drying it, he uses the tines of this cake cutter—Darnell calls it an Afro pick—to stroke the hair up and back. Darnell shows me and, man, it works. My hair is standing up tall, makes me look six foot nine. I have always disliked long hair. I don't like the shaggy, unkempt styles of the hippies or what some of the rock stars are sporting. They strike me as disordered, chaotic. But a well-kept Afro, that's a different thing. It requires constant maintenance and care, fluffing it up with the Afro pick constantly. I have to spend a half-hour some mornings to get it right.

I already know from playing Rucker League with Charlie that he's going to be the focus of our offense. And he should be, coming off the Rookie of the Year season he just completed, leading the Squires to the ABA Eastern Conference finals. The Squires had been a rebound by committee team—but what a committee!—with four players averaging over 8 boards a night and six-foot-eleven Jim Eakins leading the team with 9.3. And while Charlie had led the team in scoring, the second leading scorer, George Carter, has been traded to the Pittsburgh Condors, in part to make space and minutes on the floor for me.

In training camp, it feels a little like the Olympic development program all over again. Here I am, matching up against guys who are pros, supposedly among the best players in the world, and I am still able to get to my spots and impose my will. From the first day of training camp, I'm rebounding as if I'm back at the Cage or on the playground. Al Bianchi likes to run, and he builds his offense so that whoever gets the rebound—usually me, as I would average 15.7 rebounds a game that season—tries to hit the outlet at either the left or the right sideline between the top of the circle and the half-court. Then that player, who is usually Charlie Scott, can either pass the ball into the middle to our point guard Fatty Taylor or keep it himself. If the defenders slide over to guard him, he can throw the ball to the trailer, who would usually be me or my backup, Doug Moe, or the second trailer, who might be the center, Willie Sojourner, or the other forward, Ray Scott. As a result, Charlie gets a lot of shots within the system and will go on to shoot thirty times a game that year. I have to earn my shots on offensive rebounds—I average nearly 6 a game—or out of the half-court offense, especially when Charlie is double-teamed.

So while my game at this stage is still built around rebound, dunk, or drive, I'm also refining other elements of my repertoire. From Ray Scott, a ten-year NBA veteran, I relearn my jump shot. Ray tells me not to jump so high on my jump shot. He's right. I like to rise as high as possible before my release, perhaps a vestige of my days playing as an undersized power forward in high school and early in college. "Don't jump so high on your shot. Don't worry about guys blocking it. The main thing is keep control of your body," he tells me at the Jewish community center gym.

If I don't jump quite as high, I will jump straighter and the motion of my release will be more economical and repetitive. My jump at three-quarters maximum height is still plenty high enough to get a clear release, Ray points out. Then I can make my jump shot like a set shot, with the same release point every single time. "It doesn't matter if you jump six inches over a guy or a half inch, as long as you are over him," Ray explains.

By the end of training camp, my mid-range jumper has become an even more formidable weapon.

I believe the best test of how effective a player is at imposing his will on the game is his shooting percentage. If you are getting to those spots on the floor where you are comfortable with your shot, then you should be making a high percentage. The highest percentage shot, of course, is the slam dunk. If you can dunk the ball and you are getting the ball in a position from which you can throw it down, then you are an effective player, you are dictating the terms of the game. Wilt Chamberlain, and other dominant big men, can shoot a very high percentage because of this simple fact.

Starting in training camp, I shoot the highest percentage of anyone on the team who averages over twenty minutes: I make half the shots I take. And during the preseason, we play a couple of NBA teams, the Detroit Pistons and Baltimore Bullets, and a few ABA teams. The preseason moment that clued in Bianchi and my teammates that what I was doing in practice was going to translate into the season was a game against the Kentucky Colonels. Kentucky has the best big men in the ABA, a pair of future Hall of Famers. They already had rookie sensation Dan Issel, a local boy they drafted out of Kentucky who averaged nearly 30 a night and 13 boards his rookie season. To Issel, they added first-team All-American Artis Gilmore, who is seven foot two (maybe seven foot eight with his Afro), so tall they move Issel over to power forward for his second season. Gilmore would be Rookie of the Year that season, leading the league in rebounding with 17.8. In addition, they have Wilbert Jones, one of the four Jones boys who would play in the NBA and brother of my future Sixer teammate Caldwell. And Wilbert is a good six foot eight. This is the biggest front line I've ever seen.

I know I'm going to have to get my points from offensive rebounds or when Charlie's double-teamed. About halfway through the first quarter of that exhibition, I take the ball and I'm driving down the lane on the left side and I rise, seeing Issel and Gilmore both coming to block my shot. Then I watch Issel sort of slide down, and then Gilmore slides down, and I'm still . . . rising. I dunk the ball over both of them.

This is my confirming moment. This is the first time I ever thought of the idea of airbrakes, that I can go up and somebody will come at me and I just wait, take a breath, and I can watch their hand, as gravity will inevitably assert itself, and I stay up. It all happens in an instant but it seems like slow motion to me. I'm up there, and I wait for the hand to drop. And when I see the hand drop, it's over. Kaboom.

23.

I'm fortunate in that I can sleep anywhere. If you give me ten minutes, I can take a nap. That makes ABA life a lot easier for

me. We were always traveling on Piedmont Airlines or Mohawk Air, regional fights, tiny seats, and sometimes we have to make three connections to get from, say, Norfolk to Tampa. And about half of the flights on these regional airlines seem to turn around because of equipment malfunctions, fuel leaks, a door being open, whatever. And then we miss our connection and we're killing five hours wandering around an airport in Shreveport. There's no first class on these thirty-seat turboprops, and we're squeezing into these tiny seats, but it doesn't bother me, as I manage to catnap wherever I am. It's an essential skill in pro sports—catching up on your sleep however you can—because one of my first discoveries about life on the road in the ABA is that there are an awful lot of girls, who will cost you some valuable ZZZs.

The veteran players know girls in all the cities, they introduce me to them, and occasionally they even send them down to knock on my door, their way of showing that while I may be a new player with some moves, they still have the game off the court. And these are good-looking women, too, fast girls who are down with basketball players. I'm torn, because Carol and I are still together while she's at school and I'm a rookie in the league, but the temptations are everywhere. During our rookie training camp, I'm rooming with Willie Sojourner when this white guy in an Army uniform waving a gun around busts through our door.

"Where's Jennifer?" he's shouting. "My wife, Jennifer?"

I'm looking at Willie and he's looking at me like, What the hell is this? We got a white man with a gun accusing us of doing something with his wife. We know enough to realize that this doesn't usually end well here in the South.

"What are you talking about?"

"My wife. I know she's with one of you ballplayers."

"You can look around the room if you want," I say. "Just don't be shooting anybody."

Evidently, his wife had been with somebody on our team—to this day I don't know who. And he was probably right, his wife may just have been one of those hoochie mamas who like to flirt and go after ballplayers, some of them single and some of them not single but still available.

It's a perilous situation for a supposedly committed brother like me. I resist temptation for as long as I can, but how many times can a young man resist a beautiful woman knocking on his door and saying, "Hey, man, so-and-so told me to come by, said you needed some company." And she's a foxy woman, so I smile and say, "Really? Well, he was right."

On the road, the groupies travel in packs of twos or threes, and they are an attractive and diverse portion of the population. This is, after all, the free-love era, the swinging '70s, and I'm a pro athlete. There's money, sun, food, booze, drugs for those who might be inclined. You don't even have to look that good: if you're a basketball player there's a groupie for you.

Is there any explanation needed beyond being twenty-one and having a little money in my pocket and free time on the road? I'm flying around the country and living out of hotel rooms. I even start to experiment, to see if I can sleep with a different woman every night. For eight nights, I do exactly that, as we go from Dallas to Richmond to St. Petersburg, up to New York, down to Charlotte, over to Louisville and then back to Hampton, Virginia. A different fox every night, an Asian woman, a sister, a Caucasian, and so forth. But after a few nights, the excitement and macho thrill wear off and I start to feel empty. My conscience is getting the best of me and I

Dr. J

realize that while this is gratifying to my ego—and I am definitely making up for those lost years before I got to UMass—it
is leaving me feeling disconsolate. Once the girl leaves I am still
Julius Erving, I'm still Callie Mae's son and Freda's brother—
and I'm still in a long-distance relationship with Carol. It de-
pletes my soul, this philandering. And it bothers me that I'm
failing at my relationship.

I decide I need to talk to one of the older, married players.
In a hotel in Pittsburgh, where we're playing the Condors and
my Rucker league running mate, Walt Szczerbiak, I seek out
the oldest guy on our team, who is in his mid-thirties, happily
wedded. I've never seen this player catting around with any
groupies, which in this environment makes him a little like a
wise man on top of a mountain.

He's up in his hotel room, relaxing on his bed, watching
The Courtship of Eddie's Father after shoot-around. We're killing time before going back over to the Pittsburgh City Arena,
where the Condors play before about twelve thousand empty
seats.

I tell him my dilemma, how I've promised to be faithful to
Carol, but I'm finding the temptation of life in the pros to be
overwhelming.

"How do you do it, man?"

He gets up, turns off the television, and takes a sip of his
root beer.

"We're warriors, young man. Warriors! And we have to
overcome these temptations of the flesh, to channel all that
energy into our game. Man, you refrain, and you will make it
rain."

I'm nodding. Okay. But refrain how?

"Young man, you got to be strong! And if you know this

girl is special, that she is the great love of your life, then you will be strong. For her. That's where your strength will come from."

I guess that's the veteran approach. A sort of abstinence, like we're high priests of sport. I don't know if that's really workable for a young buck like me. But if my teammate can do it, then maybe I can, too. I want what he has, this kind of happiness that comes from a long-term, committed relationship and beautiful children. Look at him. He has this serenity about him, like he's at peace with himself. That must be what happens when you don't mess around with groupies.

"Hey, Doc," he says, before I leave. "How is that sister of yours?"

"Freda?"

He nods. "Hmm–mmm. She's fine."

"Um, yeah."

"Tell her I said hi. Maybe, if you don't mind, I'll take her out sometime."

"Aren't you married?"

He shrugs. "You're the one who asked me for advice. I never said I was faithful."

Adapting to life *on* the court is easier. We start the season winning 9 of our first 12 games. As I'm making my first stops around the league, Charlie Scott remains our big draw, but I win folks over during pregame warm-ups, when I can throw down whatever funky dunk I can imagine. I have dreams of dunks—in one dream, I see myself tossing it off the backboard, catching it with one hand making a reverse dunk—and the next night in the layup line, I do it. In games, it's not that different. In my first game against the Indiana Pacers, probably

Dr. J

the ABA's best team, I take off from the right baseline, and Darnell Hillman comes out for the block, his Afro waving, and I sort of pull the ball back and just float by him. Then Mel Daniels comes over, and I ball-fake the pass and keep floating until Roger Brown is now swooping down on me. By now, I'm beneath the basket on the left side, still floating, so I spin the ball high off the glass with my right hand. A no-look basket.

That season, Charlie and I are the highest-scoring combination in all of basketball, as we average nearly 62 points a game. Charlie leads the league in scoring at over 34 a night, and I add another 27 and pull down 15.7 rebounds and lead the league in offensive boards. But for all our scoring both Charlie and I feel that we're missing something as a team, some killer edge. We win five in a row, then lose four, and continue that boom-and-bust cycle. Until this point, through Salvation Army, high school, and college, I've never played on a team that was so inconsistent. We have the talent to beat anyone, but too often, if Charlie is having a rare off night and if I'm unable to make up the shortfall, then we get beat by determined team play. But it becomes more and more obvious to me, the more cities we pass through, and the more courts I step onto, that I have the talent to score on anybody in this league.

One of the biggest surprises about being a highly paid pro athlete is just how little money I actually have. I didn't negotiate any signing bonus, so after that first $10,000 advance on my salary—about half of which I spent on the Mark and most of the rest of which I gave to my mom and Freda—I have to live on my paychecks. After they take out the agent commissions, taxes, and the deferred money, my first check is less than $1,000, and that's supposed to last me a month. My salary is $75,000 gross, which after the $10,000 advance is taken out, then federal, state, and local taxes and insurance, and then divide that into twenty-six checks—I'm paid biweekly—that means my net pay is something like $900 a week. Don't get me wrong, that's a good salary in 1971, but I'm not exactly rich.

I ask Irwin to see if he can get me some of that deferred money. The word is out about me, and most of the folks coming out to Scope to see the team are coming to see me. (And Charlie, of course. They bill us as "Charlie 'The Great' Scott" and "Julius 'Dr. J' Erving.")

Irwin comes down to see Earl to ask about renegotiating my contract. Now that they know I'm a sure thing, Irwin says, they should make a new deal. After all, there are two leagues. I could always jump over to the NBA. We have some leverage. Earl refuses, despite the fact that Irwin tells him I wasn't fairly represented at the signing and that he thinks we can get the contract nullified. Earl isn't interested. He won't budge on the terms.

Not only does Earl Foreman refuse to pay me the deferred money, but some of the checks I am getting from him start bouncing. Now this is worrisome. Here I am. I've left college, uprooted my sister and her boys, and some weeks I don't even have a paycheck. "Irwin, man, you gotta see about getting me out of this contract." Now I like Earl, and I always give him a hug when I see him on the sidelines, but I'm starting to realize that not only is he not paying me what I'm worth, sometimes he's not even paying me what I'm not worth. But he never holds a grudge. It's just business, he says. Don't let it color our relations.

Irwin tells me I just have to play out this season, and then we'll make some moves. He says he thinks we can undo this contract because of the fact that my agent, Steve Arnold, had a

Dr. J

conflict of interest, because he was working both sides of our negotiation. In the meantime, I just have to keep playing and putting up big numbers and showing what I can do, so that an NBA team will take an interest and allow Irwin to leverage a bigger contract.

24.

Fog pushes in, thick wispy soldiers on the march up the sandy beach and down the suburban streets, a gray army overwhelming us some mornings. I wake up to windows that seem painted white. I hear the boys downstairs, eating cereal, asking Freda about when I'm getting up, their chatter deadened by the cocoon of air around the house. There are the sounds of my old friend and driver, Herman's deep voice, then the hiss of water running in the sink, the scuff of chairs sliding, shoes scraping against the wood floor. Boys on their way to school. Herman must be driving them.

The boys will need some new Chuck Taylors, the Mark needs new tires, we need a whole shopping list of food. I hear Freda moving the pans around. I know what I am, I'm the man of the house again, supporting a whole family, not even my own, and trying to stretch a too small paycheck to cover too many people. How did this happen?

"June? You hungry?"

Freda says she'll make me pancakes.

I put an eight-track into the system. Marvin Gaye sings "Trouble Man."

I come up hard baby, and that ain't cool
I didn't make it sugar, playin' by the rules

I know not to complain, not to bemoan the fact that I don't
have as much as I think I should have. But I'm twenty-one, a
boy in a big man's body, and I can't help but want the perqui-
sites of stardom. The cars, the clothes, man, I want a fine suit.
I'm not materialistic by nature, but I do feel that my success
should bring me some reward. I never want to feel like I'm
working in that jewelry store basement, no matter how grand
the trappings or how glamorous my life looks.

I am the product. I am what Earl Foreman and the Virginia
Squires organization is selling, more than any red, white, and
blue ball or dancing girls in skimpy outfits. They are coming
to see me. I am on a treadmill of capitalism.

This isn't vanity or ego. This is just my understanding of
business. The way I see it, I'm in business for myself, so I have
to figure out my worth. That's what Irwin and I talk about.

I'm standing before the mirror, still skinny as six o'clock,
with a chicken butt. I'm a boy stretched long into a ballplayer,
yet the burdens of the world are on my back. I pull on a Nik
Nik shirt, orange and brown, with a broad, deep collar, some
bell-bottoms, some platform shoes. And the Afro, man, I need
to work on that. You have to invest time in it. Otherwise, it
looks raggedy. I can't stand the disorder of a raggedy 'fro.

My Afro, jabbing skyward, scrapes the ceiling as I come
downstairs, give a warm greeting to my sister—"You okay?"
and a smile—and cut up the pancakes Freda had made for me.

The fog loosens, light cutting through in the gaps between
grounded clouds, like the sky has settled down on earth for a
spell. I figure I can drive through this, take 284 straight out of

Dr. J 209

Virginia Beach, over the inlet, down to the Admiralty Motel, where Chopper has set up his training room. He does all his taping out of the motel room. He's even got a whirlpool over there.

I pull out of the driveway, the Mark shining from Herman doing a wash and wax. I turn on the headlights and drive, past the other suburban homes, and I tell myself that this is what it feels like to be an American, to be a businessman on his way to the office, only my office is a basketball court, and what I manufacture is baskets. But this routine, this commute down 284, is a version of the life so many of you know—that time by yourself behind the wheel in the morning commute. The road cuts through Mount Trashmore and Pocahontas Village, the river birch and swamp oak trees turned rust and brown, the black-headed gulls flying inland. I brought Marvin Gaye with me.

I come up hard, but that's okay
'Cause trouble man don't get in my way

My music is loud. The fog is lifting. I'm making good time toward the estuary over the Eastern Elizabeth River when I hear a siren going off behind me. It's the state police, stopping me for the fifth time since I've moved to Virginia. Something about a black man in a car like this attracts an awful lot of attention.

"License and registration, please," the trooper asks.

"Was I speeding?"

"I'm stopping you for GP," he says.

That's what they always say. General principles. They didn't like the look of me. Something about me just seemed wrong to them, so they pull me over.

My license is valid, my registration is clean.

"What is it you do, boy?" he asks.

"I play for the Squires."

Now the Squires haven't caught on with everybody. Earl Foreman's plan to be a regional team meant we had a minuscule following spread around the state.

"What's a Squire?"

I tell him it's a professional basketball team.

"You know, officer, you guys stop me every week," I say. "I drive down this road every day, from my home to our practice facility."

He shrugs. "Don't look so suspicious." He hands me back my license and registration.

I sit there awhile. I'm a calm man, a patient man, but sometimes I feel like stepping out of the car and smacking around this state trooper. It's like the clock has been set back down here. I know the pace is slower in Virginia than in New York, and maybe because of that they hadn't caught up with the times. I mean, I'm stopped once a week. This is harassment, and it takes all my will and patience not to become a statistic out there, another black man perceived to be mouthing off or threatening an officer and then I could end up in court or worse. I don't use drugs and I don't drive drunk, so there is nothing any law enforcement can catch me at, but what they are doing is trying to provoke me into doing something, anything, so they can justify an arrest. It weighs on you, this kind of harassment. It makes you wonder about how many young men never get a chance because they can't remain calm in the face of this kind of discrimination.

The irony is, the only guy on our team who I know is

Dr. J 211

smoking weed is white, our power forward, Neil Johnson, who always has his stash in his socks. He's a little kooky anyway, so whenever he shows up late to practice, I always wonder if he's been busted. But, no, Neil would always roll in, socks bulging. Now, if he was a brother, some state trooper stopping him on a GP would have found that stash. Virginia's still some trouble, man.

25.

Meanwhile, Charlie isn't happy about playing in the ABA. I respect Charlie and I know it's his team. It was his squad up at the Rucker and he was a Squire before me. I can't help it if sometimes I show him up because of the different natures of our games. We never have an argument about whose team it is, but that's also not really my style. I see Charlie like a big brother, but we don't confide in each other. My best friend on the team is my fellow rookie Willie Sojourner. On the road, Willie and I room together. At home, Willie lives in an apartment in Norfolk, and he drives himself around town in this red Datsun Roadster. It's the damnedest thing, seeing this six-foot-eight brother driving around with the top down in this tiny little car. He looks like a big, black Shriner. But Willie and I are close, and we socialize together, going out to parties. Norfolk doesn't offer much in the way of nightlife, so we actually end up spending more time at college parties. Norfolk State, Old Dominion, and Hampton University are all local, and I'm still college age anyway, so my teammates and I end up going to lots of house parties or even the frats. The white guys and the black guys would head out together: Neil Johnson, Doug Moe, Charlie Scott, George Irvine, Fatty Taylor. If we had a night off we'd check out the college scene. Occasionally a musical act would come through Norfolk and play the Scope—Earth, Wind, and Fire, Stevie Wonder—but Norfolk isn't exactly a hot spot for black culture. It's a Navy town, with plenty of servicemen and government contractors, so as basketball players, we are definitely cultural outliers.

Maybe that's why Charlie becomes frustrated playing for the Squires. He feels he would get more exposure in the other league, where, instead of Memphis or Tallahassee or Salt Lake City, he'd be playing in Chicago, Los Angeles, New York City, or Philadelphia. He does have a point. He goes to Earl and tells him he's unhappy. Earl asks him what he wants. Charlie says he wants the Squires to sign Bob McAdoo, then a junior at North Carolina who is putting up big numbers. Charlie knows Bob from his own North Carolina days, and he tells Al and Earl that this guy is a legit superstar, a big man who can shoot from downtown, which in the ABA means 3-pointers.

Earl wants to reassure Charlie that he has big plans for the Squires, so he and Al go to watch McAdoo play at Maryland and Earl manages to sign him despite the fact that he's still a junior and has the Olympics ahead of him. But it's a secret contract, of course, that only three people know about: Bob, Earl, and Charlie. In fact, to prove to Charlie that he signed McAdoo, he shows Charlie the contract and they put it into a safety deposit box in a bank in Norfolk. Earl takes one key and gives Charlie the other.

Dr. J

26.

The ABA isn't known for its defense. The games are more fluid than in the other league, and the Squires in particular are not a lockdown team. We win by outscoring opponents rather than keeping them in check in the half-court. We allow nearly 119 points a night, which explains why as we're winding up the long season, we're barely over .500. Then, with about 9 games left in the season, Charlie vanishes. Nobody knows where he is. Al and Johnny are calling his apartment. They're asking me if I've seen him. Chopper doesn't know anything. We have a game coming up against the Condors in Pittsburgh and Charlie isn't on the flight. He's our leading scorer, our team leader, and he just doesn't show up?

"Charlie's left the team," Al tells us in Pittsburgh.

"He's hurt?" Willie asks.

"No, he's jumped to Phoenix."

"He's been traded?"

Al shrugs. Charlie just left. The Suns signed him and told him he had to get on a plane and come that night. He was at practice the day before and now he's in . . . Phoenix? The Suns indemnified him from any potential lawsuit arising from his jumping leagues.

We have 9 games left in the season. We lose six as we refocus the offense to flow through me. It's hard to make up for 33 points a night. We're the second-worst defensive team in the league. It's fun to watch, but well, what am I supposed to do now? Score 63 a night? Still, we end up in second place in the Eastern Division, going 45-39, a distant second to the 68-win Kentucky Colonels with Gilmore and Issel.

Fatty Taylor, our point guard, is warning me, "Doc, you got to save some tricky stuff for the playoffs. That's what matters. It's a different season."

Al explains that in the playoffs, the rotation shortens down to just eight guys—or seven, now that Charlie is gone—and I'll be playing almost every minute. Al is coolheaded—he's not the kind of coach who shouts in practice or screams at the referees, but I can tell even he's jacked about the playoffs. Our opening round is against the Floridians, who finish in fourth place in the East. I'm looking forward to the playoffs. Ever since those first-round NIT defeats, especially the game I fouled out of against North Carolina, I've been eager to prove myself in the postseason.

The Floridians are a team built around a couple of good guards, Mack Calvin and the very tough Warren Jabali, a famously physical player, and after playing forty minutes against him I always feel it in my rib cage. I'm not saying he's a dirty player—maybe he's just anatomically gifted with larger and sharper elbows than most men his size. Jabali has an uncanny ability to get to any spot on the floor, but he can't keep up with me. I know I can beat him with my first step, and their center, Manny Leaks, isn't much taller than I am and can't match my vertical game. My mid-range game is working, and I'm drawing the defense away from the basket, which opens up the lane. The arena is packed that night, twelve thousand fans screaming out, "Dr. J! Doctor! Doc!" and I'm loose, so loose I feel like I'm levitating, soaring up above the Floridian defenders and watching them rise and fall on my way to the basket.

I don't feel like we're missing Charlie Scott at all. George Irvine is stepping up and shooting nearly 70 percent from the field, and I'm averaging just over 30 points, 20 rebounds, and 8 assists through the first two games.

Dr. J

In game 3, I end up scoring 54, an ABA playoff record that will never be broken, and collect 27 rebounds.

We sweep.

Somehow, the New York Nets have upset the Kentucky Colonels, which means we get home court advantage in the next round and don't have to face Artis Gilmore.

The Nets have their own superstar in Rick Barry, a Hall of Famer in his prime who carries the team. Normally, he's got a great wingman in veteran NBA point guard Bill Melchionni, who is having the best year of his career. But Barry will be missing his floor general. Melchionni is out this series with a bad back.

It doesn't matter. I'm looking forward to seeing my old friend Lou Carnesecca, the coach of the Nets, and I can't wait to show him what he passed up by not signing me out of UMass.

The first two games are at Scope, and we win both easily. They don't have anyone who can stop me, and I match up pretty well against Rick Barry, forcing him away from the boards, where he's so dangerous.

I'm in that zone where I just want to keep playing. It's like Rucker League all over again: just keep the clock running. But instead of taking a night or two off, we take a nine-day break before game 3. The Nets' home arena, Island Garden, is booked for a circus and the league doesn't want to move the game to Commack. So commissioner Jack Dolph makes a decision to simply wait until Island Garden is free. We spend the week practicing and lose two of our guys, Doug Moe and George Irvine, to injuries. By the time we finally fly up to New York, over a week later, we've definitely lost all of our momentum. And meanwhile, the Nets have got Melch back from his injury.

I'm still scoring, but now Barry and Melch have the Nets believing again, and they win all 3 games on their home floor, extending the series to 7. Back at Scope, we've lost some of our swagger and Barry and Melch force us into a grind-it-out, half-court game, which isn't really our style. Still, we have a chance until Barry hits a 3-pointer that banks into the hoop in the final minute.

Even though we don't win the title, this is still a fine rookie season. While Artis wins the MVP and the Rookie of the Year award, I end up outscoring him (he finishes with more rebounds). My final numbers are 27.3 points, 15.7 rebounds, and 4 assists. Still, I don't make first-team all-ABA, as they end up picking Gilmore, Issel, and Barry as the first-team front line, and it's hard to argue with three Hall of Famers like that. I'm second-team all-ABA, but as Irwin tells me when I meet with him up in New York, I'm the guy everybody is talking about.

Back in April, while we were taking apart the Floridians, Irwin negotiated a deal with Atlanta Hawks president Bill Putnam. They are giving me a $250,000 signing bonus, and $200,000 a year with a $15,000 raise every year for five years, of which they have to pay me $75,000 up front on October 1 of each year. We also negotiate a new Jaguar XKE and an apartment in Atlanta. We're all excited about the prospect of me playing with Pete Maravich. But as part of the terms of the deal, Putnam promises to keep the deal secret until after the ABA season.

27.

As soon as the season ends, Irwin tells me, I need to get out of Virginia, literally across state lines, just in case the Squires

subpoena me in an attempt to prevent me from leaving. We pack up the Mark, and Freda, Barry, Keith, and I drive down to Atlanta. I'm excited about the move to the NBA, and the Hawks are loaded with talent. Besides "Pistol" Pete Maravich, they have Walt Bellamy and Lou Hudson. This team has some serious capital. I have my new Jaguar, the $250,000 signing bonus in the bank, and the paid-for town house in East Point. Atlanta is a real city, was one of the centers of the civil rights movement, and has an active and visible black community. I feel like I could put down some roots. And it's not far from Batesburg, South Carolina, where my people are from. And Freda likes it there, says she never felt comfortable in that old suburban A-frame.

Putnam and the Atlanta Hawks figure they aren't going to waste a first-round pick on me because they already have me under contract. They figure they'll wait until the second round to pick me. The Milwaukee Bucks, however, have two first-round picks that year, and GM Wayne Embry, who knows me from Shamrock Basketball Camp, decides to take me with his second pick in the first round. I'm now signed to two different contracts with two different teams in two different leagues, while my rights are held by a third team, a team that happens to have Kareem Abdul-Jabbar as their star. When I ask Irwin about that, he says we don't want to play with Kareem.

"Why not?"

"Because he's the star. We need for you to be the star. That's how you make the big money. And they have Oscar Robertson, another star, so you would get their third billing."

I think about my situation with Charlie, about how it seemed my success started to wear on him and may have contributed to his leaving the team. If I got into that situation with

Kareem, who do you think would be the guy who would have to hit the road? And with Oscar Robertson already there, Irwin's right, I would be the third option.

"Let's make it work in Atlanta," I tell Irwin. That's where I'm living anyway.

I drive the Jaguar back up to New York, where I'm going to play the Rucker League again, stop off to see my mom and Mr. Dan and pay a visit to Marky's grave, where I tell him about all that's happening with me. I choke up thinking about Marky and how excited he would be about all this. He would just be starting college himself.

But I'm grateful to have Barry and Keith in my life, and to be able to be a father figure and big brother to them all at the same time.

28.

I make a trip up to Amherst to visit with Carol and talk about our relationship. Carol and I have been trying to make it work. She came down to a few games, saw us suffer those tough playoff losses in Long Island. When I see her, I still have this powerful feeling that she is the woman for me. She gets along so well with my mother, with my sister. It's hard for me to imagine a future without her.

But I'm still a young man, just twenty-two now, and while the idea of fidelity to one woman seems the righteous and moral thing to do, I know enough about my own failings to recognize that it's not realistic.

Dr. J

In the car on the way up to Amherst, I think that what we need to do is test our love for each other. If we agree to see other people, to have an open relationship, then we'll know, after those experiences, whether we are truly right for each other. This seems the only logical step.

When I see her, I give Carol a big hug and we take a ride in the Jaguar. She's as beautiful as ever, and she represents to me my own history. She's more than my long-term girlfriend, she's also a connection to my past, to college, to UMass, to a more innocent time, before groupies and contracts and jumping leagues and all that. But I'm not that person anymore. Seeing Carol is both wonderful because of how easily I can fall back into being myself, into being June or Julius and not Dr. J or the Doctor. She knows me as this big goofy kid shivering on a winter afternoon in two layers of overcoats on my way to the student union, not this guy with a big Afro in a three-piece suit driving a Jaguar. She sees immediately through all this style and noise to the person she knows. The son of Mom and Tonk, brother of Marky and Freda. The other stuff, the player sleeping with a different girl every night, that's not really me, or, at least I don't want to believe that it is.

She puts a head on my shoulder and we drive.

Finally, I tell her my plan: to test our love by seeing other people.

Carol is dubious.

I tell her if we're going to be together for the rest of our lives, then we need to know, to be absolutely sure, and how can that be if we haven't experienced other lovers? It's like a test, I tell her, and if we don't pass the test, then we aren't meant to be. I don't explain that I've already been seeing other women, so my position is built on some falsehoods.

Carol is an intelligent woman. She can see that what I am actually saying is that we are . . . no longer really together.

I'm telling her, no, no baby, that's not it. This is a good thing. Positive. We're gonna be stronger than ever after this.

"Stronger? Really?"

I nod. Oh, yeah, baby, that's because we'll know, for sure, forever.

Carol wipes away tears, looks out the window at the tobacco fields we are driving past, and she turns back to me. "You're sure, Julius?"

I nod, holding back my own tears, oh, yeah, I'm sure.

But somehow, I know what I've done. I may have negotiated away the best thing I ever had.

29.

I'm moving so fast, in the Jaguar, at Rucker (I'm playing again on the Westsiders), and shopping downtown with Clyde Frazier for some new threads. With the $250,000 in the bank, the new car, I definitely feel wealthy. And I am. I buy my mom and Mr. Dan a new house, back in Hempstead over on Williams Street. I put the money down myself and arrange to pay their mortgage payments, too.

That's the very least I can do for my mother. Every place I've been, everything I've ever done, is because of her, because of how she raised me. From my first day of school, I somehow knew how to behave, and that was because of her example and ceaseless teaching.

I talk to Clyde a little bit about the NBA, about what I might expect. Clyde was the leading scorer on a Knicks team that lost to the Lakers in the NBA finals last year. He's a superstar. If anyone knows how to play in the NBA, it's Clyde. The biggest difference between the two leagues, he says, is that the NBA has bigger centers and more of them. In the ABA, unless I'm playing against Artis or Mel Daniels of the Indiana Pacers, I don't have to face the kind of skilled big men that abound in the NBA. There's Wilt, for one, and Kareem, Bob Lanier, Willis Reed, Nate Thurmond, Dave Cowens, and Wes Unseld, among others. I'm going to have to adapt my game, and that's what I work on at Rucker, figuring out how to find angles to the basket by going under guys, if I have to, or shaking a big man by using the pick and roll instead of just trying to sky over him. I'm looking forward to the challenge of scoring in the NBA.

Irwin meanwhile has filed suit in New York City to "vacate and terminate" my contract with the Squires. His lawyer, Louis Nizer, is arguing that because Steve Arnold was working for both me and the club, he "had failed to exploit more favorable opportunities." We're also suing for over $300,000 in damages. There's a city marshal in Norfolk looking for Earl Foreman to serve him with a subpoena.

The ABA, meanwhile, has a new commissioner, Bob Carlson, and one of his first acts is to sue me in criminal court, seeking an injunction against my playing for any team other than the Squires. Meanwhile, Milwaukee is insisting that they own my rights from the draft, so if I'm going to play anywhere in the NBA, I should be playing there. The NBA board of governors agrees, ruling that I have to play in Milwaukee, which prompts a $2 million lawsuit from Putnam and the Hawks, who claim the NBA draft is a violation of the Sherman Anti-trust Act.

If I'd stayed in school I would only be getting out of college now. Instead, after just a year in the pros, I'm tangled up in a legal web that I can't even explain to my mother.

Still, the only contract that I consider to be valid is the one I've signed with the Hawks, so I report to Hawks training camp in Savannah, Georgia.

30.

What nobody ever talks about with Pete Maravich is that he's a big guy. Not only is he tall, at over six foot five, but he is well built, muscular, strong. At that stage of my career, I'm still wisp-skinny, so when we meet for the first time at Savannah College and we're sizing each other up, I have maybe an inch on him but Pete is actually broader than I am. I've been hearing about Pete and watching him for years. He went pro a year before me, after scoring 44 points a game in college. I have to admit I had been a little dismissive of his college career. I always believed I could have scored a great deal more in college if Jack had let me shoot as much as Pete. Pete was coached by his dad at LSU, so I figured he had every advantage in terms of scoring. He won every award out there and was a three-time All-American. In some ways, Pete is the opposite of me. I've always been underestimated, forced to take the back door instead of being ushered through the front, transferring to Roosevelt before my freshman year, going to UMass instead of a traditional hoops power, being an alternate on the Olympic development squad, joining the ABA instead of the NBA. I've had to work for every break I've gotten, had to prove myself at each stage before I was recognized. And here I am, finally on the verge of the big stage, the NBA, and who do I find but the golden boy, the player whose name has always been up on the marquee.

It's part of my makeup that I believe I can play with anyone, anywhere. And I see Pete as no exception.

From the first day of training camp, Pete and I hit it off. He's a soft-spoken guy, sort of like me, and a little bit in his own world, but then sometimes I can seem that way, too. I'm not aloof, but when I'm playing, I get so focused that I almost seem to lose intensity when I'm actually just totally into the game. Pete is the same way.

But when you're playing with Pete, you realize that not only does he have all of the Globetrotters moves—crossover dribble, snap pass, no-look stuff—but he can do them at unimaginable speeds. He's one of the fastest players I've ever played with.

The Hawks' coach, Cotton Fitzsimmons, knows what he has in Pete and me. He's telling me, "Doc, he'll find you. In traffic, in the air, you have to be ready. He'll find you." And he's right, I've always had fast hands, and I need them playing with Pete because he has this uncanny ability to get me the ball, through narrow windows in space and time, so that I feel like I'm already in my move once the ball gets to me. Also, as Pete gets to know where I like the ball, he starts putting up these perfect lob passes, just right on my hands where I can dunk it. After I throw it down, when I'm looking for Pete to give him a nod or wink of thanks, he's already gone, running back down the floor. Fatty Taylor up in Virginia was a good point guard, but we never had the timing to do these alley-oop plays consistently—with Pete, after just a few days, we have a sort of telepathy between us. It takes some adjusting, and occasionally those passes are more flashy than good, but when they start working, I get a sense of what this season could be.

From Cotton Fitzsimmons, I learn a ton about fast-break basketball. He's a visionary on the subject, one of the gurus of the break, and he shows me more about where the guards and forwards should be positioned. Ideally, if you are fleet of foot and can get two forwards and a guard running, you can create a ton of three-on-ones or three-on-twos. I spend a month practicing this with Pete and Lou Hudson. It's a clinic in transition basketball. The great lesson I learn is that it's not how fast I run the break that matters, it's how fast *we all* run it. If, as a unit, we are faster than the other team, then we will get layups.

What is interesting is that Pete's court vision has previously been so far beyond his teammates, they're not ready for the kind of passes that he usually dishes out. I grew up imitating the Globetrotters, but I haven't had much opportunity to try this stuff in practice, or on any other court except for Rucker—whenever I tried at UMass, Jack would practically cancel practice right then and there. So running with Pete is interesting in that I feel the freedom to throw some no-look and some behind-the-back passes as well, which can catch Pete off guard.

At one point, in practice, we have a two-on-one breakaway and Pete dribbles between his legs and then hits me with a behind-the-back pass, then I dribble between my legs and hit him back with a behind-the-back pass. He is so surprised that he travels. None of his previous teammates have ever been able to match him move for move. But that establishes some kind of connection. As we were walking back down the court, he looks at me and nods. "Okay, Doc, I get you."

Dr. J

What really draws us together, however, is our work ethic. On every team I've ever played on, I'm the last person to leave the gym. If I can, I find someone who will stay after practice and play one-on-one with me. With the Squires I could convince Fatty Taylor or Ray Scott to stick around, and with the Hawks, it is Pete who stays. He's always in the gym anyway, working on his crazy shots or a new dribble.

The first time I see Pete in the gym after practice, he's shooting left-hand shots from a seated position. I've never seen anyone do that before.

I go down to the other basket and do my leaping drills, touching the rim a hundred times with each hand, then both hands, then hanging on the rim and then starting again. Finally, I go over and ask if he wants to play a little game.

"H-O-R-S-E?" he asks.

I shake my head. "One-on-one."

He nods. Just spending time with Pete is funny because he'll do these things with a basketball I've never seen before when he's just standing around, like spinning it forward, then backward, changing the direction with one flick, and it never leaves the tip of his finger.

"We'll play for dinner," Pete says.

Playing one-on-one with Pete is an experience. He's got the kind of shooting range that I've never seen before. He can shoot it consistently out to thirty-five feet, but if I'm going to go out there and defend that, then he'll cross me up on the dribble and get a layup or dunk. Pete has some great ups, and while he's not known for getting to the rim, he throws some nice dunks down in our games, his hair flapping in the hot Georgia air. One of the things that makes Pete so great is his hang time, and no one talks about that. He can leave the floor and sort of stay up there long enough to fake one way and then pass another. That's something coaches have been discouraging me from doing my whole life. I can remember only one exception: during my rookie season in the ABA we played the Kentucky Colonels, and Adolph Rupp, the legendary college coach who was working for the team as a special consultant, comes into our locker room after the game and says to me, "Young man, I've coached all my career and taught guys never to leave their feet and make decisions after they're airborne. I watched you do it tonight, and I'm changing my philosophy."

Well, Pete will make everyone change their philosophy.

We play some fierce games that summer, one-on-one battles that go for an hour after practice, and some of the guys even come out to watch after they've showered. Pete can get anywhere on the floor with his dribble and I can't stop him. But he can't keep me from penetrating, either. We play every day after practice and I think we split the bills for those dinners about in half.

Pete Maravich is the most skilled basketball player I've ever seen.

When exhibition season starts, we play the Kentucky Colonels—the leagues would regularly match up for exhibition games—and I score 28 and grab 18 rebounds. Every time I pull down a rebound, there's Pete on the wing. I hit him and then run downcourt and he always finds me in stride where I can do something with the ball. The next game, against Carolina, I score 32 on 14 of 15 shooting, thanks to Pete's passing. We win both games easily. In addition to Pete, we have small forward Sweet Lou Hudson, who can drain it from outside, and a veteran center in Walt Bellamy, who can match up in the post with anybody.

I have never looked forward to a basketball season as much as this one with the Hawks.

31.

The NBA has been fining the Hawks $25,000 for each exhibition game I play, and commissioner Walter Kennedy has vowed to continue penalizing the team until I join the Milwaukee Bucks. So for a few days, I'm thinking I'm going to have go to Wisconsin, but then a judge in New York issues an injunction ordering me to play for the Squires and insisting that we settle our contract dispute by arbitration. Atlanta has me signed, but with the NBA ruling that I have to play in Milwaukee, the Hawks are no longer interested in fighting the New York ruling, figuring they no longer own my NBA rights. Irwin and I appeal the injunction, and I go back to Hempstead to await the court's ruling. Publicly, I say I'm willing to sit out the season. I don't want to, of course, but if this gives Irwin more leverage to at least renegotiate the Squires deal, then that's the position we have to take. According to the terms of the Hawks' deal, I get to keep the signing bonus, the car, and the apartment, so we've made out financially very well for my few weeks of playing with Pistol. Irwin's earned my complete loyalty.

The season starts, and the Squires lose their first 4 games. Finally, a three-judge federal appeals court panel upholds the Squires' injunction, ordering us into arbitration, appointing as arbitrator a Harvard Law School professor named Archibald

Cox, who will later become famous as special prosecutor in the Watergate trial.

I've lost. I'm heartbroken. If I want to play basketball, then I have to go back to Virginia. Earl calls me at my mom's house and tells me he hopes I'll play for the Squires.

"You're our franchise. No hard feelings," he tells me. "It's just business."

I tell him I know. But I don't have a place to live. I gave up my house. And now it's just me. No Freda, no kids.

Earl thinks this over. "You can stay at my place." He says he's never there, since he spends most of his time in DC.

Earl has this fantastic penthouse in downtown Norfolk with a waterfront view. And I'm just one guy, basically a bachelor.

I tell him that sounds fine. I'll stay up in New York and join the team for their game at the Nassau Coliseum and then drive back down myself.

That's what I have to admire about Earl. We go through four months of bitter legal battles about where I'm supposed to play, accusing each other of cheating and saying awful things about each other in court filings. But when the judges hand down their orders, he doesn't hold any grudge, and neither do I.

The team I join is 0–4. In my first game back I score 26 and pull down 11 boards in front of my mom and plenty of my old schoolmates. The next game is back in Scope, and a crowd of nearly 10,000 gives me a standing ovation when I'm introduced. That's how loyal the Virginia fans are: they come out and show their love for me even after I've spent the summer trying to leave town. We win that night and the next two to go to 4-4. But this team just isn't the same as it was last year. Attendance is down and our club just doesn't have the same chemistry as we did the previous season. For most of the year, our number two scoring

Dr. J

option is center Jim Eakins, who shoots a high percentage but doesn't demand a lot of attention in an opposing team's game plan. Because I have to carry much more of the scoring load than before, I end up leading the league with 31.9 points a game.

About halfway through that season, however, our team gets a little more interesting when Johnny Kerr signs a nineteen-year-old kid who had been thrown out of Eastern Michigan University, a quiet, shy string-bean who can shoot like, well, like Pete Maravich. Kerr had heard about this kid through one of his old Syracuse teammates but had never seen him play. Then one day he was watching an all-star game in Michigan and he sees this six-foot-seven guard draining 25-footers like layups. That's when he decided he had to sign George Gervin.

George is so humble and easygoing I can't believe he was thrown out of college for fighting. If not for Johnny Kerr showing up at that all-star game, he may never have played pro ball. But from the moment Al brought him into practice and had him set up behind the 3-point line and shoot, I could see this kid was something special.

Faster than he looks or acts, he has this super-quick release and can get his shot off from anywhere. Plus, he can finish at the basket with either hand and from any angle. He's taking the finger roll and using it almost like Kareem uses the sky hook; it's a shot he can get in traffic whenever he wants.

One day after practice, George leaves the court. I follow him down the hall and call out to him, "Hey rook, where do you think you're going?"

He turns to me, all hang-dog shy and unsure of himself.

"We're not done practicing," I say. "We got some work to do."

And George stays after every practice with me, becoming my regular one-on-one opponent.

It's amazing, but in just a few months I've played with two of the most creative big guards in the history of basketball. I'm living the most interesting hoops clinic in history.

32.

Earl's place is in this luxury high-rise penthouse. I can park the Jaguar and the Mark down in the garage and take the elevator up to this three-bedroom aerie with panoramic views of the city and the harbor. Earl and his wife, Phyllis, had it decorated in this contemporary style, with these exposed rock walls, shag carpeting, sunken living room, wet bar, and glass-and-chrome coffee tables. The closets are filled with his and Phyllis's stuff, so it's a little odd when I'm entertaining to have to explain why there are the clothes of a middle-aged white woman in the closets. But I'm living rent-free.

Earl tells me, "No pay, just play."

Still, whenever I have girls come up, they always do a double take because they can tell that this just doesn't seem like the kind of place I'd be living in. But it works for me: it's tidy, very organized, with a cleaning lady who comes in every other day.

When George comes over, I can see him wondering how I can afford it. Earl signed George for just $100,000 over two years, so after his agent's commissions and taxes and insurance, he barely has enough to rent a modest apartment. I tell him this is the owner's pad.

George nods, and I can see him thinking that all he has to do to live in the owner's apartment is lead the league in scoring.

33.

I'm taking advantage of my new freedom with the opposite sex, dating various women, including a Squirette (those are the Squires' cheerleaders) named Rei Kelly. We were friends during my rookie season, but in my second year we become intimate as well. She's a Norfolk girl and has me over to dinner to meet her parents. We both know we're seeing other people. In fact, when the Indiana Pacers come to play, Darnell Hillman and Rei hit it off so well, she sort of becomes his girlfriend when he's in town. I don't mind. We're cool like that.

It's an interesting time for me sexually, in that I can date with a free conscience, and there are plenty of opportunities as we travel around the country. I've got a fat bankroll. I'm the star of the team. And after Carol, I am definitely not looking for another long-term relationship. The sexual revolution has finally made its way down to Norfolk, Virginia, and I'm indulging, perhaps a little too much. No matter: it never gets in the way of my game. I am aware of my role as a leader. I will never let partying or a girl impinge on practice. I make it clear to every girl I'm with that I'm not looking for any kind of long-term relationship.

But that's what I run into after we beat the Kentucky Colonels up in Richmond. Billy Franklin, a rookie on the team, said he had some girls coming up for the game. After the final horn blows, I come down the tunnel and there's Billy.

"Doc, these girls just saw you play and they really want to meet you."

They're in the backseat of a Cadillac. I bend over and look in and there's three of them, two of them sisters.

"This is Cynthia," Billy says. "This here is Cynthia's sister Camille. And that's Turquoise."

I'm not too impressed with the sisters. But I am definitely attracted to the other one, Turquoise.

I lean back down. "How you like the game?"

Turquoise smiles. My blood jumps. "Congratulations. You won."

"Yes I have." I smile.

It turns out these girls are up here from North Carolina, visiting some friends at Howard University. Turquoise's brother, James, plays at Virginia Union, so she knows a little about basketball.

Turquoise has exquisitely shaped lips, sharp cheekbones, almond-shaped eyes with tilde-shaped eyebrows, and light, almost golden-colored skin. She has Freda's coloring, actually.

She is a uniquely beautiful woman with graceful, southern manners. But I can also sense something else. There is a fierceness to her, a cunning, that radiates from her eyes, from the way she is appraising me. I like this girl. She's a Leo, just like Carol.

We exchange phone numbers.

34.

There is something wrong about how I treat women. When I went on that run of eight women in eight days, it left me feeling like I had failed at something, was in some ways a disappointment to my mother. I don't want to see women as sex objects, though sometimes I fall into that behavior and pattern. It's not how my mother raised me, I know that, but it is pretty typical behavior for young men. And now that I'm not with Carol and I'm not betraying anyone, I can convince myself that this is all in good fun. I'm always discreet, and I don't talk to the other guys on the team very much about my nocturnal activities, but sometimes, the emptiness of the pursuit gets to me. I don't want to end up alone, like Tonk, cut off from my wife and children.

I invite Turquoise to come visit me in Norfolk and stay over in the penthouse. She drives up from Winston-Salem, and by the time she arrives, I've got the mood going, a little champagne on ice, some fresh-cut flowers, some chocolates, Marvin Gaye on Earl's quadrophonic sound system, the lights dimmed so that the nighttime harbor view of ships moving in and out of port and cars moving along the expressway is all shimmering yellows, reds, and greens against black sea and through a layer of soft fog. How can a young lady resist? I'm thinking. This is almost unfair.

Then Turquoise arrives and she's with Cynthia.

We're sitting on the sectional sofa in the sunken living room: Cynthia, Turquoise, and me, and I'm thinking, How can I make a move with her wing-woman right there . . .

"You want to meet one of my friends?" I ask Cynthia.

I call the rookie, George Gervin, and tell him I have a girl for him.

"Who?"

"Cynthia," I say.

"Is she fine?"

I look her over. "Um, yeah." She's a fine person, if that's what Gerv is asking.

He says he'll come over to take her out. "She want to go to the movies?"

"You like the movies?" I ask Cynthia.

She looks at Turquoise. Turq nods.

Gervin drives over and quickly deduces that I haven't been totally frank about Cynthia's charms. But he takes one look at Turquoise and he knows why I'm so eager to be alone with her.

Once they leave, I can get my mood going again, the music, the candles, and after a few more minutes of talking, Turquoise says she's going to slip into something more comfortable.

Oh, yeah, this Doctor can operate! I am so smooth—

Then Turquoise comes back in wearing a two-piece flannel pajama suit that leaves everything to the imagination.

She makes it clear to me, no matter how slick I think I'm being, that she isn't ready to get intimate with me. "This is our first night together, and I'm not some groupie," she says.

So instead we talk through the night. She tells me she was married and has a son, a seven-month-old named Cheo. She and the father—a football player at Wake Forest—aren't together anymore. "I'm raising him on my own," she says. "He's with his grandparents tonight. But he's a big part of me, of who I am, and I want to be up front about that."

As I'm listening to Turquoise, I feel the initial powerful connection becoming even stronger. She's a feisty sister, no pushover. She's serious about life. And even though she is six months younger than I am, she has this maturity that I find almost comforting. And I am overwhelmed by her beauty.

She tells me how she wants to go back to Wake Forest now that she's had the baby, to finish up her degree.

I'm smitten, and that night, before we've even slept together, I know that this woman is something special. I'm aware, at

that point in my career, that I'm a handful. I have my habits, my desire for order, my problems with fidelity. Being with a pro athlete is not for the fainthearted. There is no training or preparation for the excessive lifestyle. A sister has to have a pretty strong ego and sense of herself to feel like she can regulate her man. And Turquoise is not intimidated or even particularly impressed by who I am. She's just like, "I have a child, I am not interested in messing around anymore."

I'm not thinking that Turquoise is the one, but I know that I want to spend more time with her than with anyone else.

Later that night, after their movie, George comes back with Cynthia and drops her off without coming inside. "I'm not feelin' her, Doc," he whispers.

Turquoise and Cynthia take one bedroom and I take another.

35.

Despite the addition of George Gervin, we finish the 1972 season 42-42 and lose to Issel, Gilmore, and the Kentucky Colonels 4-1 in the first round. I end up leading the league in minutes per game, with over 42, and for the first time in my career, the wear and tear slows me down. I miss 9 games with a groin injury, the most playing time I've missed since I tore up my knee playing sandlot football. It's disappointing to have taken a step back as a team, but it's also indicative of where our organization is going. Despite Earl's generosity in allowing me to live in his pad, I know that this is my last season in Virginia. The regional franchise strategy has not worked out for the ABA. The Floridians have finally folded, and the Squires aren't in much better shape. Earl has supposedly lost $700,000 running the Squires this year, in part because of the $200,000 in legal fees he ran up fighting my case. I know Earl is looking to sell me to a new team, which means I'll be able to renegotiate my deal.

While Indiana, led by superstar George McGinnis, beats Kentucky for their third ABA Championship, Irwin and Earl are furiously working the angles to try to trade me to the New York Nets, back on Long Island. Roy Boe, the owner of the Nets, has lost his big star, Rick Barry, to the NBA. He's looking for a gate attraction to help fill his new arena, and local boy Dr. J would be the perfect fit. I've had a fine season, leading the league in scoring and being named to the All-ABA First Team. Billy Cunningham is named MVP, scoring 24.1 points per game, 12 rebounds, and 6.3 assists, while I average 31.9 points, 12.2 rebounds, and 4.2 assists. So I can honestly say that I also had an MVP-type season. But I did miss 13 games. And the Kangaroo Kid played every game and led a Carolina team that won 57 games, so he deserves the trophy.

Billy is an NBA guy who spent the first seven years of his career in the other league before joining the ABA. He's been an all-star in every uniform he's worn. There are plenty of guys who have jumped back and forth, and that's one of the reasons why I never consider the ABA to be inferior to the NBA. The NBA does have the bigger markets, but in terms of talent, there is plenty to go around for both leagues. There are seventeen NBA teams in 1973 and ten ABA teams. (By the time you read this, there will be thirty NBA teams.) So the guys I'm playing against in Virginia are some of the best players in the world; we

Dr. J 237

just aren't always regarded that way in the media or viewed that way by the NBA. That's why we take those exhibition games against the NBA so seriously.

When we play an ABA versus NBA all-star game in 1972, the best of both leagues match up. They call it the Supergame, and NBA stars like John Havlicek, Wilt Chamberlain, Oscar Robertson, Nate Archibald, and Bob Lanier match up with ABA stars like Rick Barry, Dan Issel, Artis Gilmore, and me. The coach of the NBA team is Bill Russell and I haven't seen him since he came up to UMass to give his lecture and we spent the night talking.

Bill hasn't been following my career. As he's going over the scouting report with his players, Nate and some of the guys who know me from the Rucker League or preseason exhibition games are saying the guy Bill needs to plan for is Dr. J.

They keep repeating, "Dr. J, Dr. J."

Bill has been retired a couple of years, and he's wondering, Who is this Dr. J everyone is talking about?

So when the ABA team comes out and we're doing our layup and dunk line, he's watching me and smiling and I'm nodding back.

"I know that kid!" he shouts. "That's Julius!"

We share a big hug.

In that game, the ABA ends up losing to the NBA by 2, 106–104, but the margin is indicative of how balanced the leagues are in terms of talent. What really separates us is the lack of a national television deal. If basketball fans were able to watch the best of the ABA every weekend, the great Indiana and Kentucky and New York and Denver teams, then they would see an exciting, wide-open brand of basketball—not to mention the red, white, and blue ball, which looks great on

TV. What made the old American Football League was its TV deal with NBC. That's what brought that league to national attention and forced the merger with the NFL. We all think that sooner or later there will be a merger with the NBA, but the inability of the ABA to secure a national TV contract really holds us back, keeps the league from gaining the leverage to force a merger of equals.

Irwin is furiously trying to work a deal that will either have me playing in the NBA or for the New York Nets of the ABA. I'm talking to him by phone every day during the week when I'm back at my mom's and going down to his offices on Park Avenue where he is explaining our options. This has become one of the most complicated transactions in sports history, involving, as it does, four basketball teams in two different leagues and millions of dollars in cash that have to change hands, not to mention my own contract, which is obviously paramount in my own mind.

What is exciting me, and my mom, is the possibility that I will be playing back on Long Island. I've met with Roy Boe, who purchased the Nets back in 1969 and helped found the New York Islanders of the National Hockey League in 1972. Boe is big, tall, Scandinavian—born and raised in Brooklyn. He made his money in the fashion industry, founding a clothing company called Boe Jests that he had sold for a bundle back in the '60s. I like him immediately. He's smart enough to know that there is no reason to pursue this deal if he can't make my contract work out. He's not going to trade for an unhappy star. There is also the matter of coaches. He's getting rid of Louie after a losing season, which disappoints me personally, but I also know that Louie's style still isn't the right fit for me.

But before I can join the Nets, Irwin has to run a gauntlet

of lawyers and contracts. The Atlanta Hawks want to be paid for sacrificing their claim, and of course Earl Foreman has to get paid for selling me to the Nets so he can keep the Squires franchise going. Hanging over all the ABA guys is the fact that if they don't get this deal done, then I will be going to the NBA, and that would be awful for the league. By this point, I tell Irwin, I actually want to stay in the ABA. I have developed a certain camaraderie with the guys.

The deal we finally work out has the Nets paying $500,000 to the Hawks, with the Hawks passing along $250,000 and two second-round draft picks to the Bucks, all that to repay the Hawks for my own signing bonus and the Jaguar. The Nets also pay $1 million to Earl Foreman. To make the deal look more legit, they also trade George Carter to Virginia for me and Willie Sojourner. And the most important part of this for me: I sign a five-year deal for $2 million to play for the New York Nets.

I'm coming home.

36.

I have a new video camera, a three-quarter-inch videotape machine that weighs twenty-two pounds that I load into the trunk of the Jaguar. Turq is wearing a pantsuit and scarf, a pair of sunglasses, her hair curled and golden in the late-morning sun. Downtown Norfolk glistens from the dawn's coating of rain, now steaming back up to heaven, and we drive through the slick streets, tires growling over moist pavement, the way miraculously clear, as though Highway 264 itself had been closed for our triumphal procession of two. We are young, beautiful, powerful, irresistible, the unspoiled fruit of a nation, the gifted, the chosen, the mighty mighty. Earth, Wind and Fire sing:

> *In our hearts lies all the answers*
> *To the truth you can't run from*

The selfishness of youth, the arrogance of entitlement, the hubris of being young and fine and rich. Allow me a few moments of guilt-free bliss at our own good fortune, to be riding in a beautiful car with a beautiful woman down an open road on a warm spring day, to feel the world opening up, the options infinite, the opportunities limitless, and to have a sense that this is one more good day in what will be an unbroken string of good days. I have risen. I have taken this blessed life. We are the Bonnie and Clyde of black and sexy, the JFK and Jackie of African-American and cool.

Dr. J and Turq.

For just a few moments, I don't want to think about what my mother would say, what my sister would say. (What Marky would have said.) What you would say. Let me live free from expectations and from the constricting code of being a good Christian man, of being the son of a deaconess. Let me ride fast and hard through life and take what I can and enjoy what I can.

This fast car.

This beautiful woman.

This fast life.

The highway unspools under my wheels, a silver-slick ribbon of gray asphalt, a machine-gun burst of white lines, a dozen off-ramp gas stations and fast-food signs and promises

Dr. J

of lodging of comfort and rest. We drive on. We will not be stopped, neither by need nor the inquiring patrolmen. This morning is ours, the world pliant and beseeching: the world prostrate, begging, needing us more than we need it.

So we drive, motor roaring until we hit the ocean, the dappled Atlantic, the foaming uptide, the hissing sand, the circling birds, the diving pelicans, the walking couples on a quiet, wide beach. We park, we walk, we hold hands.

You admire. You gape. You gawk.

Everyone we pass stares at us, nods at us, admires us. We are so fucking perfect. I'm not arrogant, but let me for once be proud. God made us. God made us beautiful.

We come to a small park, where in the afternoon there will be children and parents and the swirling noise of play, but now there is no one, just us. This is our playground, and Turquoise takes a seat on a swing, and I push her, and then I walk around to the other side of her, and I videotape her, record her swinging, her head back, laughing, her gorgeous legs forward and tapering to her elegant feet. Her smile is joyous, eager, knowing, terrifying, cruel, sensuous. She swings back at me again, her face growing larger as she comes toward the lens, her finely shaped face coming into focus as she swings upward toward me.

At the time I am taping her, I think only how I admire her, how fine she is.

Later, when watching the tape, I will think I can spend my life with this one, singular woman.

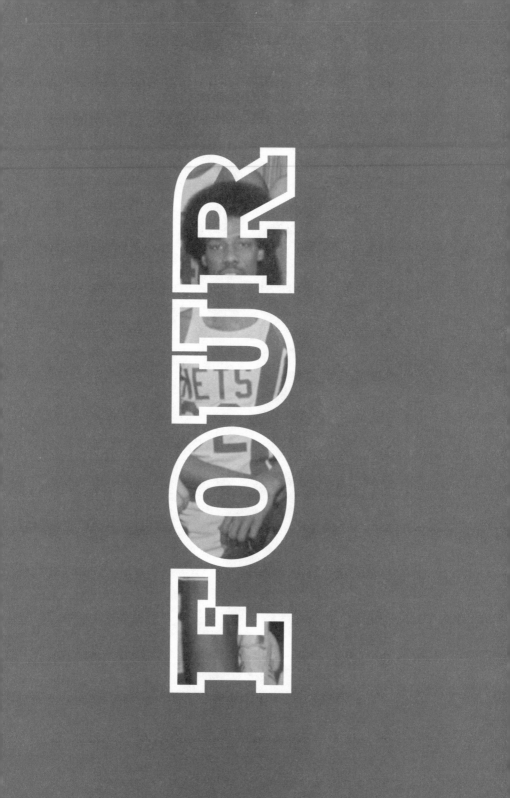

1.

It's gonna be fine, baby doll."

I'm reassuring Turquoise that my moving permanently back up to Long Island doesn't mean anything has to
change. We're at the penthouse, and I've packed the Jaguar
with my alligator skin suitcases. Two seasons in Virginia and
I'm done. I'm going to miss some of the guys, Gervin, Fatty
Taylor, George Irvine, and even big Neil Johnson and his socks
full of grass, but I am more excited about moving back home
and playing in New York again. I will not miss getting stopped
by the cops every week.

The one loose end is Turquoise, and her beautiful baby boy,
Cheo. While I've not committed to her exclusively, I've ac-
cepted that if I'm going to be in her life, I need to be a father to
Cheo. I know she's not going to let me go easily; I also know
I don't want her to.

She worries that when I move up to New York, she's going
to be forgotten.

I tell her that's not going to happen, that's not my intention. I tell her we'll make it work. But based on what I know

about long-distance relationships—look what happened with Carol—I know that this will be a challenge. I want this to work, but I've got to go.

Back on Long Island, I hire a real estate agent and we drive around a few neighborhoods and look at some houses. I decide I want to live on the beach, not far from where Marky, Freda, and I used to go swimming. She shows me a condominium in a brand-new development in Lido Beach, and I close on a modest one-bedroom next to the water, about twenty minutes from Hempstead and the Nassau Coliseum where the Nets play. I offer $50,000 and we make the deal. Irwin is pleased with how prudent I am being with my money, but I have learned from living at Earl Foreman's how little I really need in my life in terms of material possessions.

But being back in the old neighborhood raises issues. It's wonderful to be close to Mom and Mr. Dan and to be able to spend time with my extended family, all the Abneys who have moved north and gather for occasional reunion picnics over at Hempstead Lake State Park. I'm the most famous person in my family, the successful athlete, so some of my relatives come to ask me for some help, and because it's family, I'll try to do what I can financially.

With friends and acquaintances, it's another story. There are some, like Archie Rogers, my old Salvation Army teammate, who I am happy to help out with a couple of bucks, even though I know he's had his issues with the law and been in and out of prison. Still, we go way back, back to before the Sal, even. I will always be loyal to Archie.

There are some acquaintances, however, who seem to look at me like a bank, but a bank to which you don't have to repay a loan. I have to sit through so many business plans—a basketball barnstorming tour, a car dealership, a rib joint—that after a while I pass along to Irwin Weiner and ask him to take a look. Irwin will tell me, "Julius, if you want to help out a friend, then help him out, but don't count on getting this money back." I have to come up with some kind of policy here, some stock answer when these supposed friends of mine keep coming back and asking for more. I once heard Reggie Jackson say that with his various friends and acquaintances, the rule was, you could come see Reggie once. That's it. You get one bite at the apple. He also said not to make dependents out of people who should be independent, and I think about that, frequently.

I decide I'll match his policy. If we go back a ways, or if you're the best friend of my best friend, then I'll help you out. Once. I'll decide how much, and then that's it. You don't get a second bite. That's my rule and I try to stick to it. Now, if you have a legitimately lucrative business idea that makes sense to me and stands up to Irwin's scrutiny, then that's something that may make sense for the right reasons, not because we went to high school together.

Still, over the years, I probably give away $6 to $10 million to various friends and acquaintances, sometimes for business ventures or loans, sometimes just to help a brother out.

I do treat myself to one nice new perk: I buy a white Avanti sports car to drive me from the beach to the arena or into the city. Being back in New York feels like being home. And I'm returning not as some college kid on break but as a conquering hero, and for the first time I can really take advantage of the city. My wardrobe takes a serious step up, as Clyde and I head back down to his tailors on the Lower East Side. There are no names on the doors, just these old Jewish and Italian guys. I have my first fur pieces made, some wraps, some half-jackets, some three-quarter-lengths, a full-length mink, and some fur hats as well. But here's the difference between Clyde's style and mine. If he would get a suit in, say, champagne-colored velvet or some crazy print, I might get the same cut in a solid blue or gray.

2.

Can you see me now? I'm driving in my white-on-blue Avanti, wearing a mink coat with a fur buccaneer hat perched atop my Afro. I'm looking sharp, and I'm feeling good. I'm healthy, my groin injury has completely healed. Last season, I was taking novocaine shots and cortisone shots pretty regularly because the right side of my upper thigh kept tightening up. Those shots masked the pain, but as a result my injury never had time to get any better. Now, with some off-season rest, I feel like I'm pain-free and looking forward to the season.

The Nets have hired Kevin Loughery, a Brooklyn native and former St. John's man who had an all-star career in the NBA with the Baltimore Bullets. His only head coaching experience was going 5-26 the previous season running the 76ers, which was actually an improvement over the guy he replaced, Roy Rubin, who had started the season 4-47. Somehow, Roy Boe thought that a coach with a .161 winning percentage was the right man for the job. And I have to hand it to him: he was right. From my first meeting with Kevin, I like his frank style and his willingness to adjust if his plan isn't working. From the start, maybe because I've been brought in as the star player with the big contract, I feel like Kevin is trying to figure out how to use my talents and get the most out of my abilities. He's not going to try to make me conform to some abstract idea of how the game should be played. He's got a New York swagger, and he's not afraid to mix it up with the players, to grab your uniform jersey by the numbers, if he feels that's how he can make his point.

Our basketball brain trust includes Rod Thorn, a West Virginia guy who played with Jerry West and Rod Hundley and who has an encyclopedic knowledge of the game. And we've got the wise, hard-nosed veteran point guard Bill Melchionni, who is almost as old as Kevin and acts as a sort of coach on the floor.

From the start of camp, it's clear that I'm the spiritual and psychological leader of this team. The guys are taking their cues from me, and Kevin even tells me at one point that the reason the rest of the guys are working as hard as they are is because they see me doing it. We have a couple of guys I've played with up at Rucker—Billy Paultz, the big six-foot-eleven center from St. John's, and small forward Billy Schaeffer, another Johnnie. In addition to Melchionni, we have Brian Taylor, a skilled, quick guard out of Princeton. Our best shooter is John Roche, a second-year man from South Carolina. And we have two very promising rookies in power forward Larry Kenon from Memphis State and shooting guard John Williamson, a scoring machine from New Mexico State. And we have Willie Sojourner, who drives up from Virginia in his tiny Datsun Roadster.

I'm gratified when the guys vote me the co-captain, a responsibility I feel I'm ready to shoulder.

It's hard for me to compare the talent level to our Virginia squads—there's no individual stud quite like Charlie Scott or George Gervin, though Larry Kenon is close. We're all impressed with him. For a big man, he's got such grace and he's a wicked finisher around the rim. I'm looking forward to having him on the other side of the lane on fast breaks. If there is any concern I have about this team, it's that we may not be physically tough enough to get past the Kentuckys and Indianas of the ABA. On the other hand, in terms of team chemistry, there is a good, loose feeling about this bunch of guys that I've never felt before. It comes from the top, where Kevin and Rod both come out to practice in sweats and sneakers and actually scrimmage with the team, which is a great way of getting to know their players and how to make the most use of our particular abilities. One thing Kevin picks up from playing with me, and against me, is that he can use me as a defensive stopper, which he hadn't anticipated based on my reputation as a scorer coming out of Virginia.

But while Paultz is a talented center and gifted scorer, he's not known as a banger. He's not an intimidator, and in this league we need someone who can keep the Artis Gilmores and Mel Danielses from taking my legs out from under me when I'm driving. There are a couple of guys around the league, like Joe Caldwell from Carolina, who have the athleticism to give me a tough matchup. And then there are some enforcers who figure the easiest way to shut me down is to injure me. Wendell Ladner from Kentucky is a player like that, a guy whose plan to stop me seems to be to either break my legs or somehow bait me into a pair of technicals. I once tossed a stool onto the court in Virginia after I had my legs taken out from under me on a shot and no foul was called. The ref saw the stool flying past him and called a technical. I was lying on the floor, looking over at him, and shouting, "You think I just decided to lay down here? I was fouled." I know I need to be careful not to get into too many situations like this or I'll end up costing my team. But as I'm looking around the Nets lineup, I realize that we don't have a guy who I can count on to slug Wendell back if he takes a shot at me.

Maybe the only guy on our team who will go out there and throw a punch is Kevin Loughery, and he's our coach.

Otherwise, this upcoming season in the shiny new Nassau Coliseum is as promising as any in my basketball career. The only thing missing, I realize, is Turquoise. She flies up to see me over the summer, and we swim in the ocean in front of the condo. At night, we drive the Avanti into Manhattan and take a table at a restaurant or sometimes a coffee shop and people watch. For both of us, there is something so exciting about being in New York—and I don't know this yet, but these are the last few months when I can still move around without being mobbed by autograph seekers.

On one of those visits, Turquoise tells me she's pregnant.

I'm standing behind the counter in the condo. I'm holding a Coca-Cola, and for a second I flash on Ray Wilson standing outside the car, in high school, pounding the windows, telling me that kissing makes babies.

"How did this happen?" I'm asking Turq. "Weren't you using protection?"

She shrugs. "I was. It happens."

"And it's mine?" I ask.

She nods.

"How do you know?"

"I know, okay?"

It crosses my mind that this could be intentional. But it also doesn't matter because I love this woman.

Dr. J 251

I feel like if she's carrying my child, then I should ask her and her son to move up here with me.

I'm going to need a bigger condo.

3.

Once Turquoise and Cheo move up to New York, I buy the two-bedroom condo next door. I realize I have a ready-made family with one baby already here and another in the oven. I've gone from being a swinging single to being very much a family man. And I'm very impressed with how Turquoise deals with the situation. She is a powerful, calculating, confident woman, who has the tools to handle whatever life is going to throw at us. Put it this way: since I've gone pro, there are plenty of women who have decided to see if they could get with me because I'm the star player on a basketball team—and I don't say that with any intended arrogance but merely as a statement of fact about professional sports—and Turquoise is the first who has succeeded in entering my life and staying here. She loves me and is intelligent enough to realize that I'm on my way to something greater. Who could blame her for wanting a taste of that?

There is a fierce physical chemistry between us. We have a great sexual bond, but we also just like being around each other. Our personalities somehow mesh. I'm more academically inclined, perhaps more book smart, and Turq is definitely more street-smart. I'm more reserved, perhaps a little too reserved according to Turq, and she is outspoken. If she wants something, you'll hear about it. That harmonic balance, a yin and yang, doesn't necessarily make for a blissful domestic partnership—we do have our fights—but it does make for a durable one.

My mom isn't too happy about our shacking up, and it's no use telling her that we're living in a different era and there's nothing scandalous about men and women living together out of wedlock. Part of what bothers Mom, I know, is that she and Carol were very close—and both very religious—and she is having a hard time accepting Turquoise into her life. When I tell Mom that Turq is expecting, she realizes that Turq is a fixture in my life, but she'll never bond with her in the ways that I might have hoped. One thing Mom can tell is that Turquoise is a stand-by-your-man type of woman. And I can't tell my mom this, but to be the partner of a ballplayer, you have to be tough. I don't think Carol could have handled being with me.

In October, during the exhibition season, Turquoise is in the kitchen and I'm standing on the other side of the galley. She has her hair tied up in a scarf, these delicate gold hoop earrings swinging against her honey-colored skin, aglow in the late afternoon light. Her brown hair descends from beneath her scarf in delicate wisps that wrap under her ears. She has generous lips with exquisite definition, so that it looks as if she is wearing lipstick even when she isn't. And sometimes when she's smiling, as she is now, her upper front teeth are visible between those beautiful lips. She's telling me how happy she is, about where we are, about having come up to New York, and I decide that I will never find another woman like this, who combines the physical beauty, the toughness, the grace, and the intelligence of all the women I've ever admired.

Yet the chaos of our lives has been gnawing at me—the

Dr. J   253

disorder of a child out of wedlock, of living with another man's son, of cohabitating with a woman in what my mom would consider sin. I need to get my life organized, to put everything back in its proper place. The season is starting soon and I don't want to go into it having this sort of disarray waiting for me at home.

And I believe in marriage, and I want my child, and her child, to have what I never had: to grow up with a mother and a father.

I ask Turquoise if she will marry me.

Turq starts crying. "Yes! Yes!"

I nod. This makes sense. I'll adopt Cheo, raise him as my son. We'll be a family, a real family.

"Let's do it before my birthday," I say, "February tenth."

4.

My routine is I wake around midmorning. Turq prepares my breakfast and I play a little bit with Cheo if he is awake. I stroll out of the condo and into my Avanti and head over to our practice facility in Queens.

I'm getting a feel for my teammates, and they for me. In our first exhibition game, I score 42 against the Baltimore Bullets of the NBA and then play my first pro game in Madison Square Garden, a 98–87 victory over the defending NBA champion Knicks in which I go for 27 against my old friend Clyde Frazier before a sellout crowd of over seventeen thousand. I think that game serves notice to New York basketball fans that there are two championship contenders in town.

My first official game in the red, white, and blue Nets uniform is in Indianapolis at the Fairgrounds Coliseum. I put up 42 points with 18 rebounds in a losing effort to the Pacers. We win our next 4 games, including a game down in Virginia at Scope, and I begin to develop increased respect for Kevin Loughery. He's the most intuitive coach I've ever played for. He goes so much by feel, not only by who's shooting the ball well, but also who is getting a step on his man, who is posing matchup problems for the other team, and who is having trouble with his own defensive assignment. He makes some of the fastest in-game adjustments I've ever seen. He'll throw out the game plan in the first five minutes if he sees something that's not working or an unforeseen opportunity. We come into games with a certain idea about how they will progress—say, for instance, that we want to pass the ball down low to Billy Paultz to get his guy in foul trouble. Some coaches will stick with that even after it's clear that Billy doesn't have as much of an edge on his guy as we thought he would. But Kevin will make a quick switch and in crucial situations, when other coaches are drawing up plays and scribbling on their chalkboard, he'll sometimes just look at me and say, "Julius, make something happen."

What player wouldn't like that? We're such an athletic team that when Kevin lets us just play ball, we can turn the game into a track meet, which is fun for the fans but isn't always the way to win a game. In Brian Taylor and Larry Kenon and John Williamson and me, we have some players who can fly. Taylor may be the fastest guy I've ever played with. I love fast-break basketball, we all do, and we know we can score this way. But Kevin—and Al Bianchi did this as well—reinforces the notion that there are good ways to score and not-so-good ways. If you are running down and dunking the ball on the break over and over, you're just forcing yourself to play longer on defense. And you're not managing the game. Remember my idea about imposing your will? In a basketball game, of course scoring is the ultimate goal, but you want to create situations, matchups, get guys into foul trouble or break down their defensive scheme so that they lose confidence in their own ability to stop you. Our opponents are fine with me scoring 42 in a losing effort. If I'm doing that, "making something happen" in the wrong way, then my center isn't going to step up on defense and the guards might slack off. That's not because they're lazy; that's just human nature. A team leader needs to keep his team involved and motivated. I need to take care of my guys. It's a learning curve for me as well, especially after winning four of our first five and then losing nine in a row.

In one of those games, a loss to Kentucky, I decide to take matters into my own hands and call for a clear-out on the left side of the lane, a play we call Arizona. Wendell Ladner has been fouling me all game, and I go into my crouch, jab step once, and Wendell bites on the fake and I spin around him, and Wendell just grabs my shirt and elbows me in the neck.

"Come on, Wendell!"

I'm getting ready to knock Wendell out and he's looking at me all innocent, with his droopy mustache and baby-blue eyes. I realize Wendell wants me to take a shot at him, to punch him, so that we both get thrown out. I think back to Dan Ryan, at the Sal. I unleash a stream of profanities directed at Wendell while I'm stalking along the left baseline: "That is some fucking bullshit right there, Wendell. I'm fucking sick of that shit, man."

Then I run back down the court.

I always leave two tickets for my mom. And she always sits down under that basket.

After the game, we're out to dinner at a steak house in Freeport and I ask her how she liked the game. She's got a sour expression on her face, and she's been quiet since we've sat down.

"I didn't like it."

I'm wondering what's going on. Maybe it's because we lost?

"We'll get 'em next time," I say.

"Julius, I don't like it when you curse," she says. "You were cursing at that boy, and I didn't like that. I didn't like that at all. I was very embarrassed."

I nod. "Okay, Mom. I'm sorry."

And then she asks when I'm going to get my degree.

5.

Kevin calls a team meeting in his suite after we lose our ninth straight in San Diego to the Wilt Chamberlain–coached Conquistadors. Closed-door meetings are a sign of crisis, and as a team, we are all aware that our game plan isn't working. We go around the room, every player getting a chance to talk. Most of us offer the usual platitudes about where we've gone wrong. We're not rebounding. We're not committing on defense. We're giving teams second shots. We like Kevin's brand of fast-break basketball and pressing defense, but we all feel it is wearing us out more than our opponents. Kevin explains that he believes his system makes the best use of me and my abilities.

And perhaps it does, but I'm getting worn down. Kevin thinks I can run all night, and maybe I can, but not every night for an eighty-four-game season. For the first time since the Olympic development tour and those Eastern European courts, I feel my knees aching. The team agrees with me. We can't press for all four quarters and play fast-break offense all the time.

Finally, we get to one of our rookies, John Williamson, and he stands up and says, "The problem is: I'm not starting. I'm not getting enough touches. I'm not shooting enough. If you want to win, you got to get the ball to Super John."

"Who is Super John?" asks Brian Taylor.

"That's what they call me," says Williamson.

"Who calls you that?" Taylor asks.

"Everyone. Everyone calls me Super John."

We're all laughing, I'm sitting there and I look over at Williamson. "Really? They call you Super John?"

He nods.

"Who exactly is calling you Super John?" Taylor asks.

"Everyone. The fans. It's . . . it's in the papers."

"I've never heard that expression," I say. "Have you?" I look at Billy.

Paultz shakes his head. "Can't say I have."

"Super John. Super John. It doesn't ring a bell."

By now Williamson is getting upset. "Look, if you want to win, get the ball to Super John."

"Like Superman?" Taylor says.

"That's right."

"And that's you?" I say. "Let me get this straight: Super John and you are the same person?"

Williamson has a huge ego, but in some ways he does have a point. He is an emerging force, a slashing shooter who we have to better integrate into our offense. Melchionni is getting older, and he's hurt, and Williamson should be getting more minutes at shooting guard. Super John is precocious in many ways. At home, in the kitchen, he's an experimental chef whose invitations are shunned by his teammates after one meal. Chocolate-soaked chicken, anyone? He also claims to be a black belt in kung fu and that his sensei is such a fantastic leaper that he can practically fly. He corners me after practice one day and tells me, "Doc, these guys can fly. They ain't jumpin', they are *flying*. Doc, you can already fly, so if you go with me to the dojo, you will be . . . *double flying*."

I need to see this for myself, so one afternoon I drive over with him to his dojo in Uniondale. I don't see anyone flying or even jumping particularly high. What I do see is Super John getting knocked down an awful lot. I get knocked down enough on the basketball court—I'm not looking for any extra beatings. Kung fu isn't for me.

Larry Keenan is another young gun who needs more minutes. Keenan is so country, I'm not sure he ever adjusts to suburban life. He reminds me of my old freshman roommate at UMass, the vivisectionist. One afternoon I'm driving into the city with Super John and Keenan and Larry starts shouting, "Stop! Stop the car."

We're in Queens. "Why?" I ask.

"Man, look at them kids there. What are they doing?"

I look over at a school yard. A bunch of kids are playing softball.

"I never seen that," he says.

"Softball?" I say.

He shakes his head. "That's what they doing?"

Back in Alabama, where Keenan is from, he'd never seen

softball played on pavement. He finds that shocking, as if we would play basketball on ice.

Keenan is also concerned about his nickname. Since the preseason, fans and players have been calling him Dr. K, which he feels makes him seem like a second-rate Dr. J.

"I ain't no Junior Dr. J."

He suggests, as an alternative, Mr. K.

But it doesn't stick and guys on the team start calling him by his given name, Larry, which he can't stand.

"C'mon, man, call me Mr. K."

"Mr. K?" Brian Taylor says, sounding it out. "That's not a nickname, that's an . . . *abbreviation*."

Keenan broods on this for a while, before coming back with Special K, which makes us roll our eyes. Super John finally rescues him: "Man, you're just some cat, but like with a K," he says. "K-A-T."

It sticks. We call him the Kat.

6.

Kevin is smart enough to recognize that if he wants to run, he's going to have to play his young guns a little more—and allow us to play some man-to-man, sagging defense for some stretches. He begins starting Super John and Kat, and second-year man Brian Taylor. Super John and Kat are soon combining for over 30 points a game, and Keenan leads the team in rebounding that year, with over 11. Our oldest starter is Billy Paultz, and he is in his fourth year. (We call him the Whopper.) After that San Diego meeting we go on to win 19 out of 22. We are *fast*. With Kat, Super John, Brian Taylor, and me taking off on the break, there may be no team in basketball who can keep up with us. But I'm still worried we may be a little bit soft when it comes to playoff time. The game slows down in the postseason, and offenses become more methodical as defenses tighten up. If we go into the postseason with Paultz and Kat as our front line, we may not have the beef to match up against George McGinnis and the Pacers or Gilmore and Kentucky.

7.

With about 30 games left in the season, I get a call from Kevin, who tells me GM Dave DeBusschere has traded John Roche for Wendell Ladner and Mike Gale.

"Why Wendell?" I ask.

"We figured if we didn't have him on our team, he was going to break your leg the next time we played."

That sounds about right. I know firsthand how tough he is, but I wonder about him because he also holds the record for being traded the most times in one basketball season. In 1972 he got dealt from Memphis to Carolina and back to Memphis and then to Kentucky. He is built like a linebacker and he has a mustache that looks like a squirrel sitting on his upper lip. He comes from a place called Necaise Crossing, Mississippi. He went to college at Southern Mississippi and the scouts had somehow measured him at six foot nine, but when he showed

up for his rookie year in Memphis, he had shrunk five official inches.

But he's enough of a physical defensive stopper and outside shooting threat to have made two ABA all-star teams. He leads the ABA in fights started and ejections incurred. But perhaps Wendell is most famous for diving after loose balls. In Kentucky, he chased a loose ball into a glass watercooler near the Colonel's bench and had to get forty-eight stitches in his hand. I remember Billy Cunningham telling me there was blood everywhere. Supposedly, Wendell wanted to come back in and play the second half.

The first time I meet Wendell is at practice at the Cathedral College gym in Douglaston, Queens, our regular facility. Now I've been known to be vain from time to time—witness my morning Afro routine—but Wendell is something else: he actually shows up on the court with a brush so he can comb his hair during practice. But don't make any mistake about Wendell being soft. He is perhaps the most competitive basketball player I've ever played with. Even in practice, he's diving all over the place, smashing into walls and benches, knocking guys over. And every time he goes down, he gets back up, straightening his hair.

As soon as he's out on the practice floor, he and Williamson start to get into it, pushing and shoving each other.

"Don't mess with Super John!"

Wendell shrugs. "Who the hell is Super John?"

They are natural antagonists. Williamson is from Connecticut and Wendell is from Mississippi and almost every practice they get into a little tussle. He will undercut guys in practice, knock people over in a scrimmage.

"Come on, Wendell!" I'll say when he undercuts someone in a scrimmage. "This is *practice*."

"So what?"

But I appreciate the impact of Wendell on our defensive mind-set, and he gives Kevin a bench player who can instantly change a game—sometimes for the worse.

Off the court, Wendell dresses in cowboy boots, bell-bottom jeans with a buckle the size of a manhole cover, and a fringe jacket. He's the first man I've ever met who is obsessed with Burt Reynolds. I mean, we all like Burt, he's a big star coming off *Deliverance* and *The Longest Yard*, but Wendell is fixated on the man. Wendell actually does a publicity poster of himself lying down in the buff with an ABA ball strategically placed, an intentional homage to his icon. He is so exuberant and full of life that even Super John comes around and takes a liking to him, inviting him to the dojo. Wendell goes a couple of times, learns a few moves, has some photos taken of himself in a kung fu robe, and then quits, complaining that there aren't any pretty girls to spar with.

Wendell is living out of a motel near the Coliseum. Since I've bought the second condo, I invite Wendell to move into the original one-bedroom. All he has to do is pay the mortgage for his rent. It's a great deal for both of us, and it means that Wendell and I are neighbors and I end up spending more time with this big, preening redneck than with anyone else on the team. I go over to pick him up so we can carpool to practice, and he'll be listening to a Mac Davis album, or he wants to play me a new Kris Kristofferson song.

"What do you call this music?" I ask Wendell as he sings along to Mac Davis's "Baby Don't Get Hooked on Me."

I ain't ready for no family ties
Nobody's gonna hurry me

"This is my theme song, Doc."

"You ever been married, Wendell?"

He tells me he was married to his high school sweetheart and didn't want to give her a divorce, either, but was tricked into signing the papers before a game because he thought the lawyer handing him the divorce papers was a fan. He signed it, "Wendell Ladner, #33."

He loves playing in New York, he says, and of all the guys, he may well be the most successful ladies' man on the team. As a single guy, Wendell is out on the town every night, but somehow he never shows up for practice with a hair out of place on his head. At one point, Wendell says he is experiencing some discomfort in his groin area. He asks me about it, I guess because of my groin injury the previous season. When he describes the burning sensation, I tell him that his is a very different sort of issue than mine was. For one thing, this doesn't sound sports related. He goes to see the doctor and the doc tells him he's been having too much sex.

Wendell looks concerned. "You think so?"

"How many times a day do you have sex?"

Wendell shrugs. "Three or four. I don't always count."

"Well, that's excessive."

Wendell shakes his head. "It's never with the same girl."

Another time, I'm walking back to the condo and I see Wendell running down the beach barefooted, wearing only his basketball trunks.

"You jogging, Wendell?"

He trots past me. "I had to get out of there," he says, pointing at the condo. "I brought a girl back and forgot I already had one waiting for me. They're in there fighting."

He stops running. "How does my hair look?"

I'm a family man now, so I'm not out at night as much as some of the guys. Wendell and a few of our teammates—Brian Taylor, Willie, Billy Schaeffer—like to gather at a club over in Hempstead, the Salty Dog, which Billy Paultz co-owns. He's got four levels of lounges, a couple of dance floors and bars. We're heading into the disco era, and this is probably the hottest spot in Long Island. So Wendell is in heaven when he's over there, mixing and mingling with the ladies. He's always lobbying the DJs to play some Mac Davis or Kris Kristofferson, and usually failing. Once, he manages to get some Creedence Clearwater Revival onto the sound system and he starts dancing around to "Willy and the Poor Boys." Wendell actually has some nice moves out on the dance floor. You wonder how a guy who can be so graceful in dress shoes can be so wild on the basketball court.

Every game Wendell plays, you know he is going to end up in the stands, a few rows back if possible. He takes out scorers' tables, cheerleading sections, program sellers, peanut vendors, and, of course, watercoolers—sometimes on plays where it doesn't even seem diving is really necessary. He will get into fights with the other team before the game, slugging it out with Warren Jabali or Cincy Powell or John Brisker while still in his warm-up jacket. He gets technical fouls for punching opposing players walking down the tunnel before the opening tip.

In one game against St. Louis, we're losing to the Spirits by 30 and Wendell somehow slips out of his shoe and loses his man, Freddie Lewis, who is dribbling away. Wendell gets up holding his shoe in his hand, and he's chasing after Freddie. Freddie is a fast little guy, so Wendell gets frustrated and finally just throws his shoe at him, knocking the ball loose. Freddie stops, looks around at Wendell, and then just shrugs, like, What are you going to do? That's Wendell.

Dr. J 265

8.

But Wendell is the missing piece, a physically tough defender who makes every player in the league think twice before coming down the lane. And every team starts the game thinking about Wendell instead of me. With Williamson and Kenon in the lineup and contributing steadily, Paultz and Taylor having fine seasons, and my own campaign, which will win me my first MVP award, we may be the best team in the ABA this year. And one of the keys is the relationship between Kevin and me.

Kevin is an outspoken, brash coach, unafraid of criticizing a player or shouting during a practice or a game if a player is repeating the same mistakes. Remember, Kevin and Rod are often scrimmaging with us, so some of the young guys react badly when Kevin lays into them.

What gives Kevin cover is the fact that he and I have a very frank relationship. He will shout at me during practice or criticize me for not making my rotation on defense. I tend to avoid verbal confrontations, and even if I feel that Kevin could be more tactful in the way he brings up some of my errors, I also feel that he has demonstrated enough flexibility and shown me enough respect that I can let it slide if he's throwing a coaching fit, trying to make a point.

But it also stems from the fact that I can tell that Kevin respects me and my efforts. I am the player he will ask to shut down the other team's best player, or who he will ask to take the big shots, and he never questions my intelligence or desire or character. He will sometimes just start shouting, "Julius, are you ever going to rotate down to the block on that? What the hell are you waiting for?"

I do notice that he seems to shout at me at least once every practice. In a private moment, Kevin pulls me aside and thanks me for not challenging him the way so many star players would. "I ride you a little. But because you take it, the other guys, Williamson, Kenon, Taylor, they know they have to take it, too. And they need some shouting. They see that if Dr. J will listen, then they have to listen."

Kevin has us over for poker games at his place: Super John, Brian Taylor, Rod Thorn, Wendell, and a rotating cast of guys. I'm a decent card player, and tend to play more on the road or during bus and plane flights. I have a good poker face and can stay calm no matter what I'm holding. Kevin is a card shark, and he may double his salary from these poker games, especially if Wendell is playing. Wendell has no poker face. If Wendell has a big hand, he can't contain himself. His smile will light up the room.

"Wendell, keep it under your hat, brother."

"What? Aw, damn, how did you know?"

This is all part of our process as a team, this bonding. Brian Taylor even moves into a condo down the beach from Wendell and me. We're a group of really close guys and, going into the playoffs, we know we are the best team in the league, maybe in all of basketball.

9.

The challenges of life back in New York are never-ending. I need to come up with twenty to thirty tickets for every home game, since I've got so many family and friends coming to the Coliseum to see me. And Mom isn't happy about the decisions I'm making in my personal life. She accepts Cheo and loves

him as her own grandchild, but she's still vaguely scandalized by me and Turq living together out of wedlock. There is no explaining to her that we are living in a different time, that men and women are cohabitating, having sex before marriage, and all that. Still, the tension between her and Turquoise is a steady, quiet rumble in my life that I ignore at my own peril.

But I have to give Turquoise credit, because she adjusts to this new life flawlessly. She has her son, and is pregnant with our second, and still she comes to every home game and sits with the players' wives and girlfriends and immediately generates this intense interest in the fans. Everyone wants to know more about her. She has this bearing that is almost regal, and I guess that's the same quality that first attracted me down in Norfolk.

Turq and I decide to have a very quiet wedding ceremony with some family and close friends at the Americana Inn. We know that if we publicize our wedding, or if the press finds out about our plans, we will be mobbed by reporters and fans. Turq and I have done a great job keeping it quiet, and we haven't leaked to anyone, not even family. This is some serious down-low stuff. And if you ask any of the guys I've played with, I've always been good at keeping my secrets. But at a bachelor party thrown for me the night before by my teammates, I make the mistake of revealing my plans. And the next day it's all over the newspapers and on the radio, and by that night, the TV news is covering it and saying Dr. J has gotten cold feet. The truth is, I've heard about the phalanx of TV cameras that are waiting for us over at the hotel. Turquoise is already there, upstairs, and she calls me and tells me it's a circus. If I show up, I may never get inside for my own ceremony. They're stopping traffic outside. I'm thinking, Damn, this is really something. I mean, I knew I was becoming a celebrity, that my fame was starting to transcend basketball, but this was a little beyond what I had previously imagined. We need to make a move. Turquoise tells me to go to the Waldorf Astoria, that the judge will meet us there. I'm with my old friend and Rucker League teammate Dave Brownbill and his girl, Frannie Ryan, and we race over to the Waldorf Astoria where we take a suite.

When I get there, Turquoise is looking as beautiful as ever in her simple white wedding dress, holding a bouquet of flowers. She is shaking her head as if to say, What the hell have I gotten myself into?

And all I can tell her is, "I never said it was going to be easy. But it will be interesting."

The judge, August Moresca, finally turns up a little after midnight and performs the ceremony. Dave and Frannie are joined by my dentist, who just happens to walk into the Waldorf the same time as me, so I tell him to come up. (Since my job working at the bakery, I've had bad teeth, and by the time I'm twenty-four, I've already had two root canals. Believe me, inviting Dr. and Mrs. Marks is more than just an act of spontaneous generosity.) We toast with champagne and potato chips. But we have somehow managed to keep our marriage a private affair, which is what both of us wanted. As it would turn out, far too much of our lives would be played out in public.

10.

Loughery has us playing our best ball at the end of the season, as we win eleven of our last twelve to finish at 55-29, the best record in the ABA.

In the first round we take on Al Bianchi and the Squires—owner Earl Foreman has sold George Gervin to the San Antonio Spurs, so this team doesn't have the talent to compete against us. We win the first 2 games at home and then head down to Norfolk for game 3.

It's a blast being back in Scope for a playoff game, but the Squires sort of lull us into playing their game, and somehow they are leading by a point with 8 seconds left. I take the ball, drive down the left side of the lane, go up and spin the ball off the backboard, and I . . . miss. The fans seem almost disappointed that I didn't make the buzzer beater. But we take the next two to put the Squires away. This would turn out to be the last playoff game the Squires would ever play. I always wonder what would have happened if somehow Earl had kept all his pieces—me, Gervin, and Charlie Scott—together. We would have been a perennial contender in any league. The lesson here is you don't want to play for an owner who can't afford to keep a team together. I like to think that in Roy Boe we have found a guy who won't have to break up the good chemistry we're building.

In the next round we face my old nemesis, Artis Gilmore, who that season is combining with Issel for 44 points and 28 rebounds a game. They also have sharpshooter Louie Dampier and, of course, John Roche, who they picked up in the trade for Wendell. Even though we finish with a better record, it seems the media still sees Kentucky as the team to beat, in part because of the presence of their all-star big men and the fact that they have been to the finals before. I feel I have always played well against Artis, and I believe there is no defender in the league who can stop me without fouling. Artis and Issel have for a few years been the best combination in the league, and they have gotten closer to the title than I ever have. I haven't even led my team to the finals.

I've had a great regular season and win my first MVP award, as I lead the league in scoring again and finish second in minutes, third in steals, third in blocks, sixth in assists, and tenth in rebounds. I'm First Team All-ABA again, along with Artis, George McGinnis, Jimmy Jones, and Mack Calvin. But just as important for the Nets has been the emergence of Super John and the Kat, both of whom make the All-Rookie team.

But I haven't won a championship since playing for the Sal, through high school and college, and with the Squires; we have come up short at the end of the season. This year, I'm determined to change that.

We win the first two games at home against the Colonels and then go down to Louisville for game 3. Through the first three quarters, the game is a physical matchup, with both teams expending their energy playing defense and Wendell expending his energy diving after loose balls, including one notable leap where he goes over the radio broadcast crew and ends up with cables, microphones, and headsets dangling from his body like Christmas tree ornaments. Supposedly, the radio feed was out for the rest of the game. We're trailing 89–87 with fifteen seconds left, and we get the ball back. Kevin calls a time-out, and he's drawing up a play for me, with second options for a kick out to Williamson or, if Artis collapses over on me, a pass in to Whopper. I put my hand on his shoulder and I say, "Kevin, I'll take the last shot."

"Okay," Kevin is saying, "but if Doc misses—"

"I'm not gonna miss."

Kevin puts down his chalk and looks up at me. "Okay, let's get Doc the ball. Let's go."

Dr. J 271

Brian gets me the ball up near the right side of the key, about twenty feet out. I dribble to kill a few seconds and then go into my move, driving down to the right side of the foul line, as the entire Colonels defense collapses on me. I go up off my right foot, and I'm falling backward because I have to get the shot over the entire Colonels' defense.

I bank it in.

Buzzer.

After that, we know the Colonels are done, and we beat them by 13 in game 4.

The feeling among the guys is that nobody can stop us, and we act as if beating Utah is an afterthought.

The Utah Stars had started life as the Anaheim Amigos, before moving up to LA to play at the Sports Arena where they actually made the ABA finals in 1970 and then—why not? This is the ABA after all—they decamped again, this time to Utah, winning the ABA title in 1971. When they play us, several of the key pieces of that championship squad are still in place, most notably, Zelmo Beaty, an NBA and ABA stalwart who was among the first big stars to jump leagues when he signed with the Stars in 1969. Zelmo is so strong that Wilt Chamberlain has said he was the single player who gave him the most trouble—which may have been more of a dig at Bill Russell than praise for the Big Z—but is still remarkable considering that Zelmo is about three inches shorter than Wilt and played the last ten years of his career with no cartilage in his knees.

The three best scorers on this Utah team are Willie Wise, Ron Boone, and All-ABA point guard Jimmy Jones. This is a balanced, fast team, but with Big Z injured, I'm able to score 47 points at home in a rocking Nassau Coliseum, in front of friends and family. Turq is nearly at full term, but she is so fit and fierce, I can actually hear her shouting encouragement from the stands. Game 2 is even more satisfying—and more violent—as Ron Boone comes out and floors Brian Taylor, who gets up and socks Boone in the mouth. Amazingly, neither player is ejected or even receives a technical. The whole team gets involved in this win and our sagging, fast-rotating defense shuts down their three-guard attack.

We end up putting Utah away in five games and I finish the playoffs with a 28.2 average, 11.4 rebounds, and 5 assists. After we win the final game at home, we're in the locker room, pouring champagne over each other and the announcers. I give Wendell a big hug and I look around at this group of brothers and I think, These are the finest men I have ever known: Brian, Kat, Mike, Whopper, Super John, Billy, Bill, Wendell, Willie. And after I embrace Roy Boe, I sit down in front of my locker and put my head in my hands. I'm not crying, I'm just remembering Marky, and Tonk and Bobby, but also the many men who were there for me, Don Ryan and Ray Wilson and Earl Mosley and Jack Leaman. And of course my mother, Callie Mae, who taught me so well.

And then I get back up and start celebrating with my teammates. I'm sorry, Don, but this is a night for winning *and* boasting.

We end up at the Salty Dog around dawn and continue toasting each other until Wendell and I head back to the beach a couple of hours later.

Wendell says, "This feels great, doesn't it, Doc? It feels like, I don't know, it feels better than meeting a fine young lady."

I laugh. "Wendell, you need to get some sleep."

11.

The next afternoon, when I finally wake up, I can hear my mom's voice, and for a moment I'm transported back to our house over on Beech Street, and my mom is in the kitchen, making pancakes, and I've just come back from the paper route and I'm waiting for my second breakfast, and she will envelop me in warmth before I go out again into that cold day. I rouse myself and I realize she is out on the front deck, sitting in the white wood furniture on the patio overlooking the Atlantic. If the water is calm, I know, she likes to come out and drop a line off one of the boat launches into middle bay and see if she can catch some snapper or even sand dabs, which she'll cook up in oil just like they did when we would visit South Carolina when I was a boy.

If the water is too rough to drop a line, she'll just take a seat on the porch and drink iced tea and visit with Cheo. Since Turq is expecting, Mom wants to be helpful, but there is only so much Turq will let her do. I tell Mom not to take it personally, that Turq just has her own way.

I can hear Mom talking to another lady, an older white woman by the sound of her voice. I get dressed and go out to say hello and see she is visiting with Mrs. Ladner, who flew up for the finals and must be looking for Wendell. The two of them, a black lady from Long Island and a white lady from Mississippi, are chatting about fishing and catfish recipes and they might as well be on a porch down in Batesburg or Necaise Crossing, talking to their neighbors. It's a beautiful sight to see these two ladies from two different worlds getting along as if it's the most natural thing in the world.

When I say hello to both, Mom turns to me and says, "June, you know Mrs. Ladner?"

I tell her I do.

"Her boy is Wendell, your teammate."

"Yes, I know, Mom."

"She says she was supposed to come over to visit with Wendell, but he's not here. Or he's still asleep."

I'm not surprised. The sun is high in the sky, but it's still awfully early for Wendell.

"But, June, remind me, who was the young man on the team you were telling all those stories about, who is going off with a different woman every night and who has a young lady in every city you all visit? I want to make sure that Wendell knows to stay away from that boy."

12.

I wasn't there when Cheo was born, of course, so I didn't know the euphoria of that instant when a man becomes a new father. At Long Island Jewish Hospital, I watch my son Julius being born. I'm in scrubs, a surgical mask, and Turquoise is pushing, pushing, working harder than any athlete I've ever seen, veins bulging, her skin turning splotchy as capillaries are bursting on her forehead and cheeks. She is so strong, and with each contraction she pushes and struggles and Julius Winfield Erving III's crown appears and then this boy is thrust into the world. My wife is fierce and awesome and powerful, yet so full of love that as soon as the baby appears she reaches up for

Dr. J

him, and the doctor lifts him into her hands. She takes our slimy, bloody boy and holds him to her breast and that's our trophy, our prize, a second boy, another blessing in this season of blessings, in this life that God has made so full and rich that I am crying.

Fatherhood is another of life's great challenges, perhaps the greatest, but just as I was prepared for basketball through the Sal and high school ball, I have been prepared for fatherhood through being an uncle to Barry and Keith and living with them as infants and young boys. So I want to teach boys how to be good men, and I need to pass on to you what my mother passed on to me, what those strong men passed on to me, what all our ancestors passed on to me. Everything our ancestors and relatives ever did, every journey and struggle and even every basket and rebound, all of this led to you being born, right here, right now. You are the sum total of all my dreams and all of our ancestors' dreams.

I need to rise to your needs.

13.

This, then, is the American dream, isn't it? Successful athlete, wealthy, beautiful wife, loving family, sturdy sons, even a dog, a Belgian shepherd named Cain, and Turq and I are expecting another child. I'm the star player on a championship team and the toast of my hometown. Yet there are troubling signs if I look closely. Our championship series wasn't broadcast nationally. Our average attendance was below nine thousand.

Larry Bird and I had a ferocious rivalry; here I'm dunking all over him and Kevin McHale (*feet pictured in the center*). (Tony Tomsic/Getty/ Sports Illustrated)

Top and bottom

Sometimes when I went airborne I didn't even look at the basket. By the 1980s, I was more concerned about finding a way around my hero, Kareem Abdul-Jabbar. (Jim Cummins/Getty/NBA)

Top

Moses Malone was the missing piece that enabled us to win the NBA title. (Focus on Sport/Getty)

Bottom

After clinching against the Lakers, at the Forum, in 1983. (NBA/Getty)

Clockwise from top

1. My children, Cory, Cheo, and Jazmin, on the Fourth of July in 1996.
2. My family in Atlanta, 2010.   **3.** With my daughter, the tennis player Alexandra Stevenson, at my sixtieth-birthday celebration.   **4.** When I met my second wife, Dorys, she had no idea who I was: "They said you're called Dr. J. What kind of doctor are you?"

Clockwise from top
1. My hands are just as big in the boardroom as they were on the court. (Dorna Jenkins Taylor)   **2.** Barry with my late son, Cory, in 1996, four years before the accident.

This is the face of a satisfied man saying good-bye to the game.
At the Forum in 1987. (Rick Stewart/Getty)

How can Roy Boe continue to operate at this level—and to pay me—if even with the superior product he is putting on the floor every night, he can't make a profit? The rest of the league is in even worse shape. Earl Foreman and the Squires are almost bankrupt, the owners in Carolina and Kentucky want to sell, the owner of the Memphis Tams is looking to raise money by selling his hockey team, and the San Diego Conquistadors aren't going to last long playing in a high school gymnasium. More and more I am hearing that *I am* the league. I reject that. I've played with and against too many great players to think in those grandiose terms, but I do worry about the future of my contract if I keep playing in front of empty stadiums on local UHF stations, as I will through the disappointing 1975 season. Fortunately, my off-the-court income has drawn almost equal to my basketball salary. Irwin is starting to land big-money endorsements for me, with Converse, Spalding, Dr Pepper, and ChapStick. In the off-season, *Hoop* magazine flies my family down to Puerto Rico, along with Jo Jo and Deborah White and John and Beth Havlicek. Because this is an annual event for the magazine's advertisers, this also becomes a yearly vacation for us as we begin to spend our off-seasons with the Havliceks. My children, meanwhile, spend their summers in resorts around the Caribbean, instead of taking a bus to Long Beach and eating sandy peanut butter sandwiches out of a waxed-paper baggie like I did.

Irwin and I assess my financial situation—and I take a look at how crowded our condo is getting—and agree that for tax reasons, it makes sense that I step up and buy some substantial real estate. Turquoise and I find our dream house, a classic Tudor-style estate at the end of a cul-de-sac in Upper Brookville on the North Shore of Long Island. The place sits on three and a half acres of grounds, with a swimming pool, skating rink, basketball court, four-car garage, and a half dozen bedrooms. Nine thousand square feet and half a million dollars pretty clearly demonstrate how far I've come from Hempstead. We need the tax protection of a big mortgage, so I put down a hundred thousand and borrow the rest.

This is a significant move for me, a kid from the South Shore, from the Parkside Gardens projects, moving up to the North Shore, to Gatsby country. In cultural as well as financial terms, I am making a statement about how Turquoise and I see ourselves. I sometimes joke to Turq that we're like the black Kennedys, and she's like Jackie O. That's how scrutinized we feel, and now that we are living among the landed gentry, among the old-money scions and new-money dentists, I feel like we have to acclimate to a whole new lifestyle. Our kids will be going to private schools, we buy a Volvo station wagon, and navigating this new landscape will require that Turq and I learn the behavioral characteristics of an entirely new tribe: rich people.

One of my new neighbors is Kenneth I. Starr, a lawyer and accountant who, the first time he comes into my house, starts digging through the freezer, pulling out pork chops, and offering them, frozen solid, to my kids. He has a strange sense of humor, an eternal optimist with a smart answer for every question. He seems like a guy who is on his way up—like me—and has a reputation as a sharp lawyer. I start to use Ken as my attorney on most of my deals. He and Irwin become my business team. Over the years, Ken's business will grow so that he is managing money for clients like Al Pacino, Natalie Portman, Carly Simon, and Sylvester Stallone.

In the off-seasons, I start the routine of going over to the

French Riviera for a few weeks before training camp begins. I like to run from the Hôtel du Cap-Eden-Roc all the way into Antibes, and then run back, so it's about a four-mile run along the highway. There are a couple of other Americans over in France playing ball and I train with one of them, Michael Harper. (Harp will go on to play for the Trail Blazers.) There are a few outdoor courts on the beach, so we sometimes put on a little show for the locals, but the main thing I am doing is getting my legs under me, so that I turn up at camp already running a sub-six-minute mile. But I love being over in France because nobody knows me over there. I can walk the streets and they don't pay me any mind, or any more than they would any very tall brother.

Our first trip over there, we're having dinner at the Hôtel du Cap—you can only pay in cash, or bank check, or, I suppose, gold bullion, at that place—and I can hear someone loudly saying, "I heard there's some American ballplayers in here making a commotion!"

And I turn around and it's Bill Cosby.

It was Cosby who first told me about this spot. He's been coming here for years, staying a month every year, overlapping into my preseason September.

We have dinner with Bill and Camille. They invite us up to their suite, and I can see that Bill and Camille have brought over steamer trunks full of clothes, and Camille has Polaroids taken of each of her outfits so she never wears the same combination twice. Cosby is going on about how he and Camille come to the Hôtel du Cap regularly and how it's the best place on the Riviera, and that's it, I decide from now on I'm staying at the Hôtel du Cap with Cosby.

Cosby loves tennis and is urging me to play. I take up the

Dr. J 279

sport, and that becomes one of my main off-season fitness regimens, a steady and regular tennis game with Bill Cosby. We end up doing a Coca-Cola commercial together in which we say two doctors agree that Coke tastes great, and then Cos says, "You know, I was a pretty good basketball player in my days at Temple." My punch line is, "One out of two doctors agree on that."

Turq and I are moving in very different circles now, as our fame and wealth allow entrée to virtually anywhere we might wish to go. New York City in the '70s is a hotbed of African-American culture. One of the centers of it is Cosby's Manhattan brownstone in the East Fifties. He and Camille have cocktail parties and I meet everyone over there: James Earl Jones, Flip Wilson, Jesse Jackson, even Eartha Kitt and Miles Davis. Because of my nascent tennis game, Cos introduces me to Arthur and Jean Ashe, who are basketball fans and also good friends with Knick guard Dean Meminger. I invite Arthur and Jean over to Brookville, and we begin to socialize with them quite a bit. My own tennis game is improving. I'm a professional athlete in my prime, and I'm starting to think I could join Arthur on the tour!

At one point I make the mistake of challenging Arthur to a tennis match. We're at his country club down in Florida.

"You really want to do this?" he asks.

"Yeah, Art, come on. I've been working on my game."

"You want my A game?"

"Of course."

We're on the court and Arthur nods and serves and shouts, "Fence!"

I'm thinking, What is he doing? But when I try to return the serve with a forehand, it goes ricocheting off my racket and into the fence.

"Fence!"

"Fence!"

He's putting so much crazy sidespin on the serve that I can't control it.

I'm thinking I'll stick with basketball.

14.

One night I'm over at Cos's and Miles is there. We're in Cos's front parlor, and Miles takes out his trumpet and starts playing. Everyone is nodding their heads like we're all digging it, but I'm thinking, What is this guy on? Later, I will realize it's something from *Bitches Brew*, but at the time, this sounds new and alien to me, unpleasant to my ears. I look around and think that somehow, all these sophisticated people—Bill Cosby!—are digging this music. Why can't I dig it as well? I realize, there are so many levels of culture and society, too many layers of privilege, and I am just beginning to appreciate so many of these finer things. It's like, say, escargots, which we have been eating in France—or as we would have called them back in Hempstead, snails—and how at first, just hearing that we will be eating snails sounds disgusting, but after I try it and get used to it, it becomes very special.

We are changing, Turquoise and I, becoming accustomed to these moments where we glimpse how our social betters are living. We are invited into this community. I like to think it is because I am an artist as well, a painter on a canvas that is a basketball court, but that is also vanity speaking. I'm just June, an overgrown kid, and sometimes, when I'm standing in Cos's front parlor, I have to remind myself of Bobby or Marky and fishing in a canal down in South Carolina and running barefoot all summer, and, well, look at us now.

I decide one thing then, standing there with the swells and listening to Miles Davis. And that is: there are people who come here, who become part of this life, and they think that is who they are, that they are special and better than the rest, and I will never succumb to that mistaken self-love. I can't get caught up in who I'm supposed to be. I have to remain who I am.

15.

Road life in the ABA remains grueling, plenty of four-cities-in-five-days kinds of trips, regional flights to Louisville, a bus to Memphis, a flight to St. Louis and then San Antonio and then Utah, and back to New York all in one week. Most of the guys crammed into economy seats, maybe a few veterans—and by now I clearly qualify—in first class if any seats open up, breathing in that secondhand smoke, eating awful food, arriving at three a.m. for an afternoon game. Guys playing poker on fold-down tables, Wendell still getting read like a book, Super John winning pots and reminding us, of course, "That's why they call me Super John." We're still largely the same team that won the championship, with the significant difference of adding backup point guard Al Skinner, a kid I helped recruit up at UMass. A rookie like Al sits in the back.

Kevin and Rod are up front, talking over how to defend the Stars lineup and this new kid they have named Moses Malone or the Spirit of St. Louis and their amazing rookie tandem of Marvin Barnes and Maurice Lucas. Again, I owe so much of my success as a professional athlete to being able to sleep on planes, and so I arrive usually better rested than the average player. But that season, my knees are starting to feel the pounding of these hard ABA floors and the deep playoff run we made last year. Also, perhaps because of that groin injury last season, I have been favoring one knee and strained the tendons. But even after 3 games in a row, a Friday, Saturday, and Sunday, I won't take a Monday practice off. Kevin will ask me if I want to rest my legs, and I always tell him no. I play forty minutes a night, third highest in the league, and score 27.9 a game, second best in the league to George McGinnis, with whom I share the MVP award.

We fly out to San Diego after a five-day layover in February to take on the Conquistadors, who have parted ways with Wilt Chamberlain. (In fact, the entire team will soon be taken over by the ABA, as the current owners are abandoning the franchise.) After the good break and long flight, I feel well rested, my knees are fresh, and the Qs, as we call San Diego, may be the worst defensive team in the league. Their best player is probably Caldwell Jones, my future teammate in Philly.

Tonight, it doesn't matter who the Qs send out to guard me, as this is one of those games where every path to the basket seems to open up just enough for me to get there, going up and over guys or around them. On one dunk in the second half, I take the ball straight at Caldwell, going up against him chest to chest, and then I just keep rising. I finish regulation with 45 points. After four overtimes, I have 63 points, but we

Dr. J   283

end up losing, 176–166. And even more distressing, there are only three thousand fans on hand to watch the highest-scoring game in league history.

We end the 1975 season in a tie with Kentucky for the Eastern Division title. We lose a one-game playoff to Artis and Issel and the Colonels and have to face the Spirits of St. Louis in the first round. And while we beat them eleven out of eleven times in the regular season, the Spirits are a lot tougher than their 32-52 record. For one thing, in Marvin "Bad News" Barnes, they have one of the great shooting big men in the game, a guy with a McAdoo-like touch. They have Fly Williams, who led the NCAA in scoring last season, and Maurice Lucas, another physical big man who can shoot the mid-range jumper. And at the end of the season, they add Don Adams, a tough, physical rebounder who is willing to go punch for punch with the Wendell Ladners of the league and can finish any fight Bad News starts.

Marvin gets into the news plenty, for leaving the team, for threatening to jump leagues. At one point, the media reports that he has thirteen telephones in his house. Supposedly he drives around St. Louis in a Rolls-Royce. He is also famous for some questionable decisions on and off the court. One famous example is Marvin receiving the ball out on the break with four seconds left in the first half of a game and a clear path to the basket. Marvin dribbles *back* four steps to put up a three.

But at his best, he is as pure a scorer as there is in the game and may also be among the fastest big men I have ever seen. And in the first game in Nassau, he puts up 41 points, but we beat them anyway by 6 points. A few troubling trends emerge that carry over into game 2. Don Adams is playing me tough, fouling me frequently and generally getting under my skin a little bit, so that through the first three quarters, I only have 6 points and I'm getting so angry at Adams, I might floor him. Kevin takes me out to cool down but by then the result is a formality. Marvin scores 37 and gets 18 boards and the Spirits blow us out.

Games 3 and 4 are back in St. Louis and Marvin continues his rampage and we lose both. No matter, I figure we're heading back to Nassau and will even this up at home. We are actually up by a point with fifteen seconds left when I take the inbounds and get hit with a traveling call, a terrible turnover. The Spirits take the ball in and Freddie Lewis catches a pass just over the half-court line, muscles Brian Taylor out of the way, and hits a 20-footer to give the Spirits the game and series.

I can't believe it. Our season is over. And while I question the call on me, I have to take the blame. If I'm the leader of the team, then when we lose, I have to be willing to accept that burden.

In the locker room after that home loss, I'm sitting with my knees wrapped in ice, reporters gathered around me. I'm explaining how disappointing this is for me personally because I feel like I let down my team. I look over and I see Wendell, and he's already showered and changed and he's combing his hair and shaking his head.

He looks at me over the heads of the sportswriters and he mouths something.

"Wait, wait," I tell the writers. "What's up, Wendell?"

He smiles. "I'm just asking, 'How's my hair look?'"

My dog, Cain, is chewing up the leather interior of my Avanti. We've been sending him to obedience school but the dog won't stop barking, taking J's bottle, and ripping up the indoor and outdoor furniture. But when he starts getting into the leather seats of the Avanti, tearing big chunks out of the passenger seat, I start thinking, This dog has to go. I'm like, you're supposed to

be my road dog, and you're treating my car like it's a big steak bone? We try another obedience school and when I drive over to Glen Cove to pick up the dog, Cain seems chill. He's wagging his tale, happy to see me, and I'm thinking, Good, okay, now we have man's best friend coming home with me.

Two days later, he's back into the car seats, tearing up the Volvo. And he manages to gnaw through a kitchen cabinet door, which I've never seen any dog do.

I've never had a pet before, so this is new for me. Turquoise has had it with Cain, and I'm finding it difficult to build any kind of deep relationship with this hound. And with my schedule, I don't have the time to invest in really fixing whatever behavioral issues Cain might have. I do worry that this might be a symptom of the kind of home we are making here. Are Turquoise and I too busy to give a dog the kind of love he might need to thrive?

My mom says that down in South Carolina, if a dog starts acting up, well, they just put the bitch down. That's not how we do things anymore. But I can't keep him.

So I load Cain into the Volvo and drive out to Huntington where we have found a family willing to adopt him. Cain's a good-looking dog, I think, so I'm sure the family will take to him. Maybe they'll have better luck with raising Cain. I stop the car at Cain's new home, open the front door. Go on, boy. He doesn't even look back.

When I'm driving home, I'm listening to WABC and a newscaster breaks into "Why Can't We Be Friends" mid-song and says an Eastern Airlines 727 has crashed at John F. Kennedy Airport. The announcer is saying there were 124 passengers and crew on board. Wreckage is scattered along Rockaway Boulevard, a sort of ring road around the airport.

There are numerous fire and rescue vehicles at the scene. From the way he is talking, it doesn't sound like there are many survivors.

The flight had originated in New Orleans.

At home, I turn on the television and I'm watching the news. The footage is frightening. The camera crews are casting stark light on the scene and we can see what look like body parts.

I'm still watching when Kevin calls me and he says he thinks Wendell was on that plane. He was flying up from Necaise Crossing to film a commercial. (Wendell is hopeless when it comes to commercials. He can never remember his lines. Eventually, the directors and sponsors just let him talk about how much he likes potato chips or whatever it is until they feel they have something they can use.)

The TV cameras are panning the wreckage and Kevin tells me he sees what looks like a New York Nets logo on a duffel bag. But in a few hours it's confirmed that Wendell was on that flight. They ID him by his championship ring.

We all have to make the reverse flight down to Necaise Crossing a few days later to attend Wendell's funeral. Bill Melchionni and I are among the pallbearers. "He was my protector," I say in my eulogy, "my shining shield."

How does a team come back from a loss like this?

16.

I went pro when I did in part because Steve Arnold, my so-called agent at the time, was one of many who were warning

that an ABA-NBA merger was imminent and players would lose their negotiating leverage. The closest they actually came to a merger was in 1971, when an agreement was reached and ratified by the two leagues. (The only team that wasn't going to join the NBA was the pre–Dr. J Virginia Squires.) The NBA Players Association filed suit, alleging that the merger would create an illegal basketball monopoly.

That lawsuit, which was widely known as the Oscar Robertson Suit—I always think of a dignified tweed whenever I hear that expression—kept the two leagues effectively apart for five more years and allowed the Marvin Barneses and George McGinnises and, yes, Julius Ervings of the world to play both leagues off against each other and become wealthy doing it, and, if we wanted, to have over a dozen telephones in our house.

The Oscar Robertson Suit is settled in 1976, after Oscar has actually retired, and that removes the last major obstacle to a merger. But even before that settlement, there have been signs that the ABA may not be around for much longer. There are the usual ownership and financial crises around the Squires, the Conquistadors, the Stars, and whatever the Memphis team is being called this week (actually, never mind, they've moved to Baltimore, and they've been renamed the Claws). Their financial situation is so dire that when the team folds after just three exhibition games, and the players go in to the Claws office demanding what they are owed, they are told that there isn't any money but that they can take anything they want from the office. So Dave Robisch and Mel Daniels end up making off with a bunch of typewriters, telephones, and Claws swag instead of their game checks.

Adding to the sense of instability is the fact that Roy Boe and the Denver Nuggets' owners have applied to join the

NBA—I didn't even know you could do that. These are the two most successful franchises in the league, and if we go, then the ABA is essentially finished. When Roy tells me what he's doing, I feel a great twinge of sadness. I love the ABA and, like so many of the players, I have a strong sense of solidarity with the league. I didn't play at a major basketball university, I was an alternate for the Olympic development squad, I wasn't even drafted out of college. I joined a backwater franchise in the league that many—though not me—consider second rate. This is part of my identity. You never see me coming.

What we do over here, it's like a secret that only real basketball fans know about. So many of the games, some of my best moves, aren't even on tape. They are one and done. You literally have to be there or you will miss it. I once saw this documentary about Pele, the soccer legend, and how half of his greatest goals, these amazing runs where he touched the ball sixteen times and ran the length of the field, they only exist in the memories of these old guys who were at Maracanã Stadium when he was in his prime.

That's the ABA for me.

The only reason Denver and New York don't join the NBA is that the NBA wants $6.15 million from each team. Where is Roy Boe going to get that kind of money?

And for that matter, how is he going to take care of me? He has promised to raise me up to $500,000 a year. Irwin says he's not sure Roy can come through. I tell him I'll take $100,000 less to stay, figuring that means I don't have to move and pay all that resettlement cost.

But in a league where the championship finals aren't even televised, how is Boe going to come up with the commas and zeroes he needs to pay me and to join the NBA?

As it is, the league starts the 1975–76 season with just nine teams, and two of those will fold within the first 20 games.

Personally, I don't even want a merger. I'd much rather see, say, the Boston Celtics, the 1974 NBA champions, play the New York Nets, the 1974 ABA champions, in a world series of basketball. I don't know who would have won, but I have my ideas.

17.

Before the season starts, we make a big trade, sending Larry Kenon, Billy Paultz, and Mike Gale to San Antonio for Swen Nater, Chuck Terry, Kim Hughes, and Rich Jones. The idea here is to bulk up and we succeed. Larry and I were a great, high-flying combination, but we were too similar and along with Whopper didn't make for a physically durable front line. I think it's good for Larry so he can get out of my shadow a little, and he does thrive in San Antonio, where he joins James Silas and George Gervin in a dynamic lineup that will make San Antonio a perennial basketball power.

Then we trade big Swen down to Virginia for Jumbo Jim Eakins. It's a new lineup, more rugged even than our Wendell-era teams. Rich Jones especially adds a ferocious element to our defense. He's skilled with a nice shot, but he can bang. Actually, he'll take your fucking head off, he's one of those guys. And we still have Boogie Man, Tim Bassett, another tough guy. I appreciate how Kevin is trying to take care of me and lighten my rebounding load. He says that one of the reasons we faded down the stretch last year, or at least came up short in the playoffs, was that the team relied on me too much. "Doc, you can't do it for us every night." With these new additions, the New York Nets are going to be fine on the court.

The league we are playing in, however, is crumbling around us. At one point, while we are on an early season West Coast trip, and we've just beaten the Nuggets, we're hearing rumors that our next opponent, the Utah Stars, are going out of business. They're trying to sell Moses Malone and Ron Boone to the Spirits of St. Louis. This is a team that played us in the finals two seasons ago. And more urgently, where are we supposed to go? Should we fly to Salt Lake City or skip that and go on to Virginia? Or maybe not; Kevin is hearing that the Squires are also on the verge of folding.

We're sitting around in hotel rooms for days, waiting for the league to tell us who we're supposed to play. The league keeps changing the schedule, trying to stay one step ahead of the collapsing teams. With so few teams, we end up playing the Indiana Pacers and San Antonio Spurs a dozen times each. You get to know your opponents very well, on and off the court. I'm still very close with Darnell Hillman of the Pacers, and my ex-teammate George Gervin is thriving in San Antonio, and when I'm in town we always go out, along with my former teammates Mike Gale and Billy Paultz.

When Utah and San Diego fold for good about a quarter of the way through the season, the league is down to seven teams. That's not even enough to have two divisions, so now there's just one. The problem with that is how can you have an all-star game with just one division? In 1975, we played the game in San Antonio, and they gave Freddie Lewis of St. Louis, who ended up being the MVP, a horse. What does Freddie need a

horse and saddle for? So he auctioned off the horse and, sup-posedly, it died two weeks later.

But the 1976 all-star game is in jeopardy. Finally, the league decides to hold the game in Denver, as planned, only the game will feature the Denver Nuggets, who have the best record in the league and a fantastic rookie named David Thompson, against the rest of the league's all-stars. The ABA has always gone all out with all-star promotions, and for this one they've brought in Glen Campbell and Charlie Rich to do a pregame concert. The strangest idea they have, however, is something they are calling the Slam Dunk Contest. It's going to be at halftime, which means instead of a rest, five of us will have to be on the court, and it comprises five dunks from different spots on the floor, including some free-style dunks. They say they are going to judge it based on "artistic ability, imagina-tion, body flow and fan response."

Most of my dunks happen in the flow of the game, that's where I feel like I am at my most creative. But this is going to be at halftime, so we'll be jumping on tired legs. There is some prize money at stake, about $1,000 and a new Pioneer stereo system. And we're all competitive guys. Mainly we do it because they say it will be good for the league. Larry Kenon, George Gervin, Artis Gilmore, and David Thompson are my fellow dunkers.

Before the contest I'm talking to Doug Moe, my old Squires teammate who is now coaching the Nuggets, about dunking from the foul line. Jumping Jackie Jackson, who I played with barnstorming in New York City, could supposedly do it. But Doug says I can't do it. We make a $50 side bet.

During warm-ups David Thompson looks like the real competition. He's doing these cradle dunks where he is throwing the ball down through the rim with such authority that his hometown crowd is going crazy. But in the competition, despite some typically smooth Gervin moves, and a monstrous 360 degree dunk by Thompson that is actually my favorite of the whole contest, the crowd is won over when I count off the steps from the foul line back to the opposite top of the key—there is no real reason I do this, but it makes for a better show—and then I make my approach, leaping from the foul line, palming the ball up over my head, outstretched, like Lady Liberty holding her torch. I hit the mark perfectly, though Doug Moe is immediately insisting I stepped on the foul line.

I don't admit it to him then, but I will now: Doug, my foot was on the line, but that still counts as a dunk from the foul line. Nobody else was within a foot of me.

18.

With two sons at home, and we're expecting another baby in October, my outlook on the game has changed a bit. I love basketball. I view it as a sport and as an art form all in one. There is nothing more meditative for me than being in the flow of a game and finding these improvisational flourishes that seem to shift for a few moments the sense of what is possible in this universe: I grab a defensive rebound and I'm looking to start the fast break while I'm still in the air. The passing lane is blocked, I do a 360, change hands, and flip the ball left-handed to Super John. Where does that move come from? I don't know. Yet I see it also as my business, and I never lose sight of the fact that I am doing this as a job, albeit a high-paying job. When I am out there, and the fans can often lose sight of this, I am in some sense no different from a mason laying stone. That's what you are watching.

Would I play basketball if I weren't getting paid?

Of course.

Would I play several hundred games a season, practice every day, and undergo surgeries and therapies and rehabs? No.

I think I'm different from many athletes, in that as much as I enjoy the game, it does not define me. And as a father, I realize that there is one me, call him Dr. J, who is the basketball player and who lives out there on the court and in the public imagination. But there is also Julius, and he's a father and businessman trying to do what's right by his family.

Julius wants to be home with his kids, wishes he could go to every teacher-parent conference and every school play and basketball practice. I want to drive my kids to their private school in Locust Valley every day, but I can't because I'm on a plane somewhere over Ohio or sitting in a hotel room in Denver. That life, of being on the road with the guys, which can be intoxicating the first few seasons, becomes what it is, a six-month-long business trip.

It's the hardest part of being a pro baller—the weeks away from my family, the milestones, the birthdays, the first steps, the first words that I'm missing. I'm pulled toward home, and find myself resenting the time I spend on the road.

Turquoise does a sensational job at home. Our parenting roles diverge, in part because of our schedules. She is the disciplinarian, the hawk who watches their academic performance, regulates their routines, and has to oversee the everyday rigors of running a family: bandaging scrapes, cleaning up spills, enforcing bedtimes. That will change as we age and our kids grow up.

Bill Cosby once told me that his greatest challenge as a father was growing up poor but having rich children. We are always struggling to balance our own ingrained sense of scarcity with our children's reality of virtually unlimited resources. We want to give our children everything, the latest toys, the best clothes, the finest schools. And why not? Our children should be able to enjoy the fruits of my success, yet it still seems to both Turq and me that there is something wrong with all this abundance.

I think the mistakes we make are in part by trying to solve their every problem. If Cheo or J is having an issue in school, or perhaps not getting along with a teacher, instead of telling the kid to stick it out, to see it through, we are too quick to bring in specialists and counselors, to see about transferring kids from one private school to another. This seems to be what our wealthy neighbors are doing, yet ultimately, what are we teaching our kids?

So we begin the years of hushed conversations after the kids have gone to bed: The boys coming into my office hangdog because of trouble at school or a bad report card. The children playing one of us against the other. The tumult and joys of being parents and discovering all the ways we are going wrong but also the daily miracle of our children growing and becoming smarter. Because of us? In spite of us? I never know.

I am learning fatherhood as I go, as do we all, and it is more challenging than anything I do on the court. And perhaps more gratifying.

Dr. J

19.

If the ABA is in the process of collapsing, I'm more determined than ever to go out with the final ABA Championship to go along with my third straight MVP award. We finish with the second-best record in the league at 55–29, 5 games behind Denver and David Thompson, who comes in second to me in scoring as he wins the Rookie of the Year award. Even though I score over 29 a game, with 11 rebounds, 5 assists, and 2.5 blocks, we are a surprisingly balanced scoring team, with six players averaging double figures. Brian Taylor, Al Skinner, and of course Super John constitute an explosive backcourt, and rookie Kim Hughes from Wisconsin gives us a major boost on the boards.

Still, I have to be honest: the only way this team is going to win the championship is if I'm playing plenty of minutes and getting lots of touches. Kevin, though, figures out he needs to rest me toward the end of the season.

"Look, you were exhausted last year," he's telling me. "You're not going to be tired this year in the playoffs. I want you to either take a vacation or I want to play you for a quarter or so most nights. Are you okay with that?"

I'm not. I want to play. But I have to respect Kevin's basketball wisdom. It doesn't matter if we're winning or losing, I'm sitting down for the fourth quarter. It kills me, but this is something I have to do for the team. I'm still practicing hard, and as the playoffs get closer, I'm starting to think the games against the Spurs are going to be easier.

The Wednesday before the series, we're at Cathedral College in a pre-practice dunk line. I take the ball, go up and slam, and the rim comes down in my hand. It rips right off the backboard. I'm standing there with this piece of iron, sort of studying it.

"That's it!" Kevin is shouting, waving his arms. "That's it! You guys are ready. Go home."

20.

The Spurs are a dynamic team, and this turns out to be a grueling series. Kenon and Paultz and Mike Gale, all part of our 1974 Championship, are looking for revenge, and some of the players we got in that trade, especially Rich Jones, are looking to prove how wrong the Spurs were in dealing them. In game 4, after we go up 2 games to 1, Rich hard-fouls Kenon and then both benches clear and a full-blown brawl breaks out. Guys are grabbing each other and taking swings. Rich punches a half-dozen guys—he bloodies Billy Paultz's nose—and at one point he's looking to knock out Gervin, who at six foot seven weighs about 170 pounds, and Gervin just starts backpedaling and then he looks over at me like, "I ain't stupid."

Amazingly, no one is ejected and the Spurs go on to win that game. We win a tough game 7 at home, and then get a week off before we start the finals against Denver: David Thompson, Dan Issel (who they picked up in a trade from Kentucky), and the guy who is going to be guarding me, Bobby Jones, the devoutly Christian, six-foot-nine second-year forward out of North Carolina and already known as one of the toughest defenders in basketball.

Denver has had our number the last two seasons, winning 15 of 22 games we played. This is a deep, talented team.

We come out strong, however, as I score 45 in game 1 and 48 in game 2. We gain a split at McNichols Sports Arena and hold a 3–2 lead going into game 6 at home. We start the game flat, and Denver is hot. Thompson scores 42, Issel adds 30 points and 20 rebounds, and Bobby Jones is slowing me down enough to keep our team out of its offensive rhythm. By late in the third quarter, we're down by 22 and it's looking like we're heading to Denver for game 7. Kevin calls a time-out, and when I come over he says, "Thompson is killing us. Go get him." Kevin also has us play a zone press—I think of Don Ryan holding his hands up to his neck to call out our press—which is demanding of a team that has played nearly 100 games to that point. But because of the rest Kevin gave me down the stretch, I have the legs for it. No one is going to stop David Thompson in his prime, but I do keep him from imposing his will so that when our offense starts to catch fire—Super John scores 16 points in the fourth quarter and Brian Taylor and Jim Eakins both get hot and I finish with 31 points and 19 rebounds—we manage to claw back into the game and then put them away 112–106 to win the last ABA Championship.

I later heard that the Coliseum wasn't even sold out that night, but our fans were going crazy, fueling our furious come- back, and after we win, they come charging on the court. I love those Long Island fans who dig the ABA and understand what we are about. Some of the sports columnists have been writing that the NBA can't be called the best basketball league because they don't have Dr. J in it. Well, I'm in a basketball league and it's called the ABA.

Still, that epic game 6 rally? It wasn't nationally televised. And that tells the story of the ABA right there.

21.

It's not a merger, it's a capitulation. Only four teams will join the NBA—Indiana, San Antonio, Denver, and the Nets. Each team has to pay the NBA $3.2 million. The ABA teams that join get no TV money for the first three seasons in the league, and Roy is going to have to pay the Knicks an additional $4.8 million territorial fee for playing in the same market. Nonetheless, Roy has gone and signed Nate Archibald for $400,000 a year. I've still got four years left on an seven-year contract for $2 million. Roy has promised to take care of me.

"Irwin," I tell my business manager, "we need to get this done."

He's telling me I have to hold out. There's no other way we're going to get our money.

I'm at my estate in Upper Brookville. My boys come into the paneled room upstairs that I have converted into my office. Every house I live in, I have my own office, where I can keep my papers neat and organized, my books all lined up, and my pens and pencils nice and straight. Families mess things up— they *do*—so I need to have my little sanctuary where order prevails.

"What you doing, Daddy?" Cheo asks.

"I'm working."

"What you working on?"

"Business."

"You're a basketball player," Cheo says. "Why do you need to do business?"

"Because everything is a business, even basketball."

"Basketball? Nah." Cheo starts making a move, a sort of

wiggle. I've already played a little ball with Cheo. He's got some swagger. "Basketball is . . . um, you shoot the ball!"

"You're right." I take Cheo up on my lap, and J follows after him. "You shoot the ball. And they pay me to play ball. What I need to do now is make sure I get paid . . . enough."

"What's enough?"

I smile. "Now, that's a good question."

I'm one of the lucky ones, I know that, in life, in the opportunities America has given me, but also among my ABA compadres, so many of whom are finding their careers cut short now that the league has folded. Besides these four teams and superstars like Artis Gilmore, Moses Malone, Bad News Barnes, and a few others who are taken in the dispersal draft, most players will be scrambling for spots on the bench or looking for work in Europe. And the only difference between these guys and the ninth or tenth or eleventh guy riding an NBA bench is that the GM in, say, Phoenix or Chicago doesn't know his name or hasn't been watching him play for the last five seasons. I'm thinking of guys like Billy Schaeffer, my teammate on the Nets and up at the Rucker, who will never play in the NBA.

But, as I tell my boys, it's business. And I can only take care of my own business.

I don't bring my work home with me. But I do discuss with Turquoise what our options are. I have to hold out, which is the sort of move I've become used to after years of contract disputes with Earl Foreman and Roy Boe where we seem to always be playing brinksmanship. But this year, it seems different. This is hard for me because we are the ABA champs and we have the chance to show the NBA that we can win in any league. Instead, while the guys are practicing, getting ready for their first NBA season, I'm driving Turquoise to our obstetrician appointments as she heads into her eighth month with our next child. As always, I'm an excited, expectant daddy, but my heart breaks a little when the guys send me a sneaker on which they've all written notes: "Come on, Doc, we need you," from Super John; "You know you're our guy," from Tim Bassett.

I tell Turq I'm feeling like shit.

"Then go to practice," she says.

I can't. I explain what this holdout means, that Irwin has told me the problem is that Roy doesn't have the money to pay the Knicks, to sign Tiny, and to renegotiate my deal. Which means, my career with the Nets may be over. And my holdout is making me look like a bad guy in all the papers.

"Never lose sight of the fact that this is a business," Irwin is telling me, "and if people weren't going to make money off you, then you wouldn't have any leverage and this wouldn't be an issue. You'd just be this forgotten black guy in the corner."

I would consider playing for the Knicks. I ask Irwin about that. There is the possibility Roy could sell my contract to the Knicks instead of paying the territorial rights fee. How can the Knicks resist putting me together with Clyde? That's a winning nucleus right there. But apparently, according to Irwin, the Knicks are ultimately more interested in the money than I am. "But how much does Roy really care about you, Julius, if he is offering you in lieu of payment?"

Irwin has a point.

"We've just got to hold on. We'll get our deal," he says.

I agree.

"Where else would you go?" he asks.

I think about which NBA teams are close enough so that I can still live here on Long Island. I'm home. I don't want to move. There's basically Boston and Philly. But Philly is right down the turnpike, a straight shot, an hour and fifteen minutes by train, a much easier commute than Boston.

"Philadelphia," I tell Irwin.

Irwin also handles the Kangaroo Kid, Billy Cunningham, who was back playing for the 76ers where he had won a championship with Wilt in 1967, so he has good relations with GM Pat Williams and owner Fitz Dixon. Irwin also represents George McGinnis. George got a $2.5 million deal from the Sixers last year, so we know they are serious.

The Sixers are an intriguing team at that point. They won 46 games last season, led by McGinnis and Doug Collins. They have some exciting young players in Lloyd Free, Joe Bryant (who would later have a son named Kobe), and a monstrous young center named Darryl Dawkins. And from the ABA they have already signed Caldwell Jones. This is a potentially loaded lineup. Particularly attractive is the possibility of playing with McGinnis, who at six foot eight and 240 pounds is built like, well, like Dwight Howard. As Pat Williams says, "George has muscles in places where other guys don't even have places." But George is the superstar on this team, his lousy playoff performance last season notwithstanding. Don't forget, he won back-to-back ABA titles with the Pacers. If George doesn't want me, then I'm not going. George is a great player, but I'm more flamboyant, and I don't want to get into a situation where I'm resented if the fans and media are giving me more attention.

I hear from Irwin that George has told Pat Williams, "If you can get Julius, you have to."

Pat Williams comes up to New York to meet with Irwin, and eventually Irwin gets the Sixers to offer a $500,000 signing bonus, $450,000 a year for six years, plus the Sixers will pay

Roy Boe $3 million to help him pay off the New York Knicks. It breaks my heart to be leaving the Nets. I won titles with these guys—Bill Melchionni, Brian Taylor, Al Skinner, John Williamson, Kim Hughes, Tim Bassett, Jim Eakins, George Bucci, Billy Schaeffer, Rich Jones, Ted McClain. It hurts but, as I told my boys, this is a business.

As always, I read and reread every word of the contract, going over it with Irwin and making sure I understand the meaning of every clause. This is something I do to this day in my business dealings. At three a.m., I sign.

22.

In October 1976, I have a new baby daughter, Jazmin Antiqua Erving, and a new team, the Philadelphia 76ers in a new league. Here I am, coming in the side door again, sliding into the NBA from the ABA, joining a new team a day before the season opener. We have a press conference at the Spectrum, I practice that afternoon with the team and then the next night we start the season against my old ABA nemesis the San Antonio Spurs. As I'm dressing, pulling on my new number 6 jersey, George McGinnis looks at me and shakes his head. "You sure look funny in that uniform, Doc."

When we come on the court, the message board hanging down from the rafters says, "Is there a Doctor in the house?" The Spectrum is bulging with over seventeen thousand and when they introduce me, the crowd gets up and cheers for two minutes. (Do you know what that feels like? To have an arena

Dr. J

full of fans screaming for you? I never get used to it.) Then super-fan Steve Sohms runs on the court and puts a black medical bag on the Sixers logo. The place is as loud as the Nassau Coliseum when we were coming back to beat the Nuggets. And I haven't played a minute yet.

I'm rusty from five months away and finish with 17 points off the bench, in particular because of a terrible night at the foul line where I go 5 for 13.

I'm playing against plenty of my old teammates: George Gervin, Larry Kenon, Mike Gale, and the Whopper. During the game, we're all talking about how we don't like this new ball. We miss the red, white, and blue, the way you can judge the spin as soon as the ball is in the air. Caldwell agrees: this new ball sucks.

But after a year in the NBA, George assures me I'll get used to it. He scores 29 and Doug Collins scores 30. But we lose our first 2 games of the season, traveling up to Buffalo two days later and losing to the Braves, who have sitting over there on the bench a guy I remember from the ABA, Moses Malone, who they got in a trade after Portland had taken him in the dispersal draft. (Portland has another good young center, named Bill Walton.) They beat us without Moses, and two days later they trade him to Houston for a couple of future first-round draft choices.

Now "The Best Team Money Can Buy," as the papers are calling us, is 0-2.

We break through and win our first against the Jazz and Pete Maravich in New Orleans where George scores 37 and Doug adds another 25. I'm getting back into game shape and picking up the playbook—and my new coach Gene Shue has a playbook thicker than a Manhattan phone book—and the next game against Houston, I score 27 in our second win. We go on a run where we win 10 out of 13, and I am adjusting to Gene's vision for our team. His dogma is balanced scoring. His idea of a perfect team is to have 11 guys scoring 10.8 points each every night. It's clear he's not going to adjust his philosophy for me.

I get along with every coach. I listen. I follow instructions. Perhaps to a fault. It's very different with today's players, and that may be for the better. In my era, I try to conform my game to whatever system the coach has installed. My first year with the 76ers, I go from winning scoring titles and averaging 22 shots a night to scoring 21.6 points a night and shooting about 16 times a game. My field goal percentage actually goes down in Gene's offense, but that's because with George, Caldwell, and Dawkins up front, he has me playing farther from the basket. For the first time in my career, I don't average double figures in rebounds.

But Gene does everything by the book. He formulates his game plan and sticks to it, even when the players on the court are telling him it's not working. If George says, "Hey, Coach, I can beat him to the left whenever I want," Gene won't alter his offense. Instead, he'll be flipping through his playbook, looking for what he wants to run while we're standing around, waiting for him to find what he is searching for in that bloated volume.

It's a big change from Kevin Loughery, who always had this feeling and instinct for the game and was adjusting our play-calling on the fly.

During the regular season, it's not so bad, as Gene has most of the answers in that book and we're talented enough to win 50 games. I lead the team in scoring and we have six players in double figures. But come playoff time, I'm a little worried, because in those situations, as teams are cranking up their

Dr. J

defensive pressure and each possession matters more, you have to throw out the book and go with your gut.

In big games, the answers aren't in the book; a coach needs to read them in the eyes of his players.

23.

For the first few months of the season, I continue living on Long Island and get a ride down to Philadelphia for practices and games from Lloyd Free. Lloyd has a place in Brownsville, Brooklyn, and he likes to drive fast in his new Cadillac. Or sometimes, we'll take my new customized van: two captain's chairs, leather interior, seating area in the back, a TV, a folding bed, a refrigerator. Everyone on the team has a van. The situation is ideal for me because I can sleep in the passenger seat while Lloyd speeds down the turnpike. At least two times, I wake up as the car is driving down the ramp into the Spectrum, and Lloyd tells me he was stopped and ticketed by state troopers and I slept through the whole thing.

Eventually, I buy a three-bedroom condominium at the Academy House in downtown Philadelphia so that the family can come down and stay over if we have a home stand and the kids are off from school. Turquoise becomes a fixture at our games, and the TV cameras seem to seek her out. She becomes part of the news herself when she writes an article for the *New York Times* about our experiences with the Sixers. (The article is co-written by a freelance writer named Samantha Stevenson.) This is a New York newspaper, so of course she writes that we both miss New York. But Turq also has some choice words about my new team, taking the other guys to task for shooting too much, and saying she doesn't "think the 76ers will win the National Basketball Association championship."

Now, Turq is a strong woman, and she has the right to say whatever she wants. That's the kind of marriage we have. And the guys on the team don't pay it any attention. But the Philly newspapers play it up, of course. And I have to do some damage control, but I never apologize for or criticize my wife. I know better than that.

But her point is made in those few instances where the fans, as Turquoise writes, "can really see Julius play. They haven't seen all of him yet." I make the same point in interviews. If I'm not handling the ball eight or nine times down the court, then on the tenth time, it's very hard to do something spectacular with it. I've always gotten my shots in the flow of the game. I admire guys like Lloyd Free who can not only drive two hours before a game, but can put up shots at a remarkable rate. Lloyd is a shooter. He'll put it up from the locker room.

In the all-star game that year, I score 30, get 12 boards, and win the MVP award. It feels good to show the fans what I am capable of, even if I don't often get that chance in the Philadelphia offense. At least not until the playoffs.

24.

This is a team that won't shut up. Lloyd declares himself All-World (before changing his name to World B. Free), Dawkins follows by claiming he is All Universe. ("This is the Dawk and I'm ready to talk," is how he answers his phone.) Joe Bryant and Steve Mix are arguing through the media for more playing time. Doug Collins literally can't sit still long enough to complete a sentence. And there is endless speculation about whether George and I can coexist. We can, of course. There is never actually any tension between George and me. If I have any issue, it is with Gene. Why should George be taking more shots a night than Doug Collins or me if he is shooting a lower percentage? That's just not smart basketball.

But the fans don't care. We are selling out arenas all over the country—we lead the league in road attendance—and at home we're playing in front of the biggest crowds of my career. We finish with 50 wins and the Atlantic Division title, which means we earn a first-bound bye and then face the Boston Celtics in the second.

I score 36 in the first game, but we lose to my old teammate Charlie Scott and off-season buddy John Havlicek. It's a seven-game war, and Doug Collins and I take turns leading our offense against Dave Cowens and Jo Jo White. It's Lloyd Free who comes through in game 7, however, with a 27-point performance that buries the Celtics.

In the Eastern Conference finals we are facing the Houston Rockets and their imposing young center, Moses Malone. We go up 2-0 at home. In game 2 our twin towers Caldwell Jones and Darryl Dawkins hold Moses to just 7 points. In games 4 and 5, we are able to slow down Moses and hold him to just 22 total points, taking a 3-2 series lead into game 6. I score 34 in the elimination game, but we are bailed out when Jake O'Donnell calls an offensive foul on John Lucas with eight seconds left on the clock. That call could have gone either way, and on the road, I certainly didn't expect to get the benefit of the referee's doubt, but we escape Houston with a 3-point win and a date with the Portland Trail Blazers in the NBA finals.

This is my third championship series in four years, so I've been playing long seasons, leading each of these teams in minutes and scoring. I can't stress how important it is for players to get rest during the season. That's where a team's depth becomes as important as its frontline stars. If you don't have bench players who can contribute serious minutes toward the end of the regular season, then your superstars are going to get tired. They may still find a way to win—what sets great players apart is that ability to triumph over adversity—but it means you may not have the same shot at building a dynasty. Adding to our playoff problems this year is the fact that while I've increased my scoring in the postseason, averaging over 27 a game, our other superstar, George McGinnis, is struggling, averaging only 14 a night. (And his work ethic is questionable. Or at least it appears to be. Before some playoff games, he's smoking cigarettes during shoot-around.) Luckily, Doug Collins is picking up some of the slack, scoring more in the playoffs than he did during the regular season.

We're supposed to beat the Trail Blazers. But we need to play as a team, and the secret to inspiring guys to trust each other and believe in each other isn't in Gene Shue's playbook. It's something that has to be built up over a season of observing each other's strengths and weaknesses. In another era, just a few years later, the star player on the team will be the one who sets the tone. The superstar becomes the undeniable leader, in part because of the money he is making, and also because of his power to get a coach fired. At this point, I'm still living in a universe where a player takes his cues from the coach. That's

how I've been brought up, that's how I've been taught to play. I'm not the coach and I can't undermine the coach, certainly not in my first season in the league.

But maybe we are good enough to win on our individual talents. The Spectrum before game 1 is in a celebratory mood. These fans haven't seen an NBA final since the '60s and are just four years removed from the worst record in NBA history, the 9-73 team. All of us players feel some vindication at making it to the finals, given the controversy of the regular season. For me, in my first season in the NBA, this is a satisfying finale, to play for a championship, for the chance to win a title in both leagues. I start game 1 with a big dunk over my old ABA colleague Maurice Lucas and finish with 33 points. Doug adds 30 and we take a 2–0 lead. But at the end of game 2, there is a bench-clearing brawl as Lucas and Dawkins get into a tiff. Lucas never backs down from a fight, and he's a big reason the Trail Blazers are here, as he led the team that season in scoring and grabbed over 11 rebounds a game. He throws a punch at Darryl that misses Darryl but connects with Doug Collins, who is trying to break up the scuffle. Dawkins, meanwhile, is backpedaling away. I go and sit down at mid-court. The refs eject both Darryl and Maurice. Darryl goes into our locker room and demolishes our bathroom, actually tearing a toilet from the wall. He's furious, and he lets the media know how disappointed he is that none of his teammates had his back in the fight. I'm thinking, we're supposed to back up Dawk? Chocolate Thunder? He's six foot ten and 260 pounds. He is our enforcer.

More worrying is the fact that George has scored only 20 points in the whole series.

Back in Portland, Maurice, Bill Walton, Bob Gross, Lionel Hollins, and the rest of the Blazers put together a balanced attack with six guys scoring in double figures in both games as they blow us out. George scores 14 and 5. I can tell his confidence is shot, like he doesn't want to be here. I try to talk to him, to tell him that he needs to focus on his defensive play, on shutting down Maurice, on cutting off Walton's passing lanes, but he's not listening.

They beat us in game 5 at home. It's really a beat down, but we mount a furious fourth-quarter rally to cut it to 6. I score 37, but we are never really close. "It's a bad scene," I tell Turquoise after the game. We are doing everything in one-on-one situations. Portland is scoring through ball movement, keyed by Walton's post-passing skills. This just isn't how you win playoff games.

In game 6 in Portland, I score 40 points—including a big dunk over Bill Walton coming down the right side of the lane—and George redeems himself with 28, including a clutch jump shot with eighteen seconds left that pulls us within 2. Then George ties up Bob Gross on the inbounds pass, and then he wins the ensuing jump ball, tapping it to Free, who passes it to me at the top of the key. I dribble once, and put up a 16-footer with Walton in my face. I get a good look, but I miss. The ball goes out of bounds to us. In the huddle, Gene calls a play for George. I think we should run a play for Doug Collins or let me drive. But I don't say anything. I've just blown my chance to tie this up. But George misses the final shot and—

I suddenly feel like I'm invisible. There's Walton jumping up and down, Hollins tossing the ball into the air, someone stripping off Walton's jersey, and then Walton hugging Maurice Lucas. Jack Ramsay, wearing a pair of the most colorful trousers I've ever seen, is arm in arm with one of his assistants, Ramsay's blue blazer tails flapping up.

Fans are rushing past me, their fists pumping. They are climbing up on the baskets, pulling at the rims. I'm looking out over the swirl of people. Wait, wait, this isn't how it's supposed to be.

I take a deep breath and go jogging off the court, dodging delirious Trail Blazer fans. I'm thinking, I'll be back.

In the locker room, I'm sitting down and then I look over at Lloyd Free and Henry Bibby and I say, "Hey, we are good enough to win this thing. We didn't this year. That's all. But let's go over and congratulate those guys."

McGinnis shakes his head. But Lloyd stands up, and so do Bibby and Doug Collins, and we go over to the Portland locker room to shake their hands. That's what I would want my opponents to do.

And we'll be back soon. Right?

25.

After my playoff performance, the Sixer organization and the fans embrace me, and I feel the strengthening of my connection with the city. The Academy House is a new building right off Broad Street, and I become good friends with my neighbors, especially with a gentleman named Brinkley, who lives across the street. Through Brink, I become close to Teddy Pendergrass, the soul singer and an idol of mine. By then, Teddy has already gone solo from Harold Melvin and the Blue Notes and released his self-titled debut album and then one of my favorites, *Life Is a Song Worth Singing*. Teddy is a Philadelphia institution, one of the originators of the Philly Soul sound. He's also a big basketball fan, and we start to hang out whenever I'm in town.

When Teddy was just twelve his father was murdered, so there is some common ground between us in that he was raised by strong women. And we were born just a few weeks apart.

Teddy and I get along immediately. There is some mutual respect there, but also I feel like our experiences are somehow similar. Teddy—and Cos and Miles—understand the pressure of performing, of what it's like to go into the arena, night after night, even when you're not sure you have your best game or best voice in you that night. That's what it means to be a professional: to know the pitfalls, but to persevere and give the fans everything you've got.

Teddy and I talk about that. We're both in our late twenties, but somehow life on the road, in entertainment, or in sports makes you feel middle-aged before your time. It's not just the physical wear and tear, it's also the ability to be able to turn the page, to leave behind past disappointments—and coming up short in game 7 of the NBA finals is that kind of loss—and move forward without dwelling on it.

"That's right, Doc," Teddy says in his gravelly voice. "An artist has to be in the now, baby. You can't look back."

"Then how do you find the emotion you put in your songs?" I ask. I'm thinking about songs like "Turn Off the Lights" or "Only You."

Let's take a shower, shower together
I'll wash your body and you'll wash mine.

(Okay, maybe not that song.)

"That's passion, baby," Teddy says. "The passion always has to be there. I bring the passion every night."

Teddy should know. When I've been backstage at his concerts, his audiences seem like they are 90 percent women, and they can't get enough of his passion. In fact, he's starting to perform what he calls "Ladies Nights," which are women's-only concerts. My sister is calling him the Black Elvis, and he is as popular, or maybe even more so, than his contemporary R&B masters Marvin Gaye and Barry White.

That's why I will never understand his desire to use drugs.

Teddy has a bad problem. I'm standing backstage with him at the Tower Theater, and a couple of men come by and they go back into Teddy's dressing room and they are hooking him up with heroin, the needle, the whole thing. I'm like, Are you shitting me?

As a player traveling around the league, whenever I am offered cocaine, or when I see it come out at a party, then I'm leaving. That's it. Doc is gone. At one point, in Los Angeles, a Lakers player invites me to a party and we walk in and there's naked women snorting cocaine off the floor. I turn to him. "This ain't my scene."

I learn to be careful about my friends and acquaintances. With Richard Pryor, for example, whenever he's around, I know he's going to be funny, and he's a warm person who is among the most articulate and intelligent men I have ever met, yet at one point, when Richard asks me to hold his leather bag for a minute, I tell him no.

You don't ever hold Richard Pryor's bag. Whatever is in there, you know it's bad news.

About the only habit-forming proclivities my teammates seem to have is Caldwell Jones and his bathtub full of beer. I know this is reputed to be an era when the league was infested with cocaine, but perhaps because my views on the subject are well known, I don't see much of it. Or my teammates know enough to keep that stuff away from me.

26.

Pat Williams, our GM, has been with the team since 1974 and is the man responsible for our steady improvement. He is assembling our roster piece by piece, signing George and me, trading for Henry Bibby and Caldwell Jones, and drafting World B. Free and Darryl Dawkins and, soon, a point guard from West Texas State named Maurice Cheeks and another guard from the University of Seattle named Clint Richardson. He's a basketball visionary, and uniquely gifted at perhaps the GM's toughest task: serving as the axis between an impatient owner and his anxious employees. Our owner, Fitz Dixon, is a patrician Mainliner and inheritor of a fortune made a hundred years ago in the trolley car business. He lives on an estate so vast and grand that, supposedly, the flowers alone are worth $1 million. And while he is reserved, his patience for Gene Shue is apparently wearing thin.

He blames Shue for losing the championship to Portland. And 6 games into the 1977–78 season, Dixon fires him after a tough loss to Chicago. Shue spent the off-season urging Pat to trade George McGinnis, which Pat opposed because we couldn't make a good deal considering George's playoff performance. Fitz becomes impatient, so Gene is gone.

The players are happy with his replacement: Billy Cunningham. We've all played with him or against him, and he is a good communicator and has an uncanny feel for the game. He's overtly emotional while Gene was more subdued. Billy on the bench is sweating, cursing, jumping up to argue with the refs. He'll sweat right through his three-piece suits. He's a Brooklyn guy, so from the start I feel like we have good, clear communication. He's a little like Phil Jackson in that he whistles when he wants our attention.

Plus, Billy has a secret weapon. He brings in Chuck Daly, a former Pennsylvania head coach who took the Quakers to the NCAA tournament four times, including an Elite 8 appearance against North Carolina in 1972. Daly is a genius at figuring out how to motivate players and to get them to buy into Billy's system. Chuck is also the guy who can temper Billy's hotheadedness with gentle reason. And both of them have an amazing feel for who is contributing and who should be the floor. With Billy, sort of like Kevin, I feel like I can talk frankly about what I'm thinking and that, despite the intensity of those conversations, there is always a mutual respect.

Still, the season ends in another disappointment as we lose to the eventual champion Washington Bullets in the Eastern Conference finals. The Bullets are a good team, with Wes Unseld, Elvin Hayes, and Bobby Dandridge, and they take us down in six games.

Now Billy is also convinced we need to trade George McGinnis. George actually had a very productive season, averaging 22.6 points and 11.5 rebounds, though he underperformed in the playoffs again. Still, we won 55 games and broke our own home attendance record. But Billy's view is that this team, as it is presently constituted, will not win a championship. I'm all for winning, but I'm not a GM or coach. There is a chance we can get Bobby Jones, the great Denver forward who I know well from the 1976 ABA finals. Bobby is a team player, a relentless defender (hence his nickname, the White Shadow), and a guy with unique basketball intelligence. He's a decent scorer, but what is most impressive is that he is incredibly efficient. He used to lead the ABA every year in field goal percentage.

If we have a chance to get Bobby, then Pat has to do it. It takes Pat a few months, but he's dogged, and when he's done, we've added Jones to our team. And that's the same off-season where Pat drafts Mo Cheeks.

The addition of Bobby and Maurice changes the personality of our team. For one thing, the coach doesn't have to yell at Bobby and Maurice because they know the plays and are always in the right spots on the floor. I'm delighted with Maurice because now we have a guard—I'm thinking of you, Mr. Free—who will always look for me and get me the ball where I want it. In fact, Maurice looks for me so frequently that Darryl starts complaining, "Man, I see Maurice Cheeks coming down the floor and he's got his Dr. J eyes on. All they can see is Dr. J." Even Billy lights into him a couple of times. "Why are you throwing the ball to Doc?"

"Because Doc asked for it," Mo replies.

"But that's not the play I called," Billy says.

"But Doc asked for it."

That was about as mad as Billy got at Maurice.

"If Doc asks for the ball, I'm going to get it to him," says Maurice. "I know what it takes for me to stay around."

That's a smart guard. And it makes sense. If I'm bringing the ball up court, and my performance is measured in part on how many assists I collect, then I'm going to pass the ball to

Dr. J

the best finisher. If Doc is cutting, then isn't that the highest percentage option, regardless of what play is called? I think so.

The arrival of Mo makes a difference, as my scoring goes up, to nearly 27 a game in 1980, and my shots per game goes up to over 20, and I average well over 50 percent from the field.

Bobby Jones is a character as well. There are other devoutly Christian players in the league, and others who don't approve of some of the salty language athletes use. But Bobby is the first player I've been around who we actually heed. "Mother-fucker!" Dawkins will shout as he throws down a dunk.

"Will you rotate, God damn it!" Billy shouts.

Bobby will just give them that look. "You know I don't approve of that."

Maybe it's because we know Bobby is an epileptic and that it is an amazing act of courage for him to even be out here. He could have a seizure at any moment. Guys actually curtail their swearing. A little.

On the road, while the rest of us are out catting around at the nightclub, Bobby will be in his hotel room, reading his Bible, while in the next room is Caldwell Jones and his bathtub full of bottled Budweiser on ice.

Pat and Billy keep fine-tuning our team. They trade Lloyd Free to San Diego for a first-round draft pick. Lloyd can score anywhere, anytime, but Billy feels he's a one-dimensional player. Maybe he is, but that is one fantastic dimension.

The biggest adjustment we have to make as a team, however, is the declining role of Doug Collins, a great player who is missing dozens of games every year because of various injuries. We finish with 47 wins in 1979 and take apart New Jersey and my old teammates Super John Williamson and Tim

Bassett, and a great young scorer named Bernard King, in the first round.

In the conference semifinals, we're playing another former ABA team, the Spurs, with George Gervin, the Kat, and Billy Paultz. Iceman has just led the league in scoring, with 29.6 a game on 54 percent shooting. Kenon and Paultz added solid contributions.

And they take us apart at home to go up 2-0 in the series. Back home, we're not much better, salvaging a split to send it back to the Alamo for an elimination game 5. I score 32, Steve Mix, Bobby Jones, and Mo Cheeks all come through, and we blow the Spurs out at home. Then in game 6, back at the Spectrum, I have a quiet night, but Dawkins and Caldwell step up and we win a squeaker to force a game 7 in San Antonio.

San Antonio's rowdiest section of fans are called the Baseline Bums. I remember during ABA games, they would be wearing sombreros and drinking beer from pitchers, and supposedly they were dumping guacamole on opposing players and coaches. At one point, they had 10-cent beer night, so this is a fan base that gets pretty wild.

They are rocking that night in San Antonio, and the Baseline Bums are doing their level best to psych us out. In the first minute of the game, Dawk sprains his ankle and is out. With Collins already injured, Dawk is our second option on offense, averaging 16 points a game in the playoffs. Now we're without two of our three top scorers. I try to offset that by going for 34 points, but it isn't enough, as we lose 111–108. Near the end of the game, I literally hear something pop in my groin area. I play through it.

Now I'm starting to wonder if we'll ever get back to the finals.

27.

After that series, I'm driving up the turnpike and my knees and groin are hurting so bad, I have to pull in at a truck stop. I am actually thinking that this is it. I can't play anymore.

My knees have never been 100 percent since I've joined the NBA. My problems with tendonitis in my knees started after my second year in Virginia, when I began to favor one knee because of my groin injury. I played forty minutes a game that year. Chopper had kept me on the court, but that was mostly through novocaine, cortisone, and Darvon, a combination that left me able to perform but in a state where I'm not aware of how bad a pounding my knees are taking. In the off-season, my knees hurt so *much* I can barely stand to drive from New York City to Long Island. I decided after that season that I wasn't going to take any more pills or needles, and I instead switched to a regime of heat and ice. John Marshall at the Hospital for Special Surgery designed a knee brace for me, which I wore throughout my ABA career.

That was the conventional wisdom: that you brace the knee itself to create stability.

This off-season I go to work with a guy named Joseph Zohar, who is part of the evolution in sports medicine that takes a more holistic approach. He works with me to strengthen my groin and my knee. Everything around those two problem areas must be fortified—my hamstrings and my glutes. I'm doing three hours a day in the off-season, starting with just one- and two-pound weights.

I recover enough to resume swimming and playing tennis

in the off-season, and by the time camp starts, I'm almost at full strength again.

28.

Pat and Billy never stop tinkering with our roster, trying to find the combination that will get us back to the finals. By now, the mantra in Philly is "We Owe You One," based on an ad campaign the team launched after we lost in 1977. My feeling is, we owe you three, because every year we don't get to the finals, the disappointment sets in deeper. And one of the biggest differences in this league versus the ABA is how our fans keep turning out for us night after night, even when we're in a slump and the columnists are tearing us apart in the papers. The fans keep bringing their Dr. J banners and the kids want me to sign their programs. I remember going to the Garden as a kid with Don Ryan and the rest of my Sal teammates and waiting outside after the game for the Knicks players to come out and sign some autographs. We're just kids, standing in the snow, and here comes Art Heyman, a Long Island guy, and he snubs us, walks past as if we're not even there. I'll never forget that. That's why, despite being a New York kid, I never really became a Knicks fan.

I remember that feeling of being snubbed by one of my heroes. I've always taken the time to talk to my fans, and especially the kids. I don't think I deserve any praise for this. It's simply the right thing to do, as a fellow human being. It's just the way I conduct my business. I don't think there are many folks who can say they've met me or seen me in public who would think I was dismissive or rude to them. If someone comes over to me, I say hello, shake their hand, sign whatever it is they happen to be holding out, and if I'm busy with a business meeting or family, I excuse myself and that's that.

But I develop a special relationship with the Philly fans. And we are living through a great sports era in Philadelphia: the Flyers are coming off back-to-back Stanley Cups in the mid-'70s and they would make the finals again in 1980. The great Phillies teams of the late '70s made three straight National League Championship Series and then won the World Series in 1980. Even the Eagles make the Super Bowl in 1980, losing to the Raiders. This is an era when the famously fickle Philly sports fan could easily have shunned the 76ers—despite our playoff runs, we're the least successful team in town—and it's a tribute to Pat Williams and his relentless drive to improve that we not only keep the fans interested, but they never stop believing or buying tickets.

It helps that the NBA itself is undergoing a renaissance. The greatest player of my era, and maybe any era, is Kareem Abdul-Jabbar. He and I are both in our primes throughout the '70s, though he's a couple of years older than I am. I don't think there has ever been a human being that big who is as graceful and athletic as Kareem. He's the basketball player that I always measure myself against, and too often, I have to admit, I find myself coming up short.

That's why it's always a special thrill when I get the better of our matchups and throw down a dunk on him.

But in 1979, Magic Johnson and Larry Bird both come into the league. They are coming off their NCAA Championship matchup and there is a ton of buzz around this pair of rookies.

It's good for the league to have dynamic young players in Boston and Los Angeles, but I'm more interested in our rookies, Jim Spanarkel, Billy Ray Bates, and Clint Richardson.

The guy with the most talent is Bates, a third-round pick out of Kentucky State. I've never seen a player who looks better in drills than Billy Ray. He's the fastest sprinter on the team, the best miler, and he can beat you in a foot race when he's dribbling and you're running. He can shoot from anywhere. He's just an amazing athletic specimen. But you put him in a game situation, and he falls apart. He can't remember plays, he's always in the wrong spot on the floor. This goes back to the difference between the outdoor game and the indoor game. Billy Ray would be a guy I would love to have on my team up at Rucker or back in my barnstorming days. But on an NBA team, he just doesn't have the mental tools to understand the situational nature of the team game. We rely on one another. In every play and every variation of each play, depending on the defensive look we are getting, I need to be sure my teammates are going to be where they are supposed to be. And on defense, where we have to rotate or drop down to help, I need to be sure my teammates have my back. Billy Ray, the most gifted athlete on the floor, seems lost. He's gone by the second preseason game.

Later, it will turn out that Billy Ray is illiterate, and he can't read the playbook.

But Clint Richardson, a far less assuming rookie, becomes a regular contributor, and along with point guard Lionel Hollins, a leader of the Trail Blazer team that beat us in '77, who is acquired mid-season, he will be a crucial addition to our team.

It's clear, playing against Magic and Larry from the start, that they are both complete players who embody the creative flair of the outdoor game with the intelligence and discipline of the indoor game. The first time Boston comes to town with Larry Bird, it's November 1979, and he scores 22 against us. Bobby Jones guards him, and that's a pretty good showing against one of the best defenders in the league. (I score 37 that night.) What I notice right away about Larry, even as a rookie, is that not only can he get his shot—and he has amazing range for a big man—but he will make it, too. He may be the best shooter I've ever seen. And he is a smart passer, able to thread the ball through inches of daylight. And he will not stop working. At one point, after John Havlicek has retired, he's talking to me in the off-season and he says, "Man, if I knew how good Bird was going to be, I wouldn't have retired."

Bird and I have an interesting relationship on the court. When I defend him—and when the Celtics draft Kevin McHale and move Larry to small forward, that becomes a regular matchup for me—if he puts the ball down the floor, then I think I have him. I can poke the ball away and maybe get a steal. Larry's game doesn't have any weaknesses, but among his relative strengths, he's least skilled as a dribbler. When he's guarding me, he can't stay with me. But I'll be honest, I can't really stop him, either. And at that point in my career, he's a better rebounder than I am. But remember, he's ten years younger.

We have some great wars over the years. We'll match up in the playoffs four times between 1980 and 1986, with the winner going on to the finals every season. I feel like those rivalries, Sixers–Celtics, Sixers–Lakers, and Celtics–Lakers, are the most hard fought of that era. So when Larry says, as he has, that Michael Jordan was the best player he ever faced, I find it a little disrespectful. We beat them up pretty bad in some playoffs, and they got the better of us in others, but those are the toughest matchups for both of us. I don't think it's fair for Larry to say that Michael is the best based on one great playoff game, the 63-point performance in Boston Garden. But then, Larry is always playing mind games, so he's probably still trying to psych out Magic and me.

But I don't hate Larry. I never hated Larry. I hated Boston, I hated the Celtics. Larry and I do Converse commercials together, we are friendly. I'm sure he doesn't hate me, either, but I bet he hates the Sixers and hates Philadelphia. My beef isn't with Larry, it's with his team. That's how I look at it. The rivalry between Philly and Boston predates Dr. J or Larry Bird, it goes back to Wilt and Bill, to the Celtics and the Sixers meeting five straight years in the playoffs from 1965 to 1969, to even before that, with the Celtics and the Philadelphia Warriors battling three times between 1957 and 1962. Bill Russell versus Wilt Chamberlain may be the defining sports rivalry, or forget that, the defining *rivalry*, of all time. Dr. J and Larry Bird are just the latest chapter.

I remember hearing about Magic from Terry Furlow, who had gone to Michigan State and played a season with us in 1977. He was telling me about this high school junior who could play pro right now. I'm thinking, unless he's Darryl Dawkins or Moses Malone—and those were mountainous men—then I don't believe it. I remember myself at that age, I was maybe six foot two and weighed about 140 as a high school junior. So, imagine what Artis Gilmore could have done to me back then. But Terry didn't tell me this kid was six foot nine and could handle like Tiny Archibald.

Magic actually comes to see me after he wins his NCAA

title against Larry and Indiana State. He has just been drafted by the Lakers and he comes to the Spectrum to catch a Sixers game and I invite him to stay over at my condo. He's with Dr. Charles Tucker, a psychologist who is a longtime friend and mentor. Magic is this buck-toothed, smiling, happy kid, but he's also got very practical reasons for his trip. He wants to talk about the NBA and especially about how he should handle his business. He's auditioning agents, and so out of courtesy to a young draft choice I sit down with Magic and Irwin Weiner. I have no idea that he is going to become one of the all-time greats. I'm in my prime and Magic, and Larry, for that matter, they're just a couple of highly touted rookies coming into the league. No big deal. I'm more concerned with the guys I've been tangling with for years: Kareem, Elvin Hayes, and Wes Unseld.

By the end of that season, I will be thinking an awful lot about Bird and Magic.

29.

We have a great training camp. Our young players look promising. Our veterans are healthy. Even Doug Collins looks like he's going to give us a full season, which has all of us optimistic. We're all buying into the Billy C and Chuck Daly system. And I'm gratified because to a great extent, this team has been built around my skills. Pat and Billy recognize that our best chance at winning is to play through me. I'm aware that I have been given more of an overt leadership role on this team, and with that come certain responsibilities. At one point that preseason, Billy loses his cool shouting at me during a break in practice for missing an assignment on defense, telling me in typically salty language that I need to get my head in the game. I'm steaming. I'm a veteran player and I don't like being shown up like this, not in front of my teammates, not in front of the rookies, but I make a decision. I'm going to stay calm. I look at Billy, I nod, I betray no emotion.

"Okay, Billy," and I wipe my face with a towel.

That sends a message to the guys. We are going to listen to our coaches. We are going to work together and no one is bigger than the team.

We're poised for a good run, with the right mix of veterans still in their prime, and good young players like Mo Cheeks and Clint Richardson.

And we also have Darryl Dawkins.

The Sixers had taken Dawk right out of high school, back when NBA teams only drafted guys out of college. It had been controversial, but Pat Williams is willing to take chances when it comes to acquiring the best talent he can. And Dawk was a rare physical specimen, at six foot ten and 260 pounds and, supposedly, still growing.

He is always eccentric, usually in a harmless way, such as when he claims to be from the planet Lovetron, or is it Chocolate Paradise? He's definitely ahead of his time in terms of bling, wearing a few pounds of gold, diamonds, and pendants with various nicknames: Sir Slam, Dr. Dunk, and, of course, Chocolate Thunder. Less charming is his habit of shooting from long distance. Darryl actually has a good touch, but it's not as effective as when he batters his way to the basket.

Early that season, we see that power unleashed as he goes up for a dunk in Kansas City over Bill Robinzine. Robinzine isn't about to get hit with full-frontal Chocolate Thunder, so he sort of stands there and watches as Darryl dunks with such force that he pulls off the rim and shatters the backboard, raining shards of glass onto the court. I'm facing what's left of the basket and thinking, What are we supposed to do now? The game is delayed for ninety minutes while they put up a new hoop.

That's when Darryl starts naming his dunks, calling this one "Chocolate Thunder flyin', Robinzine-cryin', teeth-shaking, glass-breaking, rump-roastin', bun-toastin', wham, bam, thank you ma'am, I am jam!"

Three weeks later, back home in the Spectrum, he does it again. By then, the league has made it clear that this is frowned upon, but more important, they devise the collapsible rim so that it can't happen anymore. How many guys actually cause a change in their sport's equipment?

It becomes something Darryl can do at will. At one point we're practicing on a court over at Episcopal High School (our regular facility at Widener College is not available), and Darryl is looking up at the basket.

"Man, they got these itty-bitty rims up there." Darryl grins. "Ya'll want to go home?"

"Don't do it, Darryl," I'm saying.

He goes up and slams the ball. The rim comes right off the wood backboard.

Billy is furious. "What the fuck, Darryl? Why did you do that?"

Bobby Jones glares at him for dropping the F-bomb.

"Sorry, Bobby." Billy shakes his head. "Okay, practice is over."

We're having a fine season, on our way to 59 wins. But Boston, and Larry Bird, are doing even better, winning 61. About halfway through the season, Doug Collins tears up his foot, so we lose one of our leading scorers and team leaders. At one point, desperate for a guard, we bring in Pete Maravich, now coming off a knee surgery and riding the Utah Jazz bench. Pat is ready to sign Pistol, but Pete tells us at the last minute that he wants to also talk to Boston. He decides to join the Celtics, figuring they have a better chance to make the finals. That's when Pat makes the deal for Lionel Hollins.

I have my best season in the NBA, averaging 26.9 points a game, 7.4 rebounds, 4.6 assists, and shooting 52 percent from the field. But Kareem wins his sixth MVP award, averaging 24.8 points, 10.8 rebounds, and 4.5 assists while shooting 60 percent from the field. It's hard to argue with that, though once again, I can say I have an MVP-type season, even if I don't get the award.

In the playoffs, we sweep the Washington Bullets and take some revenge for previous seasons, then knock out Atlanta 4-1, before coming up against Boston and Larry Bird in the Eastern Conference finals. Larry has a big series, scoring 27, 31, 22 (with 21 rebounds), and 19 before slumping to just 12 points in game 5. My numbers are 29, 24, 28, 30, and 14. I average 25 a game; Larry averages about 22. Numbers last forever, and I got mine when it seemed no one was looking. That's why I can seem so obsessed with statistics.

We win game 5 by 11 in Boston due in large part to Lionel Hollins torching Gerald Henderson and Tiny Archibald for 24 points. For us, the series is a triumph of Chuck Daly's matchup scheming, as we hold Boston to under 100 points in every game.

And we are back in the NBA finals.

In game 1 at the Forum in Los Angeles, Kareem shows why he's the MVP, scoring 33, grabbing 14 rebounds, and blocking 6 shots as he effectively neutralizes our big men. But we salvage a split in LA, and I gain some measure of payback against Kareem by starting the game with a monster dunk over him.

It is easy to forget how great Kareem is. And in the years

Dr. J

since he has retired, he has been a little bit maligned, in part because he can be socially awkward. But I have the privilege of watching him work, and often working against him, for over a decade, and each time we match up, I am awed again. As tall as he is, he has amazing leaping ability. That's what makes him such a formidable shot blocker. The sky hook, of course, is what everyone justly remembers as Kareem's unstoppable shot. But he has so many moves around the hoop, up-and-unders, fall-away jumpers, and he is strong enough to back down most defenders. In this series, we ask Caldwell Jones to guard Kareem, and Kareem is able to exert his will throughout. He has a great team around him in Magic Johnson, Norm Nixon, Jamaal Wilkes, and Michael Cooper. The addition of Magic makes the Lakers almost impossible to defend, because Magic is so big that when he comes inside, backing his man down, he forces our post defenders to rotate over or we concede easy layups. When Dawk or Caldwell rotates, you can just see Kareem's eyes growing wider and wider as he knows Magic will get him the ball. The Lakers now have two dominant players at the two positions from which it is easiest to take over a game.

Game 3 back in the Spectrum is a case in point, as Kareem lays down the law, scoring 33 points with 14 rebounds, and the Lakers win to go up 2-1.

30.

I'm thinking about Miles and that evening in New York at Cosby's brownstone when he takes out his horn and just starts playing. Maybe he doesn't know what is going to come out of the horn, and it's only when he's putting his lips to the mouthpiece that a spirit moves through him and then through the horn and out into the world. That is, I suppose, the improvisational nature of jazz; the mood, vibe, the other players, even the feeling in the room that night, all influence what the musician plays.

Teddy Pendergrass tells me that's how it works. He stands there on that stage, looks out at the audience, the ladies who have come to see him, and some nights, he finds a deep, powerful, emotional voice; sometimes, it's a voice he's never heard before, with a different quality of bass, with different wind and air, and it just comes out of him and he doesn't know where it emanates from and if he will ever find it again.

I can't presume to compare playing basketball with what Miles or Teddy does, but in game 4, I have a moment where I glimpse how the artist can be surprised by the art he is making. We're in the fourth quarter and trailing by 5 when I find myself isolated against Mark Landsberger. I'm palming the ball in my right hand, and I have this sense that this is a good situation— since it's Landsberger and not Kareem who's blocking my path. I make one dribble, and I'm at full speed. I rise. I am aware that I have gathered a great deal of momentum, that I am soaring toward the basket. I'm looking for a quick dunk, but I've actually picked up so much speed that I've drifted under the basket and Landsberger has recovered and he's cutting off the right side of the hoop. So now I'm looking to make an outlet pass, to get it to the corner where a shooter would be spotting up, but there's no one in position. And here comes Kareem, and he's got his arms up and he's bellying me farther under the basket. But I have a sense that if his arms are up, then he's not in position to jump. As I'm flying behind the backboard, I'm aware that I don't have much hang time left, I'm now falling, but I see a little crevice to the reverse side of the hoop, so I bring the ball and flip it up with some backspin so that it banks in. I fall to the floor, stand back up, and run down the court.

Much is made of that move. And I want to stress, more than anything else, that it's just another move. But it's also a form of expression, and, like so much art, what makes it beautiful is that I am trying in the moment to transcend the limitations being placed upon me, by the defenders, by gravity, and by the situation, to accomplish the goal. But what also makes it interesting is that at any second the baseline move can spin wildly out of control, yet it doesn't, and so there is that tension of any number of possibilities—I get fouled, I fall out of bounds, I miss the shot, I land without shooting, I pass, I lose the ball— yet when I make the shot, that seems the only plausible result. I think when Miles plays the right solo, that solo is the only possible solo he could have played, only he has no way of knowing that beforehand.

And the best thing about that move is that it gets us back into a game that we eventually win to even the series.

31.

Game 5 in LA, however, is a letdown, as we fall behind early, and despite a furious rally and 36 points from me, we are unable to catch the Lakers. Kareem scores 40 points and he and Magic each pull down 15 rebounds. But the most important moment of the game may be late in the third quarter when Kareem steps on Lionel Hollins's foot and injures his own ankle. They take Kareem to the locker room but then he comes limping back on the floor and scores another 14 points in the fourth quarter, including a huge dunk, bad ankle and all, over me with 33 seconds left, to give the Lakers a 3-point lead.

We hear, after the game, that Kareem's ankle is in bad shape and he probably won't be making the trip back east for game 6.

We're all thinking, okay, we take game 6 and then we force it back to LA for game 7, and you *know* Kareem is going to play game 7.

Bill Russell makes the point that a team with an injured star can be a dangerous team because you can't prepare to play them the same way you did when they were intact. And this Laker team, with Magic playing center, is very loose, knowing that if they lose, they go back home where their captain is resting and getting ready for game 7.

The night before, I actually have dinner with my friends Jamaal Wilkes and his wife, Valerie. When I'm in LA, I chill out at Jamaal's, and he'll give me a ride back to my hotel the night before the game. And when we're back in Philly, I'll return the favor. People don't give Jamaal enough credit for what he does. In that game 6, he scores 37 and gives me all I can handle. (It's sort of like Clyde's game 7 in 1970 when Willis came out and jumped center with a torn thigh muscle and scored like 4 points. Clyde had 36 points, 7 rebounds, 19 assists, and 5 steals against Jerry West, and all anyone can talk about is, "The Captain was here so we won.") Magic, of course, has his MVP night, scoring 42, collecting 15 rebounds, dishing out 7 assists, and making 3 steals. The second half of this game, in particular, is like a bad dream, as we fall behind in the third quarter

Dr. J

by 10 and I can feel the Spectrum fans getting anxious. It gets quieter and quieter so that I can hear sneaker squeaks and guys breathing. We're in trouble.

Late in the fourth, we cut the lead to 2 with about five minutes left, but then Magic just takes over, scoring 9 points to win the championship.

What can I say but congratulations? I go over and shake Magic's hand.

But I feel awful for Philadelphia, and I'm thinking, What are we going to have to do to win one of these?

32.

One of the challenges of being a successful professional athlete is learning how to resist temptation. I say this not with arrogance or vanity, but just in an attempt to explain myself after succumbing too many times.

My adolescent habit of dividing females into two types—the good girl you want at home to provide and care for, and the bad girl from across the way whose only need is for me to unbuckle her skintight jeans—does not make being married to me very easy. I was twenty-three when we married. Turq made it clear that there would be no other women in my life, and for a time I stayed committed. I cut off communication with Carol and blew off some of my old friends from high school. Turq didn't want my past and tried to control my future. She'd accuse even her own friends, and me, of making flirtatious advances. At one point, when we were living in the condo in Lido Beach, she asked me to pick up a friend of hers at the airport, and by the time I got home, an hour and a half later than she expected, Turquoise was fuming. "Where ya'll been? What ya'll been doing?"

It's awkward, because this is her friend and she is our houseguest.

I tell her the truth: nothing happened. Her flight was delayed.

Doesn't matter, Turquoise stays mad at both of us the whole four days her friend is in town, which isolates us from each other. She doesn't want to hear the truth, and I don't want a fight. Turquoise is a strong woman, that's what I love about her, and that is both her greatest virtue and perhaps her greatest flaw, as she can fixate on her suspicions for months without ever telling me what it is she is thinking. She doesn't have to tell me. I know she knows I'm stepping out. But I wonder if she is, as well.

But I don't want to tell any lies, to a cop or an attorney, and I'm not certain of anything but her violent hysterics. In the beginning of our marriage, Turquoise's suspicions weren't justified. Now I hardly have a leg to stand on in a divorce.

If men in their late twenties and early thirties become aware of the passage of time—of what has been accomplished and, perhaps more important, what hasn't—a professional athlete becomes hyper-aware. We are confronted with a shorter productive peak, just a decade or so into our primes, if we are lucky. I sometimes wonder if so many of the basketball players' diversions are just that, desperate attempts to push away thoughts of the inevitable, the end of the career, the end of this life. Players drink, smoke, seek out inappropriate sex partners—we are outsized in all areas, including our appetites.

I met Samantha Stevenson in the spring of 1978, in the

Dr. J

Philadelphia locker room. She was reporting for *Sport* magazine and would later help Turquoise write that letter to the *New York Times* my first year with the Sixers. She is a smart single woman—a pretty white girl, a bit of a hippie giving off a vibe of availability. She is an unusual presence still, one of the first wave of female sportswriters who have crossed the threshold into what had previously been an exclusively male clubhouse. I like her. She's comfortable playing the flirt in pursuit of an exclusive story. A lot of players like her, and she must like the attention, too. After a while, she becomes someone who helps me unwind if I'm feeling high-strung or stressed. I can drive over and spend a relaxing evening that might even include oral sex. I'm not proud of the arrangement, but, as I said, I had this immature view of women, that there are good girls and bad girls. And she seemed a level above the buffets of easy women at Jack's place in Detroit, or Warren's in Houston, which were more or less brothels for star athletes (except you didn't have to pay).

So for months Sam is providing me with a kind of therapy, but we don't have what I consider a serious relationship. I can only remember one time that we actually had intercourse, and that was because she had just gotten this new orthodontia to straighten her teeth. With wire and gleaming metal bristling in her mouth, oral sex was not an option.

33.

I am reminded every day of what I have not yet accomplished. I'm thirty years old heading into the 1980–81 season, still in my athletic prime, hoping we can build a team that will finally get us that championship. Pat adds a great younger player in voluble shooting guard Andrew Toney out of the University of Louisiana at Lafayette. Toney, who Pat calls "cobra-quick," is a gifted scorer with a quick release and provides the kind of outside shooting touch we lacked. And for a shooting guard, he is so physically strong, he can post up any opponent in the league. Over the years, he acquires the nickname the Boston Strangler. Even Larry Bird will say that Toney is an absolute killer. "Every time he has the ball, we know he's going to score." The other notable player taken in that draft is a forward out of Minnesota named Kevin McHale, who goes to the Celtics with the third pick. The Celtics further improve by trading for Robert Parish, the Big Chief, a seven-footer who gives them a huge, talented front line.

In the conference finals last year, we had been able to wear down Boston with our twin tower attack, Caldwell and Dawk, but Boston has decisively responded to that and loaded up with an even bigger front line.

I have always believed in working on my game one-on-one. I'll remain after practice with teammates and try out new moves or refine old ones. With the Sixers, I liked to stay after with Steve Mix, my roommate on the road, and we would practice our shots by making eight in a row from different spots on the floor, and of course playing one-on-one. So much of the NBA game is based on clear-outs, on isolations, especially in this era, before there was such a thing as a technical foul for illegal offense. When four guys go to one side and leave me with the ball on the left side of the key, that's like leaving me in a little one-on-one game with my defender.

When I was a rookie in Virginia, I worked on my skills

with the older guys, Ray Scott or Fatty Taylor. And then the next year, I was the veteran playing with Gervin. And now, with Andrew Toney, I have an opportunity to be a mentor myself. Toney reminds me a little of Super John, in that he never stops talking trash—and he has the game and physical strength to actually back it up. One thing I can see is that in isolation, Toney is almost unstoppable.

And unlike most players, he is willing to listen to his coach. That doesn't mean he'll do what the coaches are telling him. But he will hear them out. When Billy starts howling his name during practice or a game—usually for ignoring whatever play Mo Cheeks has called and freelancing his own shot—Andrew shrugs, comes over to the bench, and takes a seat. "We called a play!" says Billy.

Andrew will nod. "I hear you, Coach. But just give me the ball."

With the addition of Toney, we have a sensational regular season, winning 62 games. Before the preseason, Billy said we would succeed or fail based on whether I could duplicate the previous year's performance, and I think I exceed it, scoring nearly 25 a game, 8 rebounds, 4.4 assists, and 2.1 steals.

I finally win the NBA MVP award, and while I don't attach much significance to individual achievements in a team sport, it is noteworthy in that it is the first time in seventeen years a non-center has won the award. After this, ten of the next twelve will be won by forwards or guards. I am contributing to this transformation of the game, in that the most exciting players are now playing facing the basket instead of with their backs to it. I feel like this is some vindication of my style, of the game played on the rise and above the rim.

34.

The Celtics also win 62, and the Atlantic Division title comes down to the final game of the season, played in Boston. Despite Toney scoring 35, we are outplayed by Bird and Parish, who score 24 apiece, and we lose by 4.

We have to go through Indiana and Milwaukee to get back to Boston. Milwaukee actually becomes a pretty serious rival to us during this period. The 1981 Bucks win 62 games themselves behind Marques Johnson, Sidney Moncrief, Junior Bridgeman, and Bob Lanier, who are among the seven players they have averaging double figures. It takes us until a game 7 at home to dispatch the Bucks, and we are finally flying back to Boston for what seems inevitable: another Eastern Conference final against the Celtics.

Game 1 in Boston and who else but the Boston Strangler comes through with two free throws in the final seconds. We lose game 2—Toney scores 35 but I contribute only 12—and we head home after salvaging a split. The only ominous sign is that Larry is on fire, putting up a 33-10 in game 1 and 34-16 in game 2, despite Bobby's and my best efforts.

Still, we win game 3, as we "hold" Larry to 22-13, and then we win game 4 by 2 points as Bobby, who is having a great series, makes a clutch steal at the end. We are in control, 3 games to 1, and miraculously, the Lakers have lost out west to the Houston Rockets, a team with a losing record, so the winner of this series should have a pretty clear path to the title. I can't help but think we can finally win one for Philly and our fans.

We return to the Boston Garden for game 5, and we are

Dr. J

leading by 6 with under two minutes left. This is it. Bring on the Lakers. We feel it. This is our best Sixer team yet, with a more mature Darryl Dawkins, with Andrew Toney coming on, with Bobby still providing his steely defense and sixth-man heroics. And then, I get that feeling of water engulfing me, as Bird and Tiny Archibald start to make amazing plays on both ends, and Bird in particular smothers me so I have trouble even getting my shot off. We're turning the ball over. We somehow fumble the game away and lose by 2. And Bird is definitely back on track, posting a 31–11, with 5 assists.

No matter, right? We're back home for game 6 at the Spectrum. We'll clinch it before our home fans. We go up 51–42 at the half. The champagne is literally on ice.

But we melt.

Boston takes the lead early in the fourth quarter and we never get it back.

Back to Boston for game 7.

The NBA is generally a more physical league today than it will be long after I retire. And in the playoffs, the refs swallow their whistles and let us play. And in a game 7, you know you are out there on your own with no one but your teammates to protect you. Game 7 in Boston is a war, as we again start out strong and take a lead into the old, damp, cramped Boston Garden visiting locker room at halftime. Neither team is shooting well, and every time I drive to the basket I feel like I've been thrown through a windshield. I end up with 6 turnovers, and commit 5 fouls trying to guard Larry and Cornbread Maxwell. Larry makes a typical clutch shot, banking in a 15-footer with twelve seconds left. Mo Cheeks gets fouled, hits one of two free throws. We manage to get the ball back. Billy calls time-out, we inbounds the ball to Bobby, who puts up a high, arcing pass toward the basket, which I'm supposed to alley-oop. There are so many bodies packed in around the basket that I can't get in position for a clean touch. Final score: Boston 91, Philly heartbroken.

Billy's face is creased, pale, pinched; his lips are contorted like a lasso in mid-toss. Once we're back in our locker room, he tries to find some words, something to say, but when he opens his mouth, nothing comes out but a gasp. The locker room floor is strewn with towels, torn bandages, paper cups, ice. Bobby and Andrew are sitting with their heads in their hands. Darryl is hunched over, so that his head is actually leaning inside his locker. Billy is right. There is nothing to say. We dress quickly, file out, climb onto our charter bus, and then the bus starts rocking. I'm thinking back on my senior year of high school, when we lost to Elmont and our students went over and tried to tip over their bus. Now the Celtics fans, whose team just beat us, are trying to tip over our bus? Why? They should be celebrating.

Here's the thing about Celtics fans: they're sore winners.

35.

My third son, my beautiful boy Cory, is born in 1981. We are blessed with healthy children, who mirror our own sound bodies. We are a family that is embodying the American dream. I'm a millionaire, with a beautiful wife, four gorgeous children—and a new dog—we have cars, clothes, an estate. We are an oil painting come to life, some white supremacist's nightmare, the beautiful black family that has somehow displaced English nobility and taken up their wardrobe and home. We are the wishes of our ancestors, I think, the culmination of the struggles of the dreams of Abneys and Ervings and Browns.

But American dreams always intersect with the American dream machine.

So I've starred in a film, *The Fish That Saved Pittsburgh*, a long off-season spent filming with director Gilbert Moses and actors Debbie Allen, Harry Shearer, Jonathan Winters, and the Harlem Globetrotters' legend Meadowlark Lemon. Gilbert had come to a shoot-around at the Forum before a regular season game against the Lakers and shown me the script and asked if I wanted to play Moses Guthrie, the egotistical star of the Pittsburgh Pythons, a forlorn basketball franchise that turns to astrology in an attempt to reverse its fortunes, changing its name, along the way, to the Pittsburgh Pisces. I hadn't read too many film scripts before this, but I did know enough to think this one sort of odd, but then again, this was the '70s and Gilbert said Cher had already committed to play astrologer Mona Mondieu. He said if I wasn't interested, he had Marques Johnson ready to come on board.

I showed the script to Irwin Weiner, who negotiated a six-figure fee, plus I got some back-end participation—I still get a few hundred dollars every year from *Fish*. I ended up in Hollywood, where I had to take improv classes with Meadowlark. We learned how to react to each other, how to listen to our acting partner, a lot of breaking down our inhibitions so Meadowlark and I aren't afraid to cry in front of a room full of strangers.

We spent two months shooting, one in Pittsburgh and one in Los Angeles. At one point, we're all excited that Kareem has joined the cast, playing the center of the Los Angeles Team, as the imaginary LA franchise is called. But Kareem had an argument with Gilbert over the shape of his goatee, so he knocked over his chair and stormed off the set. That's why Kareem is in the first three quarters of the championship game climax of the film, but then vanishes for the fourth quarter, probably the only time in his career Kareem wasn't on the court during crunch time.

Making movies is grueling work. And in the evening, when we were finally done with shooting, I headed back to the hotel with Jonathan Winters and he was telling jokes the whole time. If he got to the car before me, he would actually put a whoopee cushion on the seat and then wait for me to sit down. Here's the thing about whoopee cushions. They are actually funny. And when you've just been on a film set for twelve hours and watching Kareem argue with a director, to sit down on one at ten p.m. while Jonathan Winters is sitting next to you with his thumbs in his ears and his tongue is darting in and out of his mouth, well, it's pretty hysterical.

And then we would get to the hotel, which would be swarming with fans who were there to meet the film stars, and I would just be trying to get to my room while Jonathan would spend the next two hours in the lobby, entertaining the crowd with hand buzzers and puppet shows and pretending to tell people's fortunes. He had amazing and relentless energy.

There are some great scenes in the movie. I love the one where I'm sitting in a car with Toby, played by the lovely Margaret Avery. She bemoans the fact that her son Tyrone is hanging around with my character, "an overgrown adolescent who can only count in twos."

And I turn to her, take her chin in my hand, and say in my deepest, most soulful voice, "What's wrong with twos?"

I then go out on a basketball court and do a bunch of dunks

to the Spinners' "No One Does It Better." (That movie had a great sound track.)

But I decide this isn't how I want to spend my off-seasons. I'll stick with playing tennis at the Hôtel du Cap with Bill Cosby. I'm lucky I did *Fish*, however, because my family and I still get our health insurance through the Screen Actors Guild.

With a young family at home, four children under the age of eleven, I don't really have time to make movies, anyway. I am branching out into new businesses, and through Irwin I'm meeting some heavy hitters. We have dinner in New York with Bruce Llewellyn, owner of Fedco Foods and one of the richest African-Americans in the country. He says he's getting tired of operating a chain of twenty-four-hour groceries and is looking for something else.

"Too many calls in the middle of the night," he says. "Somebody's breaking into the store, somebody's slipping on the floor."

He says he's going to find an investment for us. "I want you to ride with me."

"How much?" I ask.

"Well, you put like a half-million dollars away and wait for my call."

I do a little research into Bruce. When he bought Fedco Foods in 1969, he was ahead of his time in how he financed the deal, using the kind of leveraged buyout strategy that would become famous in the 1980s. Bruce, I quickly realize, is a visionary. I'm in.

I start putting at least $50,000 of my salary away every season, thinking of it as my Llewellyn Fund. Finally, a few years later, he calls me up and says he has just the perfect vehicle.

"No matter what is happening in the economy, people always want beverages," he explains. "Coke, Pepsi, water, beer, they will always buy beverages. When people go to the grocery store, they always come out with beverages."

He tells me he's been looking to buy a bottling operation, and he's identified Philadelphia Coca-Cola Bottling Company, which controls the Coca-Cola bottling rights to Pennsylvania, New Jersey, and Delaware. This is a huge business, he explains. You can't buy Coke or Sprite or Diet Coke or any of a number of other beverages, from anyone but the local bottling company. It's like a monopoly, only legal. He needs $80 million for the whole thing. He's putting up most of it himself, but he is asking a few select individuals to come in with him, including me and Cosby. Bruce pools our money and borrows some from the bank, and we end up the owners of Philadelphia Coke. My half-million-dollar stake will eventually grow to $12 million and would pay a handsome dividend every quarter along the way. It's also a great education about how business works, how these kinds of transactions unfold, what an exit strategy looks like, how I should look to get ahead in the business world. First, I need to complete my education.

I'm not going to be a basketball player forever.

I'm also honoring my commitment to my mother by working toward my college degree. I left Amherst about thirty credits shy of graduating. UMass has a program called University Without Walls, which allows me to take correspondence courses, and throughout my Sixer career, I am taking classes. I switch my major to an area of study I'm familiar with. The primary course load is writing papers and theses about leadership and mentoring. I have these papers due constantly, and often, while the rest of the guys are out on the town, I'm in my hotel room writing a paper on, say, Martin Luther King. Or Martin Luther, for that matter. I'm also allowed to use my own experiences, my own relationships with corporations and sponsors, to write about the relationship between the spokesman and the business he represents. For example, I write a paper about Converse that explores their corporate structure, how that business works, and my role in it. I spend plenty of time in public libraries around the country, in Dallas, in Denver, working on my class papers. It's a slow process, because I only earn one or two credits a pop, three if I'm lucky, but I stay the course because of that promise I made to my mother.

36.

What is it about newborn babies that pulls you toward their cribs, even when they are sleeping? Sometimes, I go into Cory's room and bend over to kiss his soft cheeks and sometimes I just go in there and stand and sniff the air, smell his smell. It is, I suppose, the species ensuring its survival. A new baby in the house settles things down, exerts a focus and calming influence. The machine of family is working, the engine is running, the product is this: a beautiful child.

I peer in on Cory in his upstairs nursery and then walk down the hall to my office, taking my seat behind my desk, making sure my leather desk pad is parallel to the edge of my desk and my pens are in order. My drawers are neat and tidy, the top left locked like it always is. My checkbook is where it should be, inside my top drawer and flush against the bottom of the felt interior. Good.

I open my mail, sorting through the bank statements, credit

card statements, lease statements, the usual fan mail and requests from friends and acquaintances. And there is a personal letter, handwritten on yellow stationery.

It is from Samantha Stevenson, the former sportswriter, and she writes that she has a daughter, Alexandra Winfield Stevenson, and I am the father.

37.

After my customary two weeks of off-season workouts at the Hôtel du Cap on the French Riviera—running along the beach, playing tennis on the clay courts with Cosby, dining on *homard*, and drinking rosé—it is back to the grind and to attempting another climb up that mountain. I am at the absolute peak of my athletic abilities, a reigning MVP of the league, arguably the best player on the planet, but, as I said, I can hear the clock ticking. I can chart the passage of time in my sons, in Cheo, who is now—can this be?—a strapping ten-year old, and a fine athlete himself, and J, who is seven, and adorable Jaz, who is four. In beautiful Cory, the baby, who inhabits that blessed spot of the youngest and cutest, the displacer of Jaz from that role, who herself displaced J. I feel that incessant, cruel onrush of time. I need to win, now.

I'm watching great players like Doug Collins finally call it quits, after struggling to come back from numerous injuries. His body surrenders, and he retires before the season.

Pat and Billy don't make big changes in the off-season. This is a team still built around me and my abilities, with plenty of shots for Andrew Toney, who is in his second year and becoming one of the most feared scorers in the league. Cheeks has developed into a reliable scorer in addition to being a steady ball handler and gifted passer. We still have Bobby playing forward, though we have to limit his minutes because of his epilepsy, and Caldwell, Dawkins, and Catchings as our big men. This is a great shooting team, with Toney, Bobby, Mo, Darryl, and me all hitting over 52 percent—which is fortunate, because we are a terrible rebounding team, finishing twenty-second in the league in defensive boards.

It's an issue that will plague us all year. When Darryl Dawkins comes down on Mike Gminski's foot in a game against the Nets, the situation becomes so critical that Pat is talking to Wilt Chamberlain about coming back.

I tell Pat he can't be serious. "Wilt? Really? This is a publicity thing, right?"

But Pat thinks our rebounding needs are that extreme.

We have a new owner, Harold Katz, the founder of Nutrisystem, the weight-loss program, who bought the team from Fitz Dixon for $12 million. (To put in perspective how much the league has changed since 1981—or to just give some sense of inflation—there are forty NBA players in 2013 who earn that much in a single season. That's right, Nene Hillario earns enough to buy the 1981 Philadelphia 76ers.) Harold played a little ball in high school, once losing to Wilt Chamberlain's Overbrook High School 80–22. Maybe he learned a lesson from watching Wilt and spent the rest of his life believing that you need a quality big man if you want to win. This year, the Sixers just don't have that. Darryl has been an enigma his whole career. The Dawk should have been Moses Malone: he has a body that looks like it should average 20–10, but he never really comes close. I think that if Darryl had spent a year or two in college, then he could have been a smarter player—he certainly would have become better at staying out of foul trouble. Darryl was like Shaq before Shaq, the same irreverent attitude, the constant jokes—much of Darryl's material came from old black comic albums, the chitlin circuit, Moms Mabley, Slappy White. He was doing stuff he had heard growing up. He has the same whimsical approach to life as Shaq, but in the latter's case it had been refined by a couple of years at LSU where he saw what the wider world had to offer and knew how to carry himself among more sophisticated people. Dawk remained an overgrown high school kid with a juvenile sensibility. He and World B. Free were having water balloon fights while I'm trying to write my term papers and figure out how to diversify my portfolio. For basketball players, college isn't just about developing as a player, it's an introduction to the grown-up world and will give you a sense of how to cope with those adult demands. I can't imagine Dawk sitting down with a financial planner and listening to various investment strategies, but I could see him exchanging whoopee cushion tips with Jonathan Winters.

Katz was already exasperated with Dawkins when he was healthy, but now that we are getting outmuscled every night, he tells Pat that we have to get stronger inside.

38.

After reading that letter from Samantha, I sit with it for a while. I'm thinking this over. If Alexandra is really my daughter, then I have to own up to that; that's the right thing to do. I have to deal with this in my marriage and be straight with my wife.

I go downstairs and find Turq in the kitchen. She's drinking tea from a white ceramic cup. I take a deep breath and show her the letter.

Turq is a swinger, in that when she is mad, she starts throwing punches around. And the girl can hit. As she is reading the letter, she is torn between getting to the end of the letter and unleashing a haymaker.

She is pissed. As Don King would say, she is pissed to the highest degree of pissivity.

"You fucking pig," and she is pounding me, hurling punches that I'm trying to parry with my arms crossed over my chest. I'm backing up, until finally I'm against a cabinet. Then she picks up her teacup, and she's throwing that at me, along with a spoon, a pot, another pot, another cup. I need to get out of here.

Turquoise and I have some violent fights. A man can't win these fights. If I hit back, then that only enrages Turq more and she's going to start swinging harder.

I've hit her, but only in self-defense. I'm not inclined toward that kind of confrontation. I may not always be the best judge of a situation—that is, coming downstairs and handing that letter to Turq—but I don't ever touch her unless I'm being attacked. There are guys I know, ballplayers, who say, "Hey, if a girl starts a fight, slap her and she'll back down." But I know Turq. She doesn't back down from a fight. Ever. That's also what I love about her.

I get in my new Mercedes and I'm driving out east, along the Long Island Expressway, all the way to the Hamptons, where I check into a motel.

I call Irwin and we hire this hardball attorney from Philadelphia who is going to handle the paternity issues. He says we need to do a DNA test and, until we get those results, we need to sit tight. In the letter, Samantha wrote she was sure I was the father.

But I did wonder how she could be certain, since I was suspicious she'd been with another player as well as another sportswriter, but something about the letter made me believe her.

The tests come back confirming that Alexandra is my daughter.

Turquoise calls me after three days and tells me, "You need to come home."

"You're gonna hit me!" I tell her.

"Our babies need you," she says. "I won't hit you. I may kill you, but I'm not gonna hit you."

I come home. Turquoise tells me how it's going to be. The lawyers will draw up an agreement, providing support for the child—Turq doesn't care about the money—but I am to have no contact with the mother or child. Ever. It is to be a purely financial arrangement. There will be no emotional connection. The child should not even know I am her father.

What choice do I have?

We have the lawyers draw up the contract. I will give Samantha $4,000 a month until Alexandra is eighteen. She will get a car when she is sixteen and there will be private school tuition.

I'm not happy about this, but I need to work on the family that I have right here.

39.

A few years later, I'm doing a basketball clinic in San Diego, and I notice Samantha is there, standing behind a crowd of

about thirty children. I'm playing with these little kids, and Samantha comes over and she says, "You know, that's your daughter over there."

I look over and see in this crowd of kids a beautiful little girl. She looks like Jazmin, my other daughter, and my heart aches as I see this child with no father. I know what that feels like.

40.

We are having a fine season, winning 58 games, cruising through the first round, and then coming up against those always tough Milwaukee Bucks. It is the great misfortune of the Bucks of the early '80s that they happen to be sharing the league with the Sixers and Celtics of that period. These Bucks, with Lanier, Moncrief, Marques Johnson, Pat Cummings, Junior Bridgeman, Quinn Buckner, are a loaded team, coached by Don Nelson, that wins at least 50 games every year from 1981 to 1987 and never makes it to a championship final. But sorry, Don, we take your 55-win Bucks out again 4-2, winning game 6 in Milwaukee.

We've lost Lionel Hollins during the first round when he and Tree Rollins found themselves in the middle of a Three Stooges routine as Tree elbows the Train and then the Train punches the Tree in the back of his head. Tree chases Lionel behind the basket, down the aisle, into the crowd, and then back onto the floor. But no one is laughing when Lionel is diagnosed with a broken hand from punching Tree in the head.

Playing on just one day's rest after the tough Milwaukee series, we get obliterated by Boston in game 1 of the conference finals, with Larry putting up a triple-double. The biggest addition the Celtics have made is Danny Ainge, a slick playmaker out of Brigham Young, but it doesn't matter because no Celtics guards can stop Toney, who in game 2 explodes for 30. We come back to Philly and win games 3 and 4, playing smothering defense and holding the Celtics to under 100 in both. The Boston Strangler torches Chris Ford, Danny Ainge, and the other Celtics guards for 39 in game 4.

It's bothered Billy for a while that we are too nice a team. He believes that we lack a certain killer instinct, and the Boston Strangler is helping to eliminate that. But Billy also believes we have to adopt a more aggressive mind-set. He tells us he hates it when we give a hand to opponents who have fallen or been knocked over. That basic courtesy, which I've extended all my life, on the court or off, communicates that we are soft. He says we should leave them to die.

Instead, we're the ones who look to be heading for another playoff grave. For the second year in a row we have gone up 3–1, only to squander the lead and stand on the brink of losing the series. We're heading back to Boston for game 7, and, judging by our awful rebounding and terrible shooting in the last two defeats, there doesn't seem to be much hope for us to get past the bruising Bird, Parish, and McHale front line. Maybe Harold Katz is right: we just aren't big enough. And maybe Billy is right: we're not tough enough.

The *Philadelphia Inquirer* describes our situation as "Hopeless." One of the Boston papers runs a headline that reads, "WILL SIXERS CHOKE?"

We're nervous. The day before our flight to Boston, we're practicing in the Palestra, the gym at the University of Pennsylvania. Our whole team is in a funk. We've been playing center by
committee all season. Every game, Billy looks around and asks,
"Who wants to start tonight?"

And now, after 6 games, our big guys are looking at each
other and saying, "Not me."

I'm like, "Shit, man, come on!"

We need to show a little more confidence than that.

Billy and Chuck walk us through practice. But by now, after playing the Celtics twenty-three times in the past two regular seasons and playoffs, we know all their plays and tendencies
and they know ours. There is only so much the coaches can do.

Finally, Billy looks around and says, "You know what, we're
leaving. You guys need to figure out what you are going to do."

After they exit, we're standing around on the court. The
Palestra doesn't have wooden or cushioned seats, it has concrete seats, about eight thousand of them, and there is not a
soul in that building besides the twelve of us on that court. It's
like a mausoleum in there, silent, echoey; if one of us shifts his
weight, the sneaker squeak reverberates up to the rafters.

"That's it?" I say. We usually practice for about two hours.
"All right, you guys, we're going to have a team meeting."

So we go back down to the locker room and close the door
and we're all sitting there on the benches. "Most of you guys
were here last year, so you know it's going to be war up there
in Boston," I say. "Total war. We've got to bring everything
in our repertoire to win this game. And right now, I don't feel
like our team is ready. But I don't have a crystal ball. So, let's
get our feelings out there. Let's say what we're thinking, what
we're feeling."

We go around the room. Toney is talking about wanting more shots, Caldwell says something unintelligible, Darryl promises to "put something on their ass." And then we get to Clint Richardson, and he stands up and he says, "You know what? It's just us. Nobody believes in us. Nobody thinks we have a chance. Man, the coaches left. The fans gave up. Nobody in Boston thinks we can win. Nobody in Philly thinks we can win. It's just us."

Clint never says shit. But he's onto something. I repeat it. "Just us. I like that."

Mo picks it up. "It's just us!"

Dawk shouts, "Justice!"

"No, no, just us," I say. "Like, J-u-s-t u-s."

Dawk nods. "Yeah. Justice!"

But Clint has us all fired up. We're all nodding, chanting, "Just us!"

"Let's hold on to that," I say. "Let's take that to Boston."

On the bus from our hotel in Cambridge to the Garden, we're repeating that sentiment, how it's us against the world. But after shoot-around, we go back to our locker room, and somehow the Philly front office has gotten in here, and they've put all these letters up from everyone back in Philly, from janitors and secretaries and locker room attendants all the way up to team officials. There are so many of them. "We believe," "Come back with the victory," "We're all in this together." It's amazing. We're all looking at each other and reading these letters and it's like, it's not just us. It's all of us. It's all of Philly. They have been here all along, rooting for us and supporting us.

We're all inspired by that. Whoever arranged to get those letters up there is a motivational genius, because we come out of the locker room all loose and ready to kick some Celtic ass.

During warm-ups, a few Boston fans are walking around in white bedsheets with "Ghosts of Celtics Past" on the front. At first glance, when I see them, they look like the Klan. Maybe I hear Bill Russell whispering in my ear about the tortured history of Boston and black folks. I just have to laugh at my first impression.

We take them down, opening up a lead in the first quarter and never letting up. I score 29 and Toney torches M. L. Carr for 34 points. Mo Cheeks and Bobby come through with big games and we pull away in the fourth quarter, eventually winning by 14. The Boston fans show their class by chanting "Beat LA. Beat LA." And a few of them even have a red number 6 up in the stands.

I can't overstate the significance of that seventh game. It may have been the most important game of my career. Back then, those Sixer-Celtic series felt bigger than championship finals, or certainly more emotional. Those games are tougher and more mentally grueling than any others I've ever played.

That's why the finals almost seem an anticlimax. Our deficiencies on the glass were pretty clearly exposed by the Celtics, who, even in losing game 7, outrebound us by 11.

I'm not making excuses, but each of the three times we make the finals, the Lakers are waiting for us. During that period, the Celtics will make the NBA finals five times, winning three titles. But they have the good fortune to face the Houston Rockets in two of those trips instead of the Lakers. With all due respect to the Rockets, they just weren't the Lakers. The Celtics will finish the decade 1-2 against Kareem and Magic in the NBA finals, the same as ours.

The Laker team we face is a juggernaut, with four future Hall of Famers (Kareem, Magic, Jamaal Wilkes, and Bob McAdoo) and additional all-stars like Norm Nixon and Michael Cooper. Cooper doesn't start on that team and he's an eight-time first- or second-team All Defense player and eventual Defensive Player of the Year. Norm Nixon is an all-star in 1982, scoring over 17 and dishing out 8 assists a night, and he has fewer assists than Magic, who is technically their shooting guard that year. Magic actually averages more rebounds than our centers.

They get their split in the first two games, and then we go out and lose our first two in LA. These Lakers are a great running team, and they start out most games looking for fast-break opportunities. Their defenders are always leaving their men early and taking off, which puts pressure on our guards to pick up Jamaal or Cooper or Magic or whoever is running the break. They do this so often and so quickly to open games that it takes us out of our offensive rhythm, because we are already thinking about defensive matchups and getting downcourt to stop the break.

Game 6 is typical of the series, as the Lakers open up a lead with their Showtime offense, and we have to fight and claw to get back into the game. We're trailing 8–0 when I finally get us on the board with a 15-footer. Usually, the way Billy likes to run our offense is for me to defer to the other guys in the first few minutes to try to get them in the flow. Billy's reasoning is that I'm going to get my shots because I play the most minutes on the team, but to win, we need to get Andrew Toney going, and Mo Cheeks, and maybe see how Bobby's shooting the ball.

On defense, we play our matchups pretty straight up to start. But when Kareem has the ball, then we'll threaten to double-team, and if Kareem dribbles, I'll drop down, force him to pass the ball. But we can't really slow down the Laker offense, and they score 66 in the first half.

Dr. J

During halftime, Billy is furious, screaming, "Sixty-six! That's a hundred thirty-two points in a game. We can't win basketball games giving up a hundred thirty-two. We're not rebounding and we're turning the ball over. They are exploiting our exterior defense."

He wants us to stay more disciplined on offense, and to look for me down low, even if I'm covered, because that is still a good matchup for us. As it turns out, the way we begin to break down their trap is that Andrew Toney gets hot on his way to 29 points and keeps us in the game. We pull to within 1 a couple of times but are never able to take a lead. Each time we get close, then Magic gets fouled and goes to the line, or Kareem hits a big shot. We just can't impose our will, despite 30 points from me.

I am generally considered the best player on these Sixer teams, but there are significant stretches, even to close out games, where our offense goes away from me. Billy, and Gene before him, calls plays for Andrew or Darryl or Bobby (or George or Lloyd, and so on) and sometimes I don't handle the ball at all. It's the state of the game: team play, no one arguing with the coach, not even the superstars. Every scoring champion since Lew Alcindor in 1971 has come up short in the playoffs. Teams aren't designed to be top heavy.

That game 6 against the Lakers is a case in point. Down the stretch of an elimination game, our offense resembles the kind of balanced attack made famous by North Carolina's Dean Smith. Billy played his college ball in Chapel Hill, and I can't help but think he draws some of his offensive philosophy from his undergraduate experience. With five minutes to play, we're down by 3 points and over the next seven possessions, I handle the ball twice and draw one foul after the game has largely been decided.

I'm not saying I could have won that game to force game 7,

but I'm just pointing out how hard it is—and will be—to compare players from different eras (Michael, Kobe, and LeBron—my lineage—will all shoot over twenty times a game for most of their careers; I did only once in the NBA). And I'm not sure anyone could have stopped the Lakers that year. With four minutes left, Kareem makes a jumper in the lane, draws a foul, and then hits his free throw to put the Lakers ahead by 6 and we unravel from there, unable to stop Wilkes, Nixon, Magic (the Most Valuable Player for the series), and McAdoo. The Forum erupts as the Lakers win their second title in three years against us.

I've never believed in the knock on some athletes and teams, how they "can't win the big one." But now, watching Pat Riley and the Lakers celebrate, seeing McAdoo rejoice at winning his first title, and Magic grinning and hugging Kareem, I have to wonder why our team just keeps coming up a little short. I've won championships in the ABA, so I believe I know what it takes to win in these kinds of high-pressure situations. There has to be a reason this keeps happening. Bill Russell tells me that there is no such thing as a jinxed team. There are very good teams that beat other very good teams to get to the NBA finals, and then they lose to an even better team. And I have to admit, this Laker team is deeper than ours. I believe I can match up with any player in the world, but what about the rest of our guys? What about our big men? We finish game 6 with 35 rebounds. The Lakers finish with 49. We will not beat Kareem and the Lakers, never mind Parish, McHale, Bird, and the Celtics, if we can't compete on the boards.

I'm thirty-two years old. How many more shots at this am I going to get? That's why I cry in the locker room after the game for the first time in my pro career.

I don't cry when we beat Boston. I don't cry when we lose

Dr. J   359

to Boston. But this time, I feel like the window is closing. Even more worrying, the Lakers have the first pick in the 1982 draft. They're going to reload again, adding James Worthy to a championship team.

How are we going to beat these guys?

41.

My contract with the Sixers requires that I permanently relocate to Philadelphia. We sell our house in Upper Brookville, turning a nice profit. Turq and I decide on our new home: a 12,000-square-foot Normandy-style mansion in Villanova with a tennis court, swimming pool, basketball court, and huge circular drive. We pay $650,000—I'll later sell it for $3 million—and take on a permanent staff of two. This is an even more opulent home than our house in Upper Brookville, and as soon as we arrive on the Mainline, we start entertaining in an even grander style than we had in Long Island. Philadelphia has embraced me to a degree that New York never had, outside of a few communities in Long Island, and I feel that Turq is happy here in part because we are farther from my family. Turq and my mom and Freda still don't get along, and that's a source of constant tension for me. Of course my mom wants to see her grandkids, to spend time with Cheo, J, Jaz, and Cory, but Turq makes it clear she doesn't like my mom to be around. Turq's mother, Willia, whom I am fond of, and her brother James, come up and spend extended stretches as our guests. But my mom is not made to feel welcome.

To this day, if you ask Cheo or J or any of our kids about their grandmother, they will think of Turq's mom instead of mine.

I'm always trying to resolve this issue. I'm good friends with the musician Grover Washington Jr., who the year before released the song "Let It Flow" (for "Dr. J"), as a smooth jazz tribute to me. He plays it over a montage of some of my dunks, and I like to think of it as art inspiring art. I ask Grover how I can somehow connect my wife and my mother.

"You can't make two cats like each other," Grover says. "All you can do is impose your will and force them to be civil. But whether or not they like each other is not something that you can decide."

He looks at me. "But you know what?"

"What?"

"Two cats can't dig each other if one cat doesn't dig herself."

I often wonder if Turq has some issues from her own childhood or from her first marriage, but I know that I have to stay true to my commitment. I chose my wife and I didn't choose my mother. I love my mother, but I have to live with my choice, and it breaks my heart to have this enforced distance from my mom. She still comes down plenty and attends my games, but it's not the same as when we were living in Long Island. Freda and her kids have moved over to Queens, and those boys are also like sons to me, so the distance between Freda and Turq is hard for all of us to bear. I put a lot of miles on my Mercedes driving back and forth from Philly to New York.

My nephews, Barry and Keith, are old enough to take the train by themselves or even drive down for a visit. Barry is turning into a fine ballplayer himself, as well as a solid student. Keith, also a very good athlete, is more prone to get-

ting into trouble. Barry will eventually play ball at Wagner College, earning his MBA from Temple. Keith will join the Marines.

I've converted the condo at the Academy House into the office of the Erving Group, the umbrella company for my businesses. I hire my old coach Ray Wilson as my first employee. I already know this is my last pro contract, and that means I will retire, at the latest, at thirty-seven.

Irwin and I talk regularly about how I need to take the considerable fees I am paid for my endorsements and appearances, together with my NBA and ABA savings, and use these as seed money for the new businesses that can provide for me after my career. I have a lot to learn in this regard, and thankfully I have mentors like Bruce Llewellyn, Steven Wynn, Larry Magid, Harold Katz, and Bill Cosby.

It is an early off-season afternoon when the phone rings in my office. It's Freda.

"Hey, June, how you doing?"

Freda's voice embodies for me wisdom and kindness, along with the gentle judgment of being my big sister.

I stand up and walk around my desk, looking up Locust Street at the cars driving by on Broad.

"I'm sick," she says.

"You got a cold?"

She explains it's more serious than that. Cancer is a taboo subject. I don't hear many people talking about it, and then only after the fact, after someone has passed and you realize you haven't seen them in a few months or years. So when Freda tells me that she has cancer, I think that can't be right. She's so young, still not yet forty.

She says the doctors found blood clots in her stool. They did a biopsy and detected some polyps in her colon, but rather than have an operation, she is pursuing some alternative medicine that she believes is better than the surgery. She has heard about these homeopathic treatments through her church. What she doesn't tell me is that with her kind of cancer and the stage at which it is detected, the odds of remission from conventional surgery and chemotherapy are not that great anyway.

I tell her whatever she needs financially, I'll of course take care of it. She should just call Irwin and he'll make the necessary provisions.

"Have you told Mom?"

She says she hasn't.

"Gonna break Mom's heart." Like it's breaking mine.

I don't understand God's will. I don't understand His plan. The universe sometimes seems arbitrary to me, its cruelty as unthinking as a mousetrap. When Marky passed, I forced myself to keep moving forward, as I did with Bobby, Tonk, and Wendell, but when I go with Mom and Freda to Marky's grave in Rockville Centre, I think again about the substance of this life, about the extinguishing of the body and the mysteries of the soul. I always believe that Marky travels with me, and I sometimes feel him there, but I also know that this is the story I tell myself in order to soften the harsh truth of his being gone.

But could God's plan really be to take another of us so young? And a mother of two young boys? That doesn't make sense.

I call Mom and through tears we talk about what we can do for Freda. Mom is close by, so she can help out with Barry and Keith, and for now, anyway, Freda remains strong.

The homeopathic course seems to be working wonders for Freda over the next few months, as she goes into remission and

takes on a vibrancy in her life that belies her diagnosis. She continues to work as a church receptionist, frequently calling to fill me in on how the boys are doing. On my regular trips up to Long Island to stay at Williams Street with my mom, Freda comes over for family picnics and meals, and she is the same beautiful, vivacious girl I have known all my life.

When she tells me to go inside to pick up more sweet tea, I listen.

I think there is a light in her that will never go out.

Mom still has her hair salon and her friends around Long Island, and wouldn't it be nice if she had all her kids and grandkids there? I regret that I am unable to provide this for my mom, giving her only stolen moments with her grandchildren.

Everyone is always reminding me of the significance of winning a title, of basketball games. I believe there are more important things, like family.

42.

This year, before our annual trip to the French Riviera, we are joining Joe Meriweather, M. L. Carr, and a half-dozen other NBA players on a goodwill tour of China. We visit Beijing, Xian and the terra-cotta warriors, Guangzhou. Turq and I stay in the room in the Beijing guesthouse formerly occupied by Richard and Patricia Nixon. It's a strange room, featuring a urinal in the bedroom. This is before China has fully opened up to the West, and in some places we visit we are the first brothers the locals have ever seen. We have dinners with some very high-level party officials and various eminences where we are served plenty of foods we've never seen before. This is the first time I've eaten every part of a duck, and I mean every part: they serve us duck tongue, duck intestines, duck feet, and duck ass. And that's a delicacy, the ass, so they always give it to the most important person. I end up eating a lot of ass.

For most of that trip, we are out of touch with the United States. They don't have international phones in the hotels. We are left to sightsee on our own, which means that I spend an awful lot of time arguing with M. L. Carr.

I'm telling him he's lost his identity since moving up to Boston. He started out in the ABA, but since joining the Celtics he's become a towel-waving automaton.

"You forget where you came from," I tell him one afternoon as we're opening up canned peaches so we won't be too hungry at dinner.

He says I'm just bitter because I know the Celtics are going to take us apart next year.

We do get one piece of news while we're at our hotel in Guangzhou: the Sixers have traded Darryl Dawkins to the New Jersey Nets for a first-round pick next year.

"Oh no," M. L. says when he sees me, "it's over. You guys gave up your best big man!"

I feel awful. I'm marooned in the middle of China and our title chances seem to be receding further. The Lakers have picked James Worthy in the draft. The Celtics' young big men are a year older and they are about to trade for all-star wingman Scott Wedman. And what have we done? We've drafted a couple of decent college players, but in the arms race of the NBA, that's not enough to close the gap with the Lakers, much less stay ahead of the Celtics.

Dr. J

M. L. Carr is giddy the rest of the trip as I descend into a funk. He's probably in his room waving the hotel towels around as he thinks about the upcoming season.

When we finally reach Hong Kong, Turq and I check into our room and there is a message from the Sixers waiting for me. We've just signed Moses Malone.

M. L. Carr has heard the news as well, and when I see him down in the lobby, he's shaking his head. "You guys just won the title."

43.

Bill Cosby also has a house in Philly, so he and Camille become regular guests at our place. In the summers, we have parties every weekend, inviting Arthur Ashe, Grover, Teddy Pendergrass, Lynn Swann, Patti LaBelle, other Philly athletes like Mike Schmidt (Doug Collins's best friend), Harold Carmichael, Reggie White, Garry Maddox, and many of my teammates and Sixer staff. Billy Cunningham lives just up the street, so he and I are often at each other's houses, talking shop. Turq and I start to have these weekend afternoon events I call Hit, Sip, Dip, and Dine. That's a little tennis, a beverage, a swim in the pool, and then dinner.

Velveteen manicured grass that my friend John Havlicek might call Celtic green extends from the house an acre in every direction, to the stands of maples and spruce, green and going gold in the late summer. The treetops undulate in the afternoon breeze, their tips waving good-bye to the season. The oval pool, wrapped by a granite patio, is down a mossy stone path from our back deck. There are children in the pool, our own, our guests', their peals like aural confetti swirling around us. On the tennis courts behind me, I can hear a game in progress, the hollow thunk of well-struck shots, the grunt of a point lost. Turq is in the kitchen, working hard. She is a wonderful cook, her creations, usually hearty southern-style fare, are the reward after a hard day of play.

A man walks through this patio, along this deck, a glass of wine in hand, and he feels that he is somehow at the center of the world. He has beautiful children, a lovely wife, fine friends, and here around him is the evidence of that, every blade, every leaf, every splash: it is all a blessing that he never takes for granted.

But beneath that image, or around it, are the great strains of my life, and ahead of me, there is so much pain still to come. I have to admit I am no longer that shining example of promise and potential. I am now fully realized, but that means I also have to admit that this is what success is, what it looks and feels like. I appreciate its every minute, but with success come previously unconsidered problems and concerns.

One thing I am now confronting is how different my children's experience is from my own. Cosby had told me that nothing about growing up poor teaches you how to be a rich dad. My eldest son, Cheo, whom we nickname Bam-Bam for his physical strength, his nose for disruption and heavy-handed chaos, his frank boyishness and unremitting mischief, is an indifferent student, dismissive of his teachers. He's a bright boy, cat quick when he wants to be, but too rarely shows that at school, where he is a steady disciplinary problem, the concerned calls home from teachers and administrators a regular occurrence.

His younger brother J idolizes him—I wince when I realize that this is how Marky must have looked up to me. J will follow Cheo through any of his perilous, ill-conceived ventures—a plot to heist small change or record albums or candy or extra soda pop.

When Cheo is twelve and J is eleven, I get a call from my teammate, Steve Mix, saying that someone has called him and told him that my kids are smoking cigarettes behind the Friends School in Philadelphia. Now, my children are the children of a celebrity, for better or worse, and therefore are subject to constant scrutiny. That's the downside, I suppose, of being Dr. J's sons.

I call my boys into my office and ask them where they've been today.

They tell me, "Nowhere."

"How come you got home so late from school?"

"We were playing a little ball," Cheo says.

I nod. "Suppose I told you I got a call about you guys smoking cigarettes behind the school. Does that mean someone's lying on you?"

They realize they are busted. I can see Cheo running through the calculations about whether it is better to come clean or to spin another lie.

They fess up.

And then here comes the lecture. About honesty. About smoking. About drugs. About all of that, but the pattern is established. I tell them that no matter what, I will help them. I will fight for them, that Turq and I will always listen to them and try to find a solution.

Cheo nods, agrees, promises to tell the truth.

But this is something I don't understand. How he can look

me in the eye and deny what I know to be the truth? And J will nod along with him. The two of them are dissembling right through their teen years. They can never keep their stories straight. They say they are going one place and actually heading to another. And throughout their teen years, Turq and I share this frustration in understanding our boys through these lies.

I don't want to write too much about my sons' stories, out of respect for their privacy, but perhaps the greatest challenge for me as a father is to resist viewing their lives through the prism of my own adolescence. I was a different boy from Cheo and J.

As the first generation of our family to have money, Turquoise and I turn to our friends and associates for parenting advice. We consult specialists and counselors.

It is a mistake on my part to try to solve my sons' issues—as our Mainline neighbors suggest, at least by their prosperous example—by finding them a different school. They begin a labyrinthine journey through elite private schools. Their upbringing is so different from mine. I didn't have choices. If you flunked out of the local public school, well, that was it. There was no alternative. With money, however, come all kinds of options, of parenting solutions far more esoteric than my mom beating me with a switch.

I never hit my children. I break that terrible tradition. But I perhaps create a too lenient alternative where my kids are indulged. Instead of telling them, "You stick it out. You hang in there. You follow rules," I impart the message that we will change the rules to better accommodate them.

It is, I now believe, a colossal mistake.

Perhaps I am overcompensating for being absent so often. A

 Dr. J 369

professional athlete's life means extended absences. I am gone too often, and so I try to make up for it by providing in money what I can't always give in time. My job is to play basketball, and the time that demands is not optional, it is required. So I miss too much of my children's lives. I don't know that there is anything I can do about that. I am as involved as I can be. Either Turq or I will go to every parent-teacher night, to every soccer or basketball or lacrosse game, to every performance and recital.

And there is a certain amount of nature that can't be overlooked in this discussion of where my nurturing was wanting: Jazmin is a good, studious girl who stays at Episcopal Academy through high school. She's smart, steady, beautiful, and seems to thrive, despite, or perhaps because of, being my daughter.

Part of it, of course, is that Cheo and J are the boys of "the Doctor," and they have had it whispered in their ears by friends, by their peers, that, hey, they don't have to worry about anything because "your dad is Dr. J."

Like they have it made.

My dad was Tonk. I never had it made.

That may be the biggest difference right there.

But I love my children with an intensity that causes its own distortions. I'm not a stern disciplinarian, and so perhaps we are too lenient, are too soft where perhaps hardness is required. I am reacting to my own upbringing.

I play ball on our backyard court with J and Cheo, challenging them to beat me two against one. I explain to them that two should always be able to beat one, and they need to find a way to do it. I'm not allowed to shoot layups. No dunks.

We spend days on that court. Each of them tries to take me off the dribble or tries to make long jumpers instead of using the passing game to beat me.

I always tell them, "Figure it out."

Eventually they do.

But I'm very conscious of never forcing them to play sports, or in any way judging them as athletes. I know that they will be measured by too many others against the accomplishments of their father, and that's not fair.

They need to be allowed to just be boys. That's what I was before I became Dr. J.

44.

Moses Malone is the reigning MVP of the NBA, which means that we have the two most recent MVPs on this team. But what inspires confidence in training camp isn't the hardware or the statistics, it is Moses's work ethic. From the first day, he is running harder than the rookies trying to make the team. He says he's not even playing until he's sweating.

And he is a world-class sweater. I've never seen a grown man sweat so much. There is water dripping off him everywhere. It's puddling on the floor. We're hydroplaning in Moses's sweat, splattering it up into the seats and onto the backboard. He is so intense. In every scrimmage, the second team never comes close to the first team because Moses refuses to lose in practice.

We may never drop another game.

Moses makes it clear from the beginning that he feels this is "Doc's team."

"There's a lot of Indians, but there can only be one chief."

But he still leads by example.

Moses vows to go after every missed shot. He says he figures there are a hundred chances for rebounds in a game. If he fights for every one of them, then he's bound to get at least 15.

Our owner, Harold Katz, has solved our rebounding problems in a spectacular manner, by bringing in the best rebounder of all time. The only problem is that Moses was looking forward to playing with his old friend Caldwell Jones, and when he finds out that we've given CJ to the Rockets as compensation for Moses, Big Mo almost backs out of the deal. I'm also terribly disappointed to see CJ go. He's a warrior, our only player who has been willing to deal with Kareem or Parish straight up. But to get Moses, you are going to have to sacrifice something. Moses, after balking, signs, and he immediately reaches out to me and we establish the rapport that we still have to this day.

He remains one of the funniest and most perceptive individuals I know. He is shy and often speaks cryptically, and this causes many to dismiss his intelligence. But Moses has a sharp mind; he just chooses not to share it with many people.

Moses is a country boy from Petersburg, Virginia, and like Darryl, he never went to college. Only Moses didn't need to. When Moses left home at nineteen, after one of the craziest recruiting wars in the history of basketball, with sixty-five or so college coaches and scouts staying at motels and in rented rooms all through Petersburg, his momma gave him a Bible, which he carries with him everywhere.

"That's my rock," he tells me.

"The Bible?"

He nods. "Momma gave me something to put in there. That's my rock."

"She wrote in there?"

He nods.

"Okay, Mo, can I read it?"

"Nah, nah, I can't let nobody read it."

At this point in the NBA, Moses is the man. He's taken over the title from Kareem as the best center in the league. Larry and Magic are still coming into their own. I'm in my twelfth season. Moses is the alpha dog.

But he's still so country, with this arch sense of humor that comes out in flashes, like when he is checking out of a hotel in New York and the clerk hands him his bill. He studies it and says, "I just want to pay for a room, I didn't want to buy no hotel."

This is the first team I've been on since ninth grade where I'm not clearly the best player on the team. Even I have to defer to Moses. He is such a warrior down low that Billy has no choice but to run more of our offense through him. Moses takes more shots than I do, he scores more than I do. He becomes, in many ways, the physical leader of our team while I remain the verbal and spiritual leader.

And with the continuing emergence of Andrew Toney as a devastating scorer, we have so many weapons, not to mention Mo Cheeks and his steady hand at the point. Pat has signed a free agent rookie named Marc Iavaroni, a big, strong player who had preceded Ralph Sampson at Virginia before playing in Italy for three seasons. Iavaroni ends up starting, so Bobby can continue to come off the bench. Bobby still plays more minutes, of course.

At thirty-three years old, I'm picking my spots where I can

Dr. J

impose my will. I've missed 24 games in total in the previous eleven seasons, so my knees are definitely feeling the wear and tear. It is a luxury to have a guy like Moses, whose presence forces defenses to double-team. Moses has led the league in rebounding three of the previous four seasons, and last year he averaged 31 points and nearly 15 boards. And we added that to a team that was already an NBA finalist.

Throughout camp, we are scrimmaging and playing with a certain anger that has never been there before. Every guy has Moses's sneer and steely determination. I'm talking to Bobby and to Billy and to Little Mo, and we can all tell there is something different about this team. We felt great in '80 and '82, but we didn't have this kind of confidence. "Now I know what it feels like," says Little Mo.

"What?"

"Now I know what it feels like to know you can win every night."

One evening, I stop in to see Billy at his house, to talk over some issues from practice and generally to discuss the state of the team. Sometimes, if Billy and I have an issue, instead of raising it in front of the guys, we talk privately. We're practically neighbors, so it's easy to just knock on each other's door, which we do frequently.

Billy says he couldn't be happier with the way this team is performing.

I agree.

"Do you think we have enough?" he asks.

I start laughing. "I've been there three times. In 'eighty I thought we had enough. Last year, too. But this does feel different."

He nods. "It feels great."

45.

We open the season with six straight wins, including a double-overtime victory over Boston in which Moses goes for 28 with 19 rebounds, I score 28, and Toney adds 24. Moses plays fifty-six of fifty-eight minutes. We win ten of our first eleven and eventually are 50-7. Moses is the leading rebounder in the league; in fact, he has more rebounds than Dawkins and CJ combined the year before.

"Basically," Moses says, "I just goes to the rack."

In January, the Lakers come to town, and we play another overtime thriller, with Magic dropping a triple double on us, including 20 assists. McAdoo, Wilkes, Worthy, Nixon, all of them put up big games. Kareem is out with migraines. But the Lakers are still an all-star team.

But we have our own big stars now, with Moses and Andrew. I score 27, and on a deflected pass from James Worthy that I control near the half-court line, I get a breakaway with only Michael Cooper between me and kaboom. I have great momentum toward the hoop, but I want to make sure Cooper can't get at the ball before I bring it down. I know Cooper is a high flier—and a fine dunker himself—so I cup the ball in my right hand and rock it back behind me before windmilling it down for the jam. Cooper, realizing that he can't block the shot, wisely ducks beneath the backboard.

We finish regulation tied at 112, and then with twelve seconds left in overtime and the score tied at 120, Billy calls a time-out to set up a play for Moses. This seems like the prudent option. With Kareem out of their lineup, they don't have a shot blocker who can body up to Moses. But when Little Mo

Dr. J

gets the inbounds, he is trapped by the Laker guards and hands the ball off to Toney. Toney is having a good shooting night, already going 12 for 22 from the field, so he's not looking for Big Mo or me, he's thinking basket.

Billy is screaming at Toney.

Moses is already busy boxing guys out.

The entire Laker defense is converging on Toney, with Magic, Kurt Rambis, and Jamaal all closing quickly. On the left side of the key, about ten feet out, Toney stops and puts up a soft jumper, somehow clearing all those outstretched hands, and banks the shot in for the win.

As great as the victory feels, it is even more encouraging that we outrebound the Lakers 40 to 37. We sweep the regular season series with the Lakers.

In February, Billy and Pat call me into Pat's office and they ask me again, "Do you think we have enough to win it all?"

I repeat what I told them, that I thought we had enough in '77, in '80, in '82, so maybe that means you can never have enough.

They are both looking at each other. I can tell they are thinking about a specific move.

"Look," I tell them, "if there is something you can do to make this team better, then you have to do it."

That's when Pat swings a deal to get backup big man Clemon Johnson and shooting guard Reggie Johnson. Clemon is a huge piece of the puzzle, because he's basically as mammoth as Moses and almost as difficult to handle. We now have a backup center who doesn't give opposing defenses any kind of break, and with Reggie we have another bench scorer who makes up for the fact that we no longer have Steve Mix on the squad. Our younger players, Iavaroni and Earl "the Twirl" Cureton, are also making steady contributions. We are deep.

We send four players to the all-star game in Los Angeles— Big Mo Malone, Little Mo Cheeks, Toney, and me—where Marvin Gaye does his incredible national anthem, setting up the metronome, tick, tick, tick as he makes his art. (It's one of those moments, like Miles on his horn, or perhaps like one of my dunks, where it feels like it could spiral out of control, yet somehow it never does, and as he keeps singing, somehow harmonizing and working his voice into spaces in the music we didn't even know were there, it emerges as a masterpiece.) After the song, he comes over to greet the players. I've hung with Marvin a few times, though I'm closer to Teddy Pendergrass, obviously. But Marvin is one of those artists I admire.

"I got something coming out you need to hear," he says.

"Oh yeah?"

The album is officially titled *Sanctified Lady*. "They changed it up because I wanted it to be called *Sanctified Pussy*. You listen to it, but in your head, change the words to 'Sanctified Pussy.' It makes more sense."

I'm laughing. "You're crazy, man."

I am the MVP of the all-star game, scoring 25.

But Moses is the MVP of the league.

We finish 65-17.

Moses promises "Fo, fo, fo," and to this day I don't know if he meant we would sweep three straight playoff series or if he was simply promising that we will win the title. We have no doubts about the latter, as we annihilate the Knicks and Moses goes 38-17, 30-17, 28-14, and 29-14. Though he can operate out of any low-post position he wants to, Moses prefers to play facing the basket—he will end up teaching Hakeem Olajuwon many of his post-up moves during off-seasons in Houston, where the Dream is in college. "I think I'm learnin' that dude too much. He's getting too good," Mo tells me.

But in crunch time, Moses has no problem backing up to the basket for easy entry passes. And he's such a good foul shooter that there is no way for a defender to bail out by sending him to the line.

Our only playoff loss is to the Bucks. And we win game 5 at home to put them away.

Finally, we're back to the finals and the Lakers, who have won 58 games and are playing in their third championship series in four years. This is still a five-Hall-of-Famer team, and now they've added my old roommate Steve Mix to their roster.

Still, they are missing their rookie sensation James Worthy. But even if they had James, there is something different about our team this year, and I think even Magic and Jamaal can sense it. For one thing, whenever they take a lead, which they do early in games 1 and 2, we come storming back like it's no big deal. And I can see in Magic's and Jamaal's body language, they aren't as confident as in years past. During time-outs, when I catch a glimpse of them, they are looking at each other like, What do we have to do to put these guys away? In previous matchups, it would be our team that jumped out ahead and then felt helpless as the Lakers went on a tear and then put their dagger into us. Now we are in that position. They can play rabbit all they want, but with Moses down low, we are always coming back. His line this series is 27-18, 24-12, 28-19, and 24-23. We've completely reversed the rebounding situation, so that the Lakers are now struggling on the glass. Moses goes through stretches where he takes over games, going up and grabbing offensive rebounds and getting putbacks that break the Lakers' spirit.

The fourth game is typical as the Lakers pull ahead by 11 at the end of the third quarter at home. But then Moses goes to the rack and I have a stretch where I score 7 in a row in the fourth quarter.

Finally, Mo Cheeks steals the ball. I'm running downcourt ahead of him, waiting for Little Mo to set me up for the fast-break dunk, but Little Mo just keeps going. He makes one of his very rare dunks. It's over.

So this is what this feels like? The NBA title, after seven years of trying, and we are finally here, walking down the tunnel away from the Forum floor. In the locker room, I'm hugging Billy and Andrew and Little Mo. I'm up on the podium with Brent Musburger and Moses. I don't want to drink any champagne because I want to be completely, 100 percent sober in order to savor all this.

On my way to the shower, I'm hearing guys whooping and hollering when I catch a glimpse of myself in the mirror.

No matter how old I get, no matter what I accomplish, I still see a lanky fifteen-year-old staring back at me. I'm still Mom's son and Marky's brother. I'm still Junior.

Dr. J

1.

It goes by in the blink of an eye. A child is born, he grows, he rises, he becomes a man. As a father, you watch this progression, from crawling to walking to jumping, with pride at each developmental milestone but also with some pathos at the time passing, the baby, the child, repository of so many of our wishes and desires. Too quickly he is grown, gone.

You want to stop time, to freeze the frame, so you can live in that moment with that child forever, before the corrupting influences of the world rush in to besmirch innocence. The child will grow to a man. Yet in my mind's eye, when I see Cory, when I see any of my children, I still see them as the boys and girls they were. Just as I can still see in myself the boy I was.

I am riding in a convertible Cadillac down Broad Street, at the helm of a procession of Cadillacs nosing their way forward amid swirling confetti and the cheering throngs of Philadel-phians lined up a half-dozen deep, leaning out of windows and climbing up trees and lampposts. We have brought the champi-onship back from Los Angeles, and this is an exultant moment. This is a relationship between sports fans and their team, and like any relationship that works, this one is honest, our fans booing us when we let them down, bitterly complaining when we fail them. Now, when we succeed, their enthusiasm is unbridled. We owed them one but now we've paid in full.

Riding in my arms is Cory, age two, his eyes wide and bugging out at the crowd, the noise, the ticker-tape blizzard. The roar is deafening, fans running alongside the vehicles, shouting up at us. Moses Malone is behind me, holding up one finger. Billy is behind him. My children are all around me, Cheo, J, and Jaz. But my arms are around Cory. I'm sheltering him. From what? There is nothing but good intention out here today. He is still a child, so small. My instinct is to protect him.

"Daddy," he is saying, "Daddy." He is just finding his words, putting his mouth around those sounds, working a lazy tongue into syllables.

"It's loud, Cory," I tell him. "It's loud." I point to my ears.

"Daddy!" Jaz is shouting. "Daddy is a champion."

We're all champions, I want to tell Jaz. What I achieve we all achieve.

Or that's what I tell myself. I don't know that it's true. I now believe that the gifts of the father are not always passed down. Perhaps the flaws and weaknesses, but not always the gifts.

You want to protect your children, to keep harm away, to wrap them in the safe cocoon of paternal love. But I can't.

I put Cory on my shoulders. I want to put all of my children on my shoulders. I would carry them through the fires if I could.

Cory has my demons as well as my gifts. Even as a child, he is obsessed with order, with arranging his animals and matchbox cars in straight, neat rows. If J comes in and messes up the descending order of his Schleich animals, the careful logic of bunny to lion to bear to elephant to whale, Cory makes an angry scrunch, goes into a quick seethe, then he rearranges.

"Nah, nah, J, don't."

He's the only one of my boys to make his own bed, to tuck in his shirt, to pick the lint from his pockets.

As much as a father is his son's true north, his brothers, however, loom larger in his daily life. Cheo, nine years older, is in Cory's mind flawless and perfect. Millions may look up to Dr. J, but Cory worships at the altar of Cheo Erving and his lieutenant, J. And as the youngest, he is excused from the worst of Cheo's and J's cabals, but when they are receiving their regular lecture, there will be smiles and giggles in the midst of my sternest reprimands because behind me, there will be Cory, making faces, mugging, mocking my attempts at discipline. And as Cory becomes more verbal and better at arguing, he becomes Cheo's advocate. "Leave Cheo alone. Why you hollerin' at Cheo?"

Sometimes, when I see Cory, I see Marky—the same mischievous eyes, broad smile, russet skin, curly hair. I see the younger brother always in awe of the older sibling. I want to give to Cory what I never could to Marky. But Marky was studious, a hard worker, disciplined, focused. And for what?

The boy grows. He is becoming longer, leaner, the tallest of my children, a lanky boy, a good athlete, a fast runner. Yet he shares Cheo's disinterest in school, a result, perhaps, of his dyslexia, a diagnosis that sends us scurrying again to experts and specialists, to new programs and schools. By now Cheo is having his first brushes with the law, scrapes because of drinking and drugs. I've never smoked a joint, taken a non-prescribed medication, yet my boys are enthusiasts, will give over their time and, in the case of Cheo, his freedom for the

Dr. J

sake of getting high. I don't understand it. I don't know how to fix them.

So begin the steady visits to rehab centers and more counselors and sitting in treatment facilities and having family sessions with Cheo where I tell him how much Turquoise and I care about him and how he has hurt us. And the tearful confessions of dishonesty and shame, and the reconciliation, and the vows to stay clean, to stay sober, to attend meetings, to work one day at a time, and then the eventual relapse. Turq refuses to visit rehab, doesn't want to see her son that way and insists that it's not a disease, as the counselors tell us, but a damn weakness. I don't know. I only know what I am told, what the experts tell me.

And Cory's persistent defense of his brother continues, only now instead of blaming me for being too hard on his brother, he blames the world for keeping Cheo down. "Why are people always on Cheo's back? Why can't people accept him?"

Because of the decisions Cheo makes, I tell Cory, because he takes drugs and drinks alcohol and then finds himself in bad situations in bad neighborhoods. I've risen to get my children away from the culture of guns and violence that grows up around drugs, yet as teenagers, they all dabble with cocaine and marijuana. I want to understand. I try to have a dialogue on the subject.

"I'll meet you halfway," I tell Cheo. "What are you thinking?"

He's already a roughneck teen, in denim and $100 sneakers, a good-looking kid who, despite his time spent in custody and in rehabs, doesn't have a whiff of thug about him. He's still my boy. "Come on, explain your thinking?"

He nods, considering how to answer. "You know the people

in North Philly? They steal, but they steal because they have to, because they don't have anything and nobody gives them any respect and that's why and that's okay."

"Really?" I say. "You condone people breaking into homes and carjacking because they are the have-nots of the world?"

"Yeah."

"And if they came and stole from us, that would be okay?"

He thinks this over. "No, that wouldn't be okay. Not if they stole from us, but the fact that they steal? That's okay. I understand the mentality."

"Where did you learn that?"

"From being out on the street."

"And what about the law?"

He shrugs. "What about it?"

I'm trying to understand his ideas, but I disagree. This is America, the land of opportunity, and there is always some way that you can make it work, without breaking the law. Right? Always, always, right? (Or is my position somehow exceptional? Is my rise unique to me or my circumstances? I have to believe that in America, anyone can parallel my rise; it will just be in a different field or walk of life. It can be in business and not in basketball. This was my path. But it is one among many.)

I become the father always worrying over his prodigals. Those last few seasons in the league, I am compartmentalizing my life more than ever. I am asked to serve on corporate boards, I am joining civic organizations, I am a paragon of citizenship, at least by the external measures of the world. Yet my marriage is an effort, an act of will, but isn't every marriage? We get up every morning and decide we will do it again, one more day. My boys are in and out of trouble, throwing house parties when we are out of town, the police coming to raid the place. And

through this, I tell myself I am not failing as a parent, as a father, I'm trying, but why can't I get through to these boys?

During this period, I am driving back and forth to New York where Freda has fallen out of remission, where the diagnosis is dire as the cancer has now metastasized throughout her body. Irwin finds her the best doctors, a team of oncologists at Westchester Medical Center, but by the time they open Freda up, there is nothing to do but close her, the cancer marbling her lungs, her spleen. There are drugs, the doctors tell me, some experimental therapies, but Freda is fading, drifting in and out of consciousness, unable to focus on me, on her boys, Barry and Keith, both trying to be strong in the hospital room, but both frightened, their eyes wide and red with grief.

I try to manage the situation, to help make decisions. We measure time in days, then hours. Is that all she has?

My sister, who I looked up to and admired and who showed me what it is to be a good student, a good person, who led us, who was the captain Marky and I followed. She is reduced to this shattered husk on this hospital bed, the pain gripping her when she is awake. She is delirious, but still there are moments where she sees me. "June, you tell the boys to turn off the gas."

Mom is with us, sitting in a corner, her hands busy with a Bible. She is strength itself, to have buried one child and now sitting at the deathbed of another.

There is nothing I can explain to Barry and Keith as to why their mother is being taken. I could spin hokum about shortages of angels up in heaven, but these boys need her here. They know I will help them out, will do what I can.

I want Freda to know that blood will always care for blood. She knows.

She slips into a coma, her breathing steady but weak, so that when I arrive one morning where there was once my beautiful Freda, there is a frail woman attached to machines, screens blipping numbers, and nurses coming in to scribble on charts. Her fluids are measured, how much going in and out is carefully noted. Why? I don't know.

We pray. We hold hands around the bed. We remember fondly the good times, but there is no rationalizing why God would take Freda, on a rainy night in 1984, at just thirty-seven.

Turq stays away.

2.

Now, remember that bedroom back in the Parkside Gardens projects on Beech Street? There is only me, still jumping, still trying to see over that windowsill.

3.

Basketball doesn't recede in importance. Perhaps it was simply never as meaningful as it seems. It is why you know me, know my name, but it is not me. It is my profession, what I do—it's a strange profession in that those who become very good at it also become famous. Great dentists and accountants are unremarked upon when they enter a restaurant. Great basketball players are never unnoticed.

There is a fatigue that sets in after we win our championship, the accumulation of seven-game playoff series and championship finals spread over the years leaving us emotionally and physically drained. Perhaps that afflicts the Lakers when we sweep them; they are, like us, in their third final in four years. Long playoff runs tire out a team, as we are forced to return again and again to our emotional and spiritual wells. This could explain Boston's sweep the previous season at the hands of the Bucks. They were exhausted after their consecutive deep runs.

Despite the return of our front line intact, our all-star backcourt, we are taken out in the first round of the playoffs by the New Jersey Nets in a strange series in which neither team wins a home game. My knees are sore and my groin injury has recurred throughout that series, so I'm hobbled, feeling my age and playing through pain, averaging over 18 a game but never exerting my will the way I have in playoffs past.

4.

The next September, Billy and I are standing on the sideline at the Franklin and Marshall College gym watching a young player we've drafted out of Auburn, and Billy turns to me and says, "This kid is going to end my career."

I always make it a point to greet rookies, even rookies on another team. I'll go over and shake their hands and welcome them to the NBA. It's an easy gesture to make.

And it doesn't mean I won't be dunking on that rookie in the first quarter.

Charles Barkley is part of a new wave of players coming into the league. He's in the same rookie class as Michael Jordan, and both players are part of that generation of superstars who will become more powerful than coaches and general managers. They are great players who, in an era when salaries start to transform the relationship between player and organization, become so influential that they determine the course of franchises. I don't know if that's what Billy is thinking when he makes his casual comment, but he is speaking the truth. A coach's greatest skill in Billy's era is understanding and exploiting matchups and diagramming plays to take advantage of those matchups. In Billy's case, he also relies on his emotional feel for the game to figure out where he wants to go with the ball. (Also, he had Chuck Daly, who is a Hall of Fame basketball coach in his own right, as his assistant.) For coaches today, the primary talent is getting along with your superstar player, who for the first time is paid in multiples of your salary.

I am living through this transition, though I'm too late in my career to exert that kind of influence. When Barkley joins the 76ers, we have Moses, we have me, so he's not necessarily anything more than a promising rookie, a high draft pick who Pat picked up to add another rebounder. But when Charles shows up, he's a different rookie than any we've had before. He's still so country, all "yes, sir" and "no, sir," and nodding as he listens to Billy give instruction, but once he's out on the court, he just takes over. He's so intelligent that it's not a matter of not understanding or remembering the plays—or perhaps at that point in his development it is—but it's just that he's going to do things his way. If we're trying to run the break, the plan will be for Charles to get the rebound and make the outlet to Andrew or Mo, but Charles starts dribbling through traffic,

Dr. J

beats five guys, and then dunks the ball. That's what has Billy shaking his head, worrying about his career.

Charles just takes over practices, and this is a roster that has won a championship. His practice opponent is Marc Iavaroni, a starter on our title team, and Marc is a tough competitor, a Long Island guy who will stand up to anybody, but after a few days, I'm watching this with Little Mo and I tell him, "Charles is going to injure Marc."

Billy is screaming at him to give up the ball, and Charles isn't listening—because Charles can stop guys, and he can score on them, too. And that's basically the game. He's just not doing anything according to any plan that Billy recognizes. He's rocking and rolling, taking off, not giving the ball up. "Pass the ball, biscuit head," I shout at him on the break.

"Man, I can take it," and he goes up and dunks the ball over Marc. He doesn't do it the way it's drawn up, but it works.

Charles alters the dynamic of everything, so that the rest of us are scrambling to adapt to his game. I've never seen a rookie come in and do that before. But this is a different era, and Charles is ushering it in.

Charles reminds me a little of Bad News Barnes, only with the work ethic that Marvin never had. After signing his big rookie contract, he must have gone out and bought a half-dozen new cars, Mercedes, a Porsche, some huge SUV, a couple of BMWs. I only notice this because he's driving a different car to practice every day.

At one point, I stop Charles as we're walking back to our cars.

"How many cars do you have, Charles?"

"I got six."

"You don't need six cars, man."

"How many do you have?"

"One," I tell him. "You don't need six fancy cars to be somebody. With one car, everybody knows it's me behind the wheel. It's not about the car, it's about the brother driving it."

I tell Charles to be careful with his money. There are too many cases like Bad News Barnes who wound up broke, too many multimillion-dollar contracts that end up with a player deep in debt.

I hope I'm getting through to him.

I tell Billy, maybe it's like with our kids. "You have to meet this guy halfway."

5.

This is still a team built around Moses and his rebounding, but Charles has arrived and he quickly displaces Iavaroni in the starting lineup. And we win 58 games that year, finishing behind Boston and their 63 wins, including an early season 130–119 pasting the Celtics hand us in Boston, during which Larry Bird and I get into a famous fracas. At the time, the whole dispute seems unremarkable to me. It's office politics, the squabbles of men at work, a situation that escalated because the game was being officiated by only one referee, Dick Bavetta, because the second, Jack Madden, was forced to sit out with a knee injury.

Quinn Buckner of the Celtics is bringing up the ball. Larry and I get entangled as we're running along the left side of the court around the 3-point line. We're both pulling and tugging

at each other, and Bird hits the floor. Bavetta calls the offensive foul on Larry, and I don't think anything of it and run back up the floor, taking up position on the left side of the lane. I'm aware that Larry is upset, telling Bavetta he thinks it's a "bullshit call," and he's still steaming as he runs down the court. I can see by his expression and the way he is squaring up that he's not really getting into defensive position. He looks like he's getting ready to take a swing. Or at least that's what I think, so I reach out, just wanting to make sure that Larry can't clock me. I end up with my right hand on his chest, and my fingers around his neck, which infuriates Larry, who swings upward, trying to break my hold. It feels like a punch to me, so then I start swinging and it's on.

My teammates have my back, and it's Charles and Moses who quickly come over and grab Larry from behind.

Then M. L. Carr puts down his towel and grabs me and the benches have cleared. I'm not a fighter. I remember Ray Wilson telling me that if I get in a fight and get ejected, I've just let the other team impose their will. But sometimes, as the team leader or coach or even a bench player, you just have to take one for the team.

Larry and I are each fined $7,500. But Larry and I harbor no hard feelings because of it, and it never gets in the way of our working together in commercials or to promote the One on One: Dr. J vs. Larry Bird video game that will come out in 1983.

The only time we'll ever talk about it is when we both decide we aren't going to sign photos of the fight. That's not who we are.

Moses has his usual stellar year, averaging 24.6 points and 13.1 rebounds. I score 20 a night, and Toney contributes nearly 18 a game but is starting to struggle with the foot problems that will eventually end his career. It's a shame because Andrew is one of the great clutch players of all time, and had he stayed healthy, he would have been a Hall of Famer. Charles has a very good rookie season, averaging 14 points on 55 percent shooting and 8.6 rebounds in just twenty-eight minutes a game.

We have a deep playoff run, sweeping a 59-win Milwaukee team before losing to the Celtics in 5 games in another conference finals. I average only 17 a game, and against Boston I realize that at this point in their careers, the front line of Larry Bird, Kevin McHale, and Robert Parish is simply too strong for us. Mo and I are a little too old and Charles is a little too inexperienced. And the addition of Dennis Johnson slows down a hobbled Andrew Toney enough to put the Celtics over the top.

Billy quits after the season.

6.

You can look at our roster the next season—Moses Malone, Charles Barkley, Julius Erving, Maurice Cheeks, Andrew Toney, Bob McAdoo—and say, How is it that this team doesn't contend for a title? Under Matt Guokas, we win 54 games and get to the second round of the playoffs before Don Nelson and the Milwaukee Bucks finally exact their revenge. We're an old, slow team, and it becomes clear as the season goes on that Charles is the future of this franchise. Charles and Moses can't coexist. They both need real estate near the rim, and they both

collapse defenses, but there are only so many post plays we can run for both of them. At this point, Charles is outrebounding Moses 12.8 to 11.8 and averaging 20 a game while shooting 57 percent.

But more important, Matty wants a faster, more wide open offense, which doesn't suit Moses at this stage in his career.

Owner Harold Katz trades Moses to the Washington Bullets for Jeff Ruland, which is sort of like trading the best center in basketball for a knee problem. I mean, Moses will play through any injury. As long as he can—and sometimes even when he can't—he will get you 20 and 10. If I need one player to build my franchise, and Kareem isn't available, then the next call I'm making is to Moses Malone. I don't care if he's eighteen years old or thirty.

As for the thirty-six-year-old Dr. J? Maybe that's not a call I would make. (The twenty-two-year-old Dr. J is another story.) I spend my final season playing shooting guard. My knees are bothering me, my groin injury is acting up all season, but I am still a steady contributor to a 45-win playoff team.

One of the greatest challenges to playing as long as I have is the generation gap that develops with the younger players. The guys coming into the league are kids, with the concerns of teenagers, while my concerns are so often *about* my teenage children. I'm thinking of how to get from practice to my daughter's ballet recital while the younger players are thinking of where they can go to meet women. The Sixers and Matty make a special dispensation, allowing me to get to games on my own. I don't always travel with the team that last year, making my own arrangements and meeting the team in Milwaukee or New York or Chicago for shoot-around, playing the game, and then going about my business, which could have me making my own way to our next city.

The league throws a season-long farewell party for me that is unprecedented. Every city we play in that final year has a ceremony for me. I remember when John Havlicek retired, that there had been plenty of speeches and pregame festivities, but this was of a different magnitude. Each night on the final road trip, the home team is presenting me with plaques, banners, trophies; it's a remarkable outpouring and this is from opposing fans. Since coming into the NBA eleven years ago, I've managed to make even the fans in Boston somehow sad to see me go. That's the greatest tribute I can imagine as an athlete, more important than MVP awards or scoring titles or any of that, even more important than championships. That's what I'm thinking as the fans in Milwaukee and Chicago are cheering for me and I give them my little speech thanking them for the memories. I gave them something. I made them feel something.

I'm not sure why me and not some other players. Why am I the one who touches them? Is it physical ability? Certainly that's a part of it. But it goes back to what Leon told me years ago when we were barnstorming. Somehow, when people watched me, they got a taste of what it was like to be me. I bring them with me as I rise.

They talk about how I transformed the horizontal game and made it into a vertical game. But that was bound to happen at some point. While I am studying for my degree, I read about Martin Luther and the demands he nailed to the church door in Germany. One of the points the author made is that eventually someone was going to start the Reformation; it just happened to be Martin Luther. The tides of history were moving that way. Does that diminish Martin Luther's achievement?

I'm not comparing myself to the great German monk.

Dr. J

But basketball was moving in a certain direction. The playground game was coming indoors. Connie Hawkins and Elgin Baylor were transforming the sport, taking it airborne. What I was doing was simply refining the new version of the game we were all playing. It was going to happen eventually. I am just the player who nailed it.

7.

In my final home game at the Spectrum, I score 36 points. My last basket, an eight-foot turnaround, puts me over 30,000 for my career. Only Wilt and Kareem have reached that plateau at the time I retire. I averaged 24.2 points and finished eighth in games played with 1,243, seventh in career minutes, third in field goals, and fifth in field goals attempted, for a lifetime shooting percentage of over 50 percent. I even finish the all-time leader in steals.

There are eighteen thousand there that night. They have made a sign that says, WE'LL NEVER FILL YOUR SHOES, DOC. THANKS FOR THE MEMORIES.

I think to myself, Wait, it's not like I'm dying. As I tell the fans in every city, "Don't be sad, you should be as happy as I am happy, as my family is happy, that we are able to walk away from this beautiful game. . . . I'm going to take the time to understand myself better, to understand my family better and my family's needs and not volunteer to get into any situation that would be as consuming as this profession has been. . . . I'd like to be freed so that God's hand can work for me and my family in my life after basketball. I don't know what I'll do, but I'm going to allow my creator to tell me what's next."

8.

Shortly after I retire from basketball I honor my mother, and Marky and Freda, by completing my bachelor's degree.

9.

It has been a blessing. To escape from the jewelry store basement of life, and to be given a chance to travel, to see the country and the world, to make friends high and low, to have visited the White House three times, to have met presidents and First Ladies, artists, intellectuals, actors, musicians, the voices and leaders of my generation, and all through a game I play. I rise from those projects to these great heights, never forgetting where I am from or who I am—as if my mother would ever allow that to happen—and yet when I am finished with the game, I am almost surprised at this long ribbon of life still ahead of me, ahead of us, my family.

I sometimes go see Sixers owner Harold Katz up at his office building in North Philadelphia. Harold has built Nutrisystem into the second-largest weight-loss business in the country. I like to talk to him about how he got his start and just generally understand the mind-set of a successful entrepreneur. He tells me that he feels he has become a victim of his own success, that his business demands that he be there every day, that the success or failure of it depends on his micromanaging, and that's a big mistake. It sounds like a grander version of the old jewelry store back in Rockville Centre. I don't want that.

I have been preparing for this day for my last few seasons, knowing I will transition into business. My investment with Bruce Llewellyn in Philadelphia Coca-Cola has been lucrative, and with my degree in hand I am offered numerous seats on corporate boards, learning firsthand how the upper echelons of capitalism function. This, too, is one of the blessings of my rise, that I make connections with captains of industry, am invited to join them on the golf course and tennis courts, am called to take my place in society, another suburban dad, balancing children, wife, family.

I don't retire with the $100 million or more a modern-day star of my stature might walk away with. My highest salary was under $2 million a season, a fortune for a kid from Hempstead, and when I leave the game, I have about $4.5 million in cash and another $4.5 million in assets. Additionally, the NBA and David Stern pay me a few hundred thousand dollars a year to work for the league as a goodwill ambassador, helping to promote the game globally, talk to rookies and international players about the transition to playing in the NBA, and appear on behalf of the league in corporate and cultural settings. Still, I know this is transitional work for me, a perquisite of completing a successful career.

I fully plan to work every year for the rest of my life.

I've started the Erving Group to oversee my investments and centralize the managing of what we now call the Dr. J brand. I've always loved one-on-one basketball, believing it is a terrific way to hone my skills. It's been a part of my practice routine my whole career. And I remember those matchups with Pistol Pete and George Gervin as some of the highlights of my career. Why not share that with the fans and see if we can make some cash doing it? David Wooley, a Philadelphia business associate of mine, and I conceive the Clash of the Legends Pay Per View Event. The system is already in place, so we are just providing the content. If just 5 percent of the pay-per-view audience buys it, that's $18 million in revenue. Donald Trump has built a reputation by televising boxing and wrestling, and I have a good relationship with him. We plan three matchups at the Trump Taj Mahal in Atlantic City, Rick Barry versus Connie Hawkins, Tiny Archibald versus George Gervin, and for the main event, Kareem Abdul-Jabbar versus Dr. J. Kareem and I are guaranteed six-figure paydays, while the rest of the guys get a little less and we are all going to share in the pay-per-view sales. The event is going to be produced like Wrestlemania, with fire pots and smoke and loud music. And if this works, we can expand it, make it a regular event: Magic versus Bird, Michael versus Drexler, who knows?

One thing I don't consider is that one-on-one basketball is not as much fun to watch as it is to play. While the event generates plenty of buzz and media coverage, the actual PPV buy is disappointing as only fifty-five thousand fans pay to watch Kareem beat me 41 to 23 in four five-minute quarters. I won't defend the business decision, which definitely overestimated the amount of interest in one-on-one basketball, but I will defend my result, saying that Kareem had more time to prepare, since I was working so hard on putting together and then promoting the event.

Still, I have to give Kareem credit. He's the greatest.

Dr. J 401

10.

I'm inducted into the Basketball Hall of Fame in 1993. It's an honor to go in with Calvin Murphy, Walt Bellamy, and old, worthy adversaries Dan Issel and Bill Walton. As I am inducted, I feel Marky and Freda there with me.

My children Cheo, J, Cory, and Jaz are there. So is Turq.

Have I earned your love, all of you? No matter, I have to earn it every day again. That's what Ray and Earl and Don taught me. That's what my mom taught me.

11.

Every famous athlete retires twice, first from the game and then from talking about the game. The familiar career for the ex-jock is to take my place behind a desk, to sit with Bob Costas, Bill Walton, Peter Vecsey, Hannah Storm, and other pundits and players and spout wisdom and platitudes about the game. It takes a certain knack, a quickness of mind, and an ability to say nothing while sounding like I am saying something. I have to learn to speak while a producer is talking into my ear, giving me some statistics that I can use in support of a vacuous thesis about the first half of a basketball game that will be forgotten tomorrow. During the season I travel every weekend up to New York City to work at the NBC studios in Rockefeller Center, and then for the NBA finals I fly to the host cities, where I sit with Walton and Costas and Vecsey at our desk in the stands where we weigh in during halftime on how the Houston trapping defense is slowing down Penny Hardaway or Nick Anderson or how Hakeem is getting the better of Shaq down low. I find the analyses numbing. It is remarkable to me how we can fill hours, days even, of television talking about basketball, and yet I always feel that we are failing to communicate the truth of the game. Even here, in this book, I worry that I am not up to the task of explaining the essence of basketball as it is played at the highest levels. I feel that it is like trying to explain music through words or to describe a painting through text. You can give a feeling of the work, or compare it to something else, but you can't re-create the *actual* feeling of being on the court, or making that move, of imposing your will, of the precise moment that you realize you can reach the front of the rim. Because it is not a moment, it is a sense, an instinct, a flicker of insight and nerve so sudden that you have to act on it before it is a thought. What do you see? A subtle shift of weight, a lowering of the hands, a leaning forward, a glance, and that is enough to set off a chain of events. They are actions that stem from a thousand tiny instincts. But from where we are sitting above the court, we are unable to explain the game through these small moments, and instead talk about the Bulls' second chance scoring and the Rockets' bench production. I understand the need to do that, I have done some of that in this book, but I also know that we are simply describing a simulation of the game, rendering a three-dimensional activity in two dimensions. The truth, I think, is two men facing each other on a playground somewhere, and one of them senses the other is leaning to his left, only the defender isn't actually leaning, he is trying to force the ball handler to his own left, and so on, the game spiraling

Dr. J

upward in complexity and reaction and twitch and rise, from asphalt to high school, college gymnasiums to NBA parquet, and finally to here, where I sit behind this desk, talking about all of this as if it is nothing more than just those two kids in that school yard.

But as I make that drive every weekend up to New York to take my place behind the TV desk, or to fly down to Orlando or Houston or Chicago or Seattle or wherever the NBA finals are, I am reminded of something, of that boy riding his English racer bicycle along Sunrise Highway to work at Goldy's Jewelry Store. I'm a grown man in a fine suit behind the wheel of an imported automobile on the New Jersey Turnpike, but the feeling is exactly the same: I am headed back into that mailroom.

I don't want this. I don't want to spend the rest of my life talking about basketball.

12.

When Pat Williams of the Orlando Magic asks me to join him in Orlando as executive vice president of operations, I'm drawn to the position in part because it's not the typical ex-player job, but a real business position. Pat and John Gabriel, another former Sixers employee who would become Executive of the Year as Magic GM, coax me down to Orlando with a $1 million-a-year contract and the opportunity to work building up the team's off-the-court business opportunities.

I appreciate Pat and John believing in me as a businessman.

And I'm eager to move on from NBC, so I decide to move down to Orlando.

Turquoise wants to stay in Philly. We talk it over. We've been through so much together, so much betrayal and reconciliation, the worried nights talking over what to do with our kids. The joy of Jazmin graduating high school and going on to Spelman College, and the disappointment over Cheo getting arrested and ending up in a state penitentiary. J and Cory are finding their way; however, both have their issues with substances, sometimes following Cheo's lead. But through each of our hardships—and my own failings as a husband are part of that—we somehow pick up and carry on. We go through hell together. Somehow, there are enough good times to more than balance that out.

This time, however, Turq says she's not coming with me. Cory is still in school, and she wants him to finish in Philadelphia. It's not the best thing for the relationship, I know that.

"Are we separating?" I ask. We've been together over twenty-five years.

Neither of us is sure of what exactly we are doing. But we are certainly leaving the traditional marriage space, if we've ever really been in it. This is trouble. If I'm living on my own for a month, and I have an urge, then I'm likely to do something about it. Not every man is like that, so I have to acknowledge that this is my issue. Every man has his own time frame when he might stray, but for me, I know that going to live on my own in a new city is likely to be trouble.

Yet the relationship is durable. When Cory graduates high school, Turq moves down to Orlando and we pick up again. She is a soldier, I have to give her that. Cory has moved down with us as well, and he has struck up a friendship with young

Dr. J

Orlando Magic player Corey Maggette. The two of them are the same age, and I'm pleased by this relationship. Corey is a good influence, a Duke alumnus who is focused and disciplined. My son Cory, at nineteen, is still growing and I think he sees in Corey a role model. And removed from Philadelphia and some of his old influences, Cory is thriving down in Orlando. I tell him if he's not going to school, then he's going to have to get a job, and he gets part-time work at a Panera Bakery, and he's also starting back up at a junior college in Lake Mary, Florida.

I have a policy with all my children: if it's school, they know I will support their effort financially and emotionally. I believe in education. If they are looking for help with a business venture, then I need to look at that strictly as a dollars-and-cents issue, with the obviously more generous view that I'm inclined to make toward my own flesh and blood.

My middle son, J, or Julius Erving III, has gone on to become successful in his own right, building the music management firm Erving Wonder along with Troy Carter and selling that to the British management company Sanctuary. J has developed and worked with acts like Angie Stone, Floetry, Tyga, and Nelly. He's an unquestioned success in his field and if leveraging the Julius Erving name has helped him, then I'm both proud and impressed, because sometimes even I struggle to leverage that name.

After college, Jaz was in sales at Saks Fifth Avenue before starting her own events planning company, Jazmin Tea. Jaz now lives in Los Angeles, where she is pursuing a master's degree in psychology.

Cheo still breaks my heart, as he has been in and out of prison. He's even told me he doesn't mind prison, that he appreciates the routine. I don't always understand him, and we may not always be friends, but we will always be family. A father's love for his son transcends understanding.

13.

Occasionally over the years I hear about Alexandra. I know she's a promising tennis player. In that world, the pro tennis circuit, there are already plenty of rumors circulating about who her father is. I run into the tennis legend Pancho Gonzalez down in Miami, and he starts talking to me about Alexandra, about what great strokes she has and the way he's saying it, it's obvious that he knows she's my daughter. And at one point I'm walking with John McEnroe through LaGuardia Airport—we're actually on our way back from Michael Jordan's golf tournament—and he's telling me about Alexandra, how good she's getting, how she's turning pro. So, among tennis people, my paternity is well known.

Still, I'm caught off guard in 1999 when Alexandra turns pro two weeks after graduating from La Jolla Country Day School and makes a great run at Wimbledon. She's the first woman qualifier in the Open Era to make a semifinal. The English are going crazy over her play and her dainty curtsies as she acknowledges their applause after another victorious point. But the speculation is becoming rampant about who her father is. A sportswriter from a local newspaper has been calling me repeatedly, asking questions about Alexandra, which I'm careful to dodge. But when Alexandra makes the semis, the

paper publishes a story that I've denied being her father, which I never do. I simply refused to corroborate his story.

I have no choice but to release a statement confirming that I am the father and asking the media to give her space on this issue. I'm hoping that will put the story behind her before her semifinal match against Lindsay Davenport.

I also have to tell my other children that they all have a sister they haven't known about. I've paid a terrible price for my sins, I suppose, and there is some justice in that. But why should Alexandra have had to pay any price? What sin did she commit?

Samantha obviously did a fantastic job as a single mom raising her daughter, and I have nothing but praise and admiration for both of them. As I said, there are facets of my life that are less than heroic. This is an area where I wish I could have done it differently. I wish I could have been there for her from the start, to have fought harder against Turquoise's ultimatum about how this was to be handled. (I can't blame Turq, of course. She was just protecting our family.) There is no villain here, though I would say—and this is my book—that there is one person who is more at fault in this affair than the rest, and I raise my hand.

Alexandra and I have since reconciled and have spent plenty of time trying to forge a relationship after over twenty years of a vacuum. She knows her brothers and sisters, and they know her. I'm trying to encourage those relationships. She's had some problems with injuries. As she's making her comeback, she's asked me to come watch her play, and I did, going to a tournament in Hilton Head. I've given her substantial financial support as she tries to revive her tennis career. She's a wonderful athlete and deserves that opportunity.

But she's also got to be sensible. Is it really worth spending several thousand dollars in air travel, accommodations, and additional expenses only to come in third and win $900? At one point in Los Angeles, we sit down and have a talk.

"I want to be involved in your life," I tell her, "but I don't want it to just be a financial arrangement."

She nods.

"I want us to be father and daughter," I say, "and that means more than you calling me and asking for checks."

Relationships with grown children are complex, and perhaps ours was bound to be even more complicated because of all the time we missed. How could it not be? But at least we have a relationship.

I miss her. I always missed her.

14.

Turquoise and I are planning a dinner party. We've always thrived in social settings, in many ways getting along better in public than we do in private, which in a lifestyle such as ours is not as superficial as it sounds. We spend a great deal of time in public as Julius and Turquoise Erving. A dinner party, a fine meal with some good friends, is an important step for us in reestablishing our bond, in figuring out how we are together.

Turq is in the kitchen, working, and she asks Cory if he'll run out to get some bread from Panera Bakery. He's done this plenty of times. It's a bread run, like my going up to Mrs. Pete's back in Hempstead. He gets into his black Volkswagen Passat,

carefully pulls his seat belt over his dress shirt so as not to wrinkle it, and he's gone.

When Cory was eighteen, we visited former NBA point guard and head coach John Lucas's rehab facility in Katy, Texas. (John was the point guard on the Bucks team that knocked us out of the playoffs my last season in the league.) I had taken Cory down there because of his dabbling in drugs, and after a few days, John called me and said he didn't think Cory was an addict. Yet he was definitely prone to experiment with drugs, but then there are doctors and lawyers and NBA players who do that and aren't considered addicts. First with Cheo and now with Cory, I've tried to find the right approach: rehab, tough love, counseling, therapy, I don't know. I do know that a drug addict is going to use until he hits bottom, and that bottom is very often jail, or an institution, or worse.

Along with Cheo, Cory had been detained by the police when he was seventeen for being in possession of a crack pipe and burglarizing a car over in Altamonte Springs. But it was easy for me to rationalize that he had been under Cheo's influence.

As I watch Cory drive off that evening, I try to tell myself, as I have at least a dozen times before through his life, that this time maybe it's different; this time maybe he really has changed.

But when he doesn't come home that night, Turquoise and I do our best to struggle through a social evening while exchanging knowing glances that Cory may be out on a drug run. I'm angry, first that he could be so irresponsible about an errand we've asked him to do, and so thoughtless as to his family and our worries about him. We go to bed that night, sharing our frustration that Cory hasn't become more responsible, more mature, and when he is still not there the next morning,

I'm thinking of what I have to do to make Cory grow up. I had been hoping that being around mature young men like Corey Maggette would wake him up, but now I see that I was naive.

In my office that Monday, I'm trying to focus on work, but throughout that day, there is a rising sense that something is very wrong, that Cory isn't out partying. I check in with Turq at home a couple of times. This is not like him. He doesn't just drop out of sight. Or if he does, he will be with Cheo or some of his other friends, and maybe they are up to no good, but we have an idea of where he is. To just get in his car and drive away? This doesn't sound like Cory.

Finally, after another long night, we call the police. They retrace his steps, confirm that he stopped to buy bread, and subsequently stopped at a fitness center in the same shopping complex. That was the last anyone had seen of him. From there, it should have been a straight shot back to our house. Because of the circumstances, and Cory's own history, the police start to suspect foul play. After a few days of news reports about Cory's disappearance, we have thousands of tips: someone who has seen Cory in a 7-Eleven, another who saw him buying drugs down in Altamonte Springs, another who saw him at a movie theater. None of them pan out.

I remember the feeling of our team falling behind in a conference finals or NBA finals, that sense that we are simply not doing enough to win, that despite our efforts, Boston or Los Angeles is pulling away. However intense those feelings were, they are nothing compared to what I am going through now, this sense that Cory is out there, somewhere, perhaps in pain, perhaps suffering, and there is nothing I can do to help him, there is nothing I can do to even find him. This is what defeat feels like, forget losing a basketball game.

Dr. J

There are advantages to being Dr. J, and one of them is that I can use to my advantage the same media that sometimes is so bothersome. I appear on *Larry King Live* to talk about Cory and to ask America to help find him. President Clinton, whom I met a few weeks earlier at a Medal of Freedom ceremony for Nelson Mandela and F. W. de Klerk, sends Secret Service agents to help with the investigation. We're having prayer meetings, vigils. We hire a psychic who handles some of Cory's possessions and tells us she sees him surrounded by water. We have local lakes and rivers dragged. But nothing. We're checking every body of water in the area.

There are mornings when I sit in my car and cry, when I can't bear to look at Turq because it reminds me of what we are missing. A hard silence descends on our house. Cory's brothers and sister come, and then go, after a few days of searching with no results. What can they do? To drive around aimlessly, calling his name out a car window as if looking for a missing dog? There is nothing but to stumble through our daily routines, of answering calls, of going to supermarkets, all while wondering where he is.

There is a break in the case after thirty-eight days, when a gate attendant at a neighboring development says that Cory used to come driving past his guardhouse all the time, taking a sort of back road to our place to the west. The attendant actually thought Cory lived in that development instead of Alaqua.

There is a cat road that cuts over, through some land that is being cleared for development. The development is marked by some cones and pilings from freshly cut trees. The cones and pilings are moved around by the crews, depending on where they are working and how much progress they are making. Next to this cleared area is a retention pond.

The police look at aerial photographs of the area and notice the pilings had been shifted, so that previously there had been room to drive between them and the pond, but about a month ago, they were so far to the right that the road actually went to the left of the pilings. This is an open area, a sort of depression before a slight rise, and if you are driving fast, you would use the pilings to set your course, the pond being almost invisible as you approach.

The pond is only eight feet deep and they find Cory's car barely submerged. Cory's body is in the passenger seat. He drove right into the water, his engine pulling the car down, the water pressure preventing him from opening the doors.

I listen to the sheriff explain how Cory died. The details about how cars sink, about how Cory was thrown forward when the car hit the water. I think about the panic he must have felt, the car sinking, my boy struggling to open the door, the slow suffocation. I think about the fear, about how his last feeling must have been fear.

About how alone he was.

15.

I look at photos of my children and I can barely remember: When did I play with them? What did we play? Go fish? Memory? Checkers? We must have played. I look at photos of Cory. He's a beautiful boy. Did I play enough with him? Did I spend every minute with him I should have? Why didn't I stop everything, drop all plans, hold all calls, cancel all subscriptions,

and turn off all televisions, shut down computers, switch off cell phones, turn off engines, and tell the post office to hold my mail. Why didn't I quit basketball, quit society, quit the world, and quit everything and everyone so I could play one more game of checkers with Cory, tell him once more that I am his father and I care about him, sit with him just one more time and lie to him that everything will be all right?

16.

Marky, Freda, Bobby, Wendell, Tonk, Cory. Our lives are also the stories of our loved ones' deaths.

But our lives must also be the celebration of those lives.

17.

The years after Cory's passing are a blur, a period of mourning during which I try to fulfill my professional obligations. I'm physically present, at work, in my marriage, but emotionally, I'm gone.

We survive infidelity, lies, fights, disdain, disrespect, and cruelty. But Turq and I can't make it past the death of our son. Like so many before us, we become a statistic and end up filing for divorce.

18.

I take into my business life the same philosophy I tried to take through my basketball career. The words of Don Ryan, Earl Mosley, and Ray Wilson continue to be those that I apply in my daily life. I don't believe in those *Art of War* mantras that so many modern executives seem to try to do business by. I'm trying to build a legacy by doing things the right way, making deals and investments where I can leverage my name while also trying to make a difference. With Bruce Llewellyn, we build the Philadelphia Coca-Cola Bottling Company into one of the largest minority-owned businesses in the United States, with over twelve hundred employees and $540 million in annual revenue. I'm a co-owner and board member. And from Bruce I learn to empower employees and incentivize them so that their interests are aligned with the business.

Bruce shows me the way in so many areas. In 1985 we join together with Essence Communications' founders Edward Lewis and Clarence Smith, and several other investors to buy a television station in Buffalo from Capital City Communications, who got a substantial tax benefit by selling to a minority buyer. As a result, Bruce was able to put up less for WKBW, and when we turn around and sell the station to Granite City, I more than double my investment.

After my retirement, he puts together another syndicate to buy the New York Times Cable Company, which serves over 170,000 homes in New Jersey. Bruce and I are part of a team that puts up $55 million in cash as part of the $420 million purchase. We get in and get out within five years, again making a great return.

One of my proudest achievements is starting the first minority-owned NASCAR racing team, with former football great Joe Washington. The Washington-Erving Motorsports team includes drivers like Mark Green and Tony Roper.

I am a member of the board of directors of Converse, EA Sports, Saks Fifth Avenue, Darden Group, and Sports Authority. I continue to work with and appear in endorsements for a number of brands, including Dr Pepper, Crown Royal, and Converse.

We are always seeking out new investments, with varying degrees of success. Yet one of my biggest investments turns out to be my costliest. I first met Chuck Watkins at Kathryn Crosby's golf tournament in North Carolina—she's Bing's widow—and we hit it off and he became a close family friend. I partner up with Chuck, and we buy a prime golf course up in Tucker, Georgia, called the Heritage, a beautiful twenty-seven-hole operation with old-growth trees and rolling hills. I'm going to be putting up $3 million and borrowing the remaining $11 million from the bank. (At the peak of the market, this place was valued at $22 million.) But even if it never gets back to those numbers, the course makes sense operationally. I have Ken I. Starr review the deal and he says it looks kosher to him. It will turn out that Ken was preoccupied with some other matters, as he was soon to be indicted on twenty-three counts of fraud and money laundering. Luckily, none of my assets were tied up in that scandal.

The golf course revenue model is both private memberships and daily play. Chuck knows his way around a golf course, so this business seems like a smart way to leverage capital, investing $3 million to add a desirable $14 million property to my portfolio, and one that will more than pay for itself. The idea is that Chuck will put in sweat equity and also raise some private placement investors from his circle of contacts in Atlanta.

Well, we run into some problems pretty quickly, and I'm lucky that I have a new partner, my true life partner, my wife Dorys.

19.

I'm standing at baggage claim at Orlando International Airport for over forty minutes waiting for my bags. That's a long, long time, but as I'm looking around at my fellow passengers, I see a beautiful brunette and I figure I might as well kill time as pleasantly as possible by striking up a conversation. I admit that I'm making a little bit of a move, but hey, those bags are taking an awfully long time.

I introduce myself and give her my Orlando Magic card and extend a standing invitation to an Orlando Magic game. "Get some friends. Call me if you feel like coming."

A few weeks later she calls me. She's not a basketball fan so she had no idea who I was when I gave her my card. She's since shown it to her friends. "They said you're called Dr. J. What kind of doctor are you?"

She comes to the game with a few friends, and I visit with them at halftime, and after the game I ask Dorys if she would like to go the movies.

A few nights later we go to see the movie *Soul Food*, and we hit it off.

Dorys is an independent woman. She left Honduras at six-

 **417**

teen to model in Europe and then lived in Canada for a couple of years. She worked in a jewelry store for a while in Orlando before starting her own gift shop in one of the hotels downtown. She's a serious, driven woman, and gorgeous as well. That's a combination that always worked on me.

I'm not looking for a serious relationship, yet I find that Dorys becomes a part of my life.

Let me be honest here: I meet Dorys while I'm still with Turq, during that period when she is living in Philadelphia and I am in Orlando. We have our first son, Jules, before Turq and I split up for good. I'm not proud of that—I am, of course, fiercely proud of Jules—but that's the truth and I've promised to tell my whole story. Whatever shame I feel at having sired children out of wedlock is balanced by the fierce pride I take in them, in all of them.

When Turquoise moves down to Orlando, I tell her about Dorys and Jules, and I make arrangements to take care of them, but I know it makes reconciliation that much more difficult.

As I say, mine is an American life, fully lived, and I am not above reproach for my shortcomings. I hear my mother's stern voice and still feel her disappointment.

In the bad winters of the '90s, I encourage my mother to move down to Florida. In 2000, she finally closes down her hair salon and leaves Long Island for good.

Mom moves in with me and spends the last few years of her life living in Orlando. She's in and out of the hospital with respiratory problems. She has bursitis, arthritis, all the itises that happen to our seniors. Over a period of two years, from ages seventy-eight to eighty, she deteriorates before my eyes. I lose my mother in 2004.

20.

Marky, then Freda, then Callie Mae.

Now there's only me.

21.

I'm living in St. George, Utah, with Dorys and our children. In addition to Jules, there is my younger son, Justin, and his little sister, Julieta. Julieta was born a year after Callie Mae passed. She has my mom's soul. My new family, my second wave of children. I am present for these kids in a way I never could be while I was an active basketball player. The only rivals for their affection are the golf course and my business. Dorys is a fierce, proud, intelligent woman who is homeschooling our children. I am the father I could never be with my older children. I'm more mature, more present, more aware of the passing of time, of how precious these years with young children are. I have the harsh lessons of Cory (and Marky), of how fleeting a life is and how each day with our children is unique, because by tomorrow they have become someone new, still beautiful, but new.

We moved to St. George, nestled against the Nevada border, because I wanted to try living in the American West. I'm one of two African-Americans in town; the other is former Utah Jazz forward Thurl Bailey, and I find the climate and area agreeable. And for my young children, it's suburban in ways

that remind me a little of Hempstead, but Hempstead when I was a boy, not today.

This could be the life, a beautiful wife, great kids, and a steady income from the golf course and my other investments. That's the plan, anyway, only I start receiving phone calls from Chuck asking me for additional capital.

"Additional capital?" I say. "There isn't any additional capital."

He tells me that he can't make payroll, can't make the note on the lease.

I'm thinking, What the hell is going on there?

Dorys knows Chuck, and she's a keener judge of character than I am, and she immediately senses that this is trouble.

I send Ray Wilson up to see what's going on. Ray is pushing seventy, but he's still sharp and he goes up there and he immediately suspects that Chuck isn't being straight. For one thing, Chuck has bought a new $900,000 house. And where would he get the down payment for that? It turns out, as he admitted to me and to the district attorney, that he took it out of our corporate funds as an advance compensation.

Also, we have a large Korean and Japanese clientele, and these guys like to pay cash. Chuck has been setting that cash aside and it never makes it into our corporate accounts.

Ray tells me what's going on and I fly to Atlanta to confront Chuck, laying out the details of what we know.

He explains that all of this, the cash, the down payment on the house, that was advance compensation. Our deal was that he gets $4,000 a month to run the place and a substantial equity share in the business. There was no provision for advance compensation.

I call the district attorney, and we set up a meeting, where we tell Chuck that he has two options: either relinquish all claims of ownership or go to jail.

And in this meeting, Chuck is still arguing that this is advance compensation, that it was all legit, and I'm like, Chuck, we got you by the balls, now walk away.

We have to move to Atlanta to run the golf course. Dorys doesn't even blink. Her attitude is that we roll up our sleeves and make this thing work. It's our money, it's our family's future.

Now I'm stuck running a golf course—I feel like I'm back in that jewelry store basement—and I don't know the first thing about it. Chuck has let the place fall apart, the bank is hounding us for its note, suppliers and vendors are already fed up with our operation, and the staff has long since given up on us. I have an office on-site, I bring in a few trusted associates, sons and nephews of former teammates, and even Cheo comes in and becomes our gardener.

I'm there every single day for two years. Dorys is right there with me. But we just can't make it work. The numbers don't add up. Additionally, another supposed friend of mine has run out on a $150,000 debt he took out in my name. He was a member of my church. Dorys and his wife are good friends. His children and my children are playmates. When I was looking for a line of credit for the golf course, he introduced me to a bank that set up the collateralized loan. My friend asked me to cosign a loan for another $150,000. I thought, This guy is a friend, a fellow churchgoer. What could go wrong?

He never pays his debt. And that gets thrown on my balance sheet. Now I'm financially upside down with a failing golf course that has me owing $3 million to the bank. The bank forecloses. I'm underwater. I'm living month to month.

I feel so ashamed at how I've let my family down. But Dorys won't take any pity on me. She fixes me with that fierce expression. "Don't worry, honey, we're gonna be all right."

I leave the golf business and find myself with a negative net worth, but I make a commitment to myself to pay all my debts. I will pay all my debts.

Basketball saves me, as we take my trophies and medals and rings out of storage and auction them and raise nearly $4 million, pay down our debts, and buy a new house in Buckhead. I never displayed any of that stuff, so it was a blessing to be able to share it with the fans all around the world in the most successful athlete's memorabilia auction ever.

Now I'm starting over. With my nephew Barry, and my attorney Dorna Taylor, we're building up Dr. J Enterprises. The main revenue stream right now is through my various endorsement contracts and a new role with the 76ers as a strategic consultant. Last year, our revenue was over $1 million. And now we are joint-ventured in other areas, including cell phone tower development and founding a cord blood bank.

I always knew I would work for the rest of my life.

22.

In the mornings, I drive my children over to Lifetime Fitness in Buckhead with indoor basketball courts. Julieta does gymnastics, spinning cartwheels by the side of the court. "Daddy, look at me."

I watch her rise.

Justin and Jules like to play pickup games with their friends. Both are fine young players. Jules, at six foot three and in eighth grade, already has the height and talent to fulfill his potential and may possibly carry on the legacy, having recently enrolled at a private high school basketball power.

When they're done playing pickup, I'll challenge them to a game of two against one, repeating that two should always beat one. The same rules: no layups, no dunks. At sixty-three, I'm not much of a dunker anymore, but give me some time to limber up and a warm gym, and I'll still throw some down. Jules is already dunking.

Jules has gotten more confident, more aggressive, and obviously is looking forward to the day he can dunk on his dad.

Our games are spirited, as I'm not ready to get posterized by my own son.

Jules takes a pass from Justin, he faces me, he jab-steps and goes for the rim.

He rises.

I rise.

We rise.

Dr. J

Acknowledgments

FROM Dr. J

Everything I have accomplished in life has been due to the loving support of those people closest to me: my parents, Julius Sr. and Callie Mae; my stepfather, Dan Lindsay; my siblings, Alexis Alfreda and Marvin Vincent; the Abney family and the Erving family, including my wife (Dorys) and children (Cheo, Julius III, Jazmin, Alexandra, Jules, Justin, and Julieta), my grandchildren, aunts, uncles, cousins, nieces, nephews, and in-laws. They were and are the source of my ability to soar and score and rebound from improbable circumstances that arose during my sixty-three-year journey. Without their love and support, there would be no me.

In the course of working on my autobiography, I found myself dependent on trusting a number of people to get to the finish line. Karl Taro Greenfeld tops the list because he brilliantly captured my voice and transformed our conversations into tales for generations to enjoy. Dedicated and patient describe David Hirshey and Barry Harbaugh, who managed to keep the project moving after numerous setbacks and who brought experience and editorial input to our collaboration. My team, Dorna Jenkins Taylor, Esq., Barry Bookhard, Val Small, and

Ray Wilson, provided legal, business, and personal support every step of the way. Alan Rubin and Matt Guma assisted in making my first publishing deal the win-win that it ultimately became. I sincerely thank all of them.

Additionally, I would like to thank the following people who have been and are still profoundly instrumental in my journey through life (in alphabetical order by first name):

Al and Mabel Erving, Al Bianchi, Al Domenico, Al Williams, Albert and Doris Taxin, the Albert Boys (Marv, Steve and Al), Alexandra and Samantha Stevenson, Allen J. Bernstein, Alonzo Somerville, Andy Haggerty, Annie Meyers-Drysdale and family, Archie Rogers, Artie Hecht, Artis Gilmore and family, Artise Irving, Barry Bookhard, Beatrice Turner, Bennett and Judie Weinstock, Bill Cosby and family, Bill Zaruka, Billy Crystal, Billy Cunningham, Billy Melchioni, Bob and Peggy Corrao, Bob Beamon, Bob Billingsby, Bob Brown, Bob Chopper Travaglini, Bob Costas, Bob Elliott and family, Bob McCullough, Brad Martin and family, Brady Speler, Brenda Sabino, Brian Alchermes, Brian and Maryann Thompson, Brian Taylor, the Brower family, Bruce Blackwell, Burdette and Mica Hawkins and family, the Burgess family, Buster Wolosky, Caldwell Jones, Carl Spider Lockhart, Carol Bromery, Catherine Costa and family, Cecil Watkins, Celia Sabino, Charles Barkley, Charles McIlwain and family, Charlie Scott, Cheo Erving, Chloe and Charles Turner and family, Christine and Grover Washington Jr. and family, Chuck Daly, Clem Ballas, Clemon Johnson, Clente and Ojetta Flemming and family, Clint Richardson, Clyde Drexler, Cousin Gladys Simmons and family, Craig Drake, Dan Lindsay, Dan Napier, Dana Napier, Danielle Triplett, Danny Meachum and family, Dave Chapman, David Keith, David Porter, Debbie Mazer,

Debra Carroll, Dick Gregory, Don Massman, Don Ryan, Donna Skinner, Dorna and William Taylor III and family, Dorys Erving, Dot Farmer, Doug Duncan, the DuVal family, Dr. Ed and Raydelin Guindi, Earl Cureton, Earl Mosley and family, Eileen and Robert Irving and family, Elaine Wynn, Elgin Baylor and family, Enrique McPhail and family, Eric Dickerson, Ernie Cambridge, Estell and Brunson Abney and family, Ethan and Marisol Penner and family, Franco and Dana Harris, Frank Hairston, Frank Lenny Carter, Fred Leidman, Fritz Massman, Gabriella Vallerdares, Garry Saunders, Gary Brokaw, Gary Leavitt and family, George Gervin, George Rigopoulis, George Tinzley, Marie Henderson, Gerhard and Sigrung Von Heeson and family, Grace Fenton and family, Greg and MaryAnn Coleman, Gus Williams, Hannah Storm Hicks, Harith Wickrema, Harold Katz and family, Hempstead Salvation Army teammates, Henry Bibby, Herb and Stormy Washington, Herman Curtis, Hershal Smith, Hwa Wu, Irwin Weiner, Isadore and Adele Becker and family, J. Bruce Llewellyn, Jack Adias, Jack Leaman, Jack Smith, James Brown Jr. and family, Janie Smith and family, Jari and Silvia Vallerdares, Jason Williams, Jazmin Erving, Jeffrey Haller, Jeffrey Osbourne, Jennifer Bragg, Jennifer Thompson, Jerome Riggs, Jerry and Sandra Simmons, Jesse Jackson, Jim and Fran Gray, Jim and Monique Brown, Jim Chestnut, Jim Eakins and family, Jim Hill, Jim Kelley, Jim Lagagne, Jim Wade, Jimmy and Marguerite Maggette and family, Jodi Williams, Joe and Meadowlark Washington, Joe Farmer, Joe Smith, John Butch Purcell, John Cardone, John Clark, John Gabriel, John Hannah, John Kilbourne, John Lucas, John Smoltz, John Tedesco, John Williamson and family, Johnny Green, Johnny Red Kerr, Joseph Zohar, Jr. Bridgeman, Juanita Hayden, Jules Erving, Julieta Erving, Julius Erving III, Justin Erving, Karen and Bob Natkin and family, Karen Ramos Coleman and family, Karen Russell, Keith Bookhard, Keith Williams, Ken Jr. and Melissa Griffey, Kenneth Ira Starr, Kenny Leon, Kenny Smith, Kevin Loughery, Kim Hughes, Kim Willis, Kira Clifford, KT Schaefer, Kwaku Leon and Afie Saunders and family, Lafeea Watson, Larry and Mickey Magid, Leah Lally, Lee Elder, Leroy Brinkley, Lionel Hollins, Lisa Borders, Lloyd Pinkie Gardner, Luz Gonzales, Lynn Swann, the Mackey family, Magic Johnson, Marc Reisman, Marcus Allen, Marcus Iavaroni, Margaret Washington, Martha Korman Zumival and family, Martha Ramirez, Marty Sloan and family, Marvin Gaye, Pastor Marvin Moss, Maryann and Gregory Coleman and family, Maurice Lucas and family, Mel and Joan Davis, Mel Speler, Dr. Mel Stanley, Melissa Springate, Melvin Abney Jr. and family, Michael Jordan, Michelle Williams and family, Miguel and Rosalia Sabino, Mike Rogers, Mike Storen, Monjur Ali, Moses Malone, Murray Bullock, Miles Davis, Nancy Lieberman, Neill Wright, New York Nets teammates, Oprah Winfrey, Pat O'Brian, Pat Williams, Patti LaBelle and family, Peter and Wendy Corry and family, Peter Broaca, Peter Lev, Phil Jasner and family, Philadelphia 76ers teammates, Prospect School teammates, Quinn Buckner, Rachel Tran, Ramon Bardales, Ramond Floyd and family, Mr. and Mrs. Randolf Bromery, Ray and Gloria Wilson, Ray Leonard, Ray Scott, Re Kelly and family, Reggie Jackson, Reggie Whitehead, Ric Wilson, Rich De Voss, Rich Jones, Richard Dent, Rick Barry, Rick Vogeley, Robert Mayrant and family, Robert Pollack and family, Rodney and Takata Harrell, Roger Morningstar, Roland Fatty Taylor, Ron Bectal, Ron Wilson, Ronald Abney and family, Ronnie Rabina and family, Ronnie White, Roosevelt

High School teammates, Rosalin and Curtis Springate, Sean Lynch, Shahara Llewellyn, Sharon Dunn and family, Shelly Hatton, Sherman Brown, Shivani Desai, the Sloan family, Sonny Hill, Spike Lee, Stedman Graham, Dr. Stanley and Dorothea Lorber, Dr. Steve and Dari Alchermes, Steve and Maryalice Mix and family, Steve Wynn, Teddy Pendergrass and family, Terry Tyler, Tim Bassett, Tom and Bruni Reed and family, Tony and Lorriane Ferdinand and family, Ukee Washington, UMass teammates, Val and Garfield Small and family, Victor and Ester Green, Virginia Squires teammates, Warren Moon, Wendell Haskins, William F. Russell, Williard Sojourner, and Yvette Beauchamp and family.

PEACE AND BLESSINGS,
Julius Erving

FROM Karl Taro Greenfield

Much appreciation to my Harper starting five: Barry Harbaugh, David Hirshey, Gail Winston, Maya Ziv, and Jonathan Burnham. Also, gratitude to David Kuhn, Becky Sweren, Stanislaw Radzicki, David Bar Katz, and Ptolemy Tompkins. My family, Esmee, Lola, Silka, Foumi, Josh (and Noah) were, as always, along for the ride. And finally, Julius Erving is the most gracious subject and collaborator I have ever worked with. Thank you.

About the Authors

JULIUS ERVING is one of the greatest professional basketball players of all time and an American icon. He lives in Atlanta with his family. This is his first book.

KARL TARO GREENFELD is the author of six previous books, including the acclaimed memoir *Boy Alone* and the novel *Triburbia*. His fiction has appeared in *Harper's*, *The Paris Review*, *Best American Short Stories*, and the PEN/O. Henry Prize Stories. He is a longtime writer for *Time* and *Sports Illustrated*, among many other publications, and his nonfiction has been collected in *Best American Sports Writing* and *Best American Nonrequired Reading*.